Czech Plays

CZECH PLAYS:
SEVEN NEW WORKS

Martin E. Segal Theatre Center Publications
New York

Martin E. Segal Theatre Center Publications
Daniel Gerould, Director of Publications
Frank Hentschker, Executive Director
Jan Stenzel, Director of Administration

CZECH PLAYS:
SEVEN NEW WORKS

by

Lenka Lagronová
Egon Tobiáš
Jiří Pokorný
Iva Klestilová Volánková
David Drábek
Ivana Růžičková
Petr Zelenka

translated by

Petr Onufer and Mike Baugh
Sodja Zupanc Lotker and Howard Lotker
David Short
Alex Zucker
Don Nixon
Ivana Růžičková
Štěpán S. Šimek

Martin E. Segal Theatre Center Publications
New York
© 2009

Library of Congress Cataloging-in-Publication Data

Czech plays : seven new works / by Lenka Lagronová ... [et al.].
    p. cm. -- (Czech plays in translation)
ISBN 978-0-9790570-6-9
1. Czech drama--21st century--Translations into English. I. Lagronová, Lenka, 1963-
PG5145.E5C94 2009
891.8'62608--dc22
                                    2009020332

This book is made possible by support from the
Arts and Theatre Institute (Prague) and the Czech Center New York

Copy-editing and typography by Christopher Silsby
Cover design by Bohumil Vašák/Studio Najbrt
Cover photo by Josef Ptáček

Table of Contents

Foreword

"A Seismograph of the Times"
The Czech Tradition in Modern Drama

Modern Czech theatre, which begins in 1918 with the creation of independent Czechoslovakia in the aftermath of World War I, is held in high esteem throughout the world because of its intellectually daring playwrights who have championed human rights and freedom of thought in the face of totalitarian threats to their very survival. Two dramatists, Karel Čapek and Václav Havel, are the best known Czech cultural figures of the twentieth century. They enjoy the sort of prestige usually accorded to patriots and statesmen and are regarded as embodiments of social conscience and commitment to fearless truth-seeking. Taken together their careers cover the different eras of modern Czech theatre in the twentieth century.

Using their lives and works as focal points, I intend to trace the development of what can be called the Czech tradition in modern drama, which, as the result of wars, military interventions, political coups, and revolutions, has often had its continuity violently disrupted, producing a recurring pattern of revival and regeneration followed by interdiction and repression. But since Čapek and Havel, no matter how exceptional they may be, are representatives of broader currents, I need also to discuss their most talented contemporaries and co-workers and place these outstanding figures in the social and artistic contexts out of which they emerged.

The first Republic of Czechoslovakia—a new political and cultural entity created in 1918, which would last only twenty years—was favorable to the development of a genuinely popular and democratic avant-garde theatre of great vitality and variety. Centrally located between East and West, Prague was open to the multiple influences of the many international artistic movements being freely circulated in a Europe temporarily at peace. It had access to the theatrical avant-garde of all of Europe. Russian Futurism was propagated in Czechoslovakia by Mayakovsky's friend, the linguist Roman Jakobson. The Italian Futurist designer and director Enrico Prampolini spent several months in Prague in 1921, bringing with him sets from the Teatro Sintetico Futurista, whose principles of simultaneity influenced subsequent Czech staging.

In the interwar years, when dictatorship and repressive regimes spread throughout Europe, Prague was an artistic beacon and cosmopolitan place of asylum for artistic refugees fleeing from tyranny in their home lands. Despite Slovak discontent, problems with ethnic minorities, and the growing menace of German Fascism, the new republic prospered under the presidency of Tomas Masaryk. The Czech half of the country was an advanced liberal democracy with a large educated bourgeoisie, the natural breeding ground and primary source of support for the avant-garde.

The arts in Prague flourished in an atmosphere of tolerance. The best known Czech playwright of the period, Karl Čapek, was avant-garde in his orientation; he and his painter and stage designer brother Josef introduced Cubism, with its multiple perspectives, to the Czech public. Karel Čapek's apocalyptic *R.U.R (Rossum's Universal Robots)* in 1921 about the dangers of modern industrial technology, was an exciting science fiction melodrama of ideas in its form, making it accessible to broad popular audiences at Prague's National Theatre and insuring its instant world-wide success. Karel Čapek was the first Czech writer to enjoy international reputation. Following his example, the modern Czech playwright has often assumed the role of a public figure confronting challenging social and ethical issues and awakening the national consciousness.

The mordant and satirical *Insect Play* (1922), which Karel Čapek wrote with his brother Josef, is a philosophical allegory of human destiny. The Čapek plays are parables of the human condition and the future of man featuring fantastic plots and archetypical characters in a style akin to expressionism. They defend the ordinary individual facing the growing mechanization and dehumanization of life caused by the technological and scientific revolutions.

In contrast to Prague's large state-financed institutionalized theatres, there flourished dozens of small avant-garde theatre studios pursuing anti-realistic, anti-illusionist, anti-stylized, and anti-expressionist programs, first under the banner of constructivism, then of poetism, or pure poetry, and finally of surrealism. A decisive influence on the development of Czech avant-garde theatre in the interwar years was played by the leftist arts group Devětsil (Nine Forces, or Nine Muses), consisting of young poets, critics, writers, painters, directors, musicians, and sculptors. Devětsil's revolutionary manifesto of 1922 contained a theoretical piece on the proletarian theatre by the communist intellectual (and future semiotician) Jindřich Honzl, a director known for his staging of mass choral recitations of workers' poetry and a major figure in the shaping of the Czech avant-garde. By 1924 the heavy rhetoric of Marxism was abandoned for a new conception of theatre: poetism devoid of propaganda and even of thought. Drawing upon architecture, film, dance, technology, circus, and music hall, the theorists of poetism argued that the stage should be a place of fancy and free association, expressing the joy of life and dreams of beauty through images, words, and movement.

Honzl, who had visited the Soviet Union and fallen under the spell of Meyerhold and Tairov, opposed a literary conception of theatre and considered the text only as a starting point for the director's blending of words, music, rhythmic recitation, and visual effects. In the mid-1920s Honzl joined forces with Jiří Frejka, a director known for his improvisatory commedia productions, to found the Liberated Theatre as part of Devětsil. Based on the postulates of Soviet constructivism, the Liberated Theatre was a small experimental stage, devoid of decoration and scenery where the harmony of word, gesture, music, dance, pantomime, and visual effect created a pure theatrical spectacle. The texts Honzl staged were French surrealist and proto-surrealist works by Ribemont-Dessaignes, Apollinaire, and Jarry as well as Czech plays by poets, such as Vítězslav Nezval's lyrical *Telegrams on Wheels* (1926). As typified by the work of the Liberated Theatre, the Czech avant-garde was a playful autonomous poetic experience, governed by rhythm and musicality and collectively created by writer, actor, and director.

In 1927 two former law students, Jiří Voskovec (1905-1981) and Jan Werich (1905-1980), created the Vest-Pocket Revue, which quickly became the most popular avant-garde theatre in Czechoslovakia. The duo were soon sponsored by the Liberated Theatre, which they eventually took over, calling it the Liberated Theatre of V + W and moving into larger quarters. Voskovec and Werich wrote, produced, and acted in their own "jazz revues," which consisted of partially improvised comedy and social satire, plus song and dance numbers presented by the rest of the company. The best young actors in Czechoslovakia appeared in supporting roles. The jazz-inspired music was by Jaroslav Ježek, and Honzl directed the shows. The circus and silent movie slapstick and the parodies of famous films and theatre sequences created irreverent fun in a "camp" style that appealed to the younger generation. After Hitler's rise to power in 1933, Voskovec and Werich directed their satiric barbs against the fascist threat. The caricature of Hitler in *Ass and Shadow* (1933) called forth protests from the German Embassy in Prague, and *Executioner and Fool* (1934) led to riots in the theatre between rightist students and the majority of the spectators. The last two productions, *Big Bertha* (1937) and *A Fist in the Eye* (1938) were their most complex and combative; both alluded to the Sudetenland crisis that the Nazis used as a pretext for dismembering Czechoslovakia. After the betrayal of the Republic at Munich in 1938, the Liberated Theatre was closed by the police, and Voskovec and Werich escaped to America.

In 1927 Frejka had formed his own Theatre Dada and invited the composer, musician, and actor Emil Frantisek Burian (1904-1959) to join him as co-director. It was then that Burian gave the first production of his Voiceband, a form of choral recitation and chant to his own syncopated music, using thirty-two players, mostly amateurs. In 1933 Burian created his own small avant-garde theatre collective, D34 (D from Divadlo [theatre]), plus the number of the year changed annually). Music became the organizing element in the performances which were conceived as a montage of poetry, movement, and light that united acting and dancing. Burian effected a radical simplification of theatrical structure by the use of light and music which he composed himself. He often wrote his own material, such as *War* (1935), a poetic antimilitary scenario set in a Czech village and based on old folk songs and popular ballads. Burian regarded every text as a libretto which he then must execute as composer, orchestrator, and conductor. In 1935 he invented a "theatregraph" that combined live actors and film projections in a poetic fashion anticipating the Laterna Magika of the 1950s.

After the crash of 1929 and the growing threat of Fascism, the avant-garde became more directly engaged politically, as also did the institutionalized state theatres. All theatre artists were united in the defense of Czech culture and the Republic. The National Theatre joined the struggle with its productions of Čapek's last two plays, the anti-totalitarian *White Plague* (1937) and *Mother* (1938). Following the Munich Agreement, the right wing government that was then installed vilified the playwright. Although he was number 3 on the Gestapo's most wanted list, Karel Čapek refused to flee to England. He died in December 1938, three months before the Nazi soldiers entered Prague. His brother Josef died in the Bergen-Belsen concentration camp in 1945.

During the Nazi occupation significant Czech theatre came to a virtual standstill, and the vibrant artistic life of the interwar came to an end, except for underground organizations like Group 42, an association of writers, poets, intellectuals, and artists. After the war, from 1945 to 1948 there was a period of limited democracy and relative artistic freedom while the fate of Czechoslovakia hung in the balance. Immediately after the liberation, as part of the strong anti-German backlash, Soviet drama enjoyed great popularity both with artists and much of the general public. An important playwright, critic, and theorist who began writing in this transitional period was the Slovak communist writer Peter Karvaš; his science-fiction drama, *The Meteor* (1945) uses an elemental natural disaster that almost destroyed the human race to explore ethical issues raised by the fight against fascism, *Antigone and the Others* (1962) transposes the Greek myth to concentration camp, and *The Scar* (1963) portrays the persecution of the innocent under the cult of personality. Karvaš was purged after 1968. Plays of an allusive, allegorical nature proved durable. An anti-collaborationist parable, *Playing with Devil* (1945/6) by Jan Drda, originally staged as an attack on the Germans, was revived in 1968 as a denunciation of the Russians.

Following the 1948 coup that turned Czechoslovakia into a Soviet satellite, Moscow-directed rule, which lasted a dreary fifty years, severely restricted freedom in all the arts, particularly in theatre, regarded as central to the building of communism. The centralized state theatre system was designed to serve communist ideology and further propaganda goals of creating an internationally acclaimed cultural show case. From 1948 to 1953 while Stalinism reigned, Čapek and other pre-war avant-gardists were forbidden, and officially prescribed socialist realism became the only permitted theatrical style, leading to a glut of factory plays showing the heroic accomplishments of the new socialist man in fulfilling production quotas. Young audiences were bored and stayed away.

By the mid-1950s, as a consequence of Stalin's death and the slight loosening of controls that followed, a cultural thaw began to make itself felt. Previously banned works of Čapek were reprinted and revived, and Western writers like Beckett, Ionesco, and Dürrenmatt started to be known and published. Progressive Czech authors began a mild rebellion against the neo-Stalinist regime by writing satirical plays that attacked abuses of the system without yet daring to challenge the regime itself.

Most important of all, new theatrical spaces became the home for previously undreamed of cultural freedom. In reaction to the monumental "stone" theatres—official state-run and state-financed institutions that were firmly controlled by dictatorial centralized power—young artists sought out urban places where they could perform non-traditional works in informal settings, giving rise to a proliferation of small experimental stages. Because of their diminutive size and off-beat locations, these inventive little studio theatres managed to escape intrusive surveillance and became the breeding ground for a new generation of Czech theatre artists and theatre audiences. In 1950s Jan Werich, back from America, returned to the stage and became director of the small ABC Theatre, where he revived the repertory of the original Liberated Theatre, blending political satire with surrealist poetry and jazz.

In this fashion, continuity with the past was re-established. The twenty-three-year-old Václav Havel, at loose ends having been denied a university education because of his wealthy bourgeois class origins, got his first job in the theatre in 1959 as a stagehand at the ABC with Werich. There the young playwright-to-be discovered the tradition of free humor, poetic shorthand, and clowning that came directly from the small avant-garde stages and cabarets of the interwar period.

Years later, looking back at his formative years working in the Prague studios of the 60s, Havel theorized that the theatre was "a seismograph of the times," "a place of self-awareness," "an area of freedom, an instrument of human liberation." The concept of community was the key to the creation of the show, because, according to Havel, both performers and young audiences experienced a "very conspiratorial sense of togetherness" and engaged in a collective act of existential freedom by their active presence and participation.

The Czech theatrical renaissance from 1956 to 1968 was also impelled by dynamic interaction among the arts, as had been the case in interwar Prague. Composers, painters, poets, filmmakers, playwrights, directors, and actors made common cause, ignoring boundaries and sharing secrets. The model collaboration was between playwright Havel and director Grossman at the Theatre on the Balustrade, the first and most important of the Prague little stages. In the early 1960s the brilliant drama critic, theoretician, and translator Jan Grossman became the artistic director of the Balustrade and staged his own adaptation of *Ubu Roi*, works by Beckett and Ionesco, and Kafka's *Trial*. He also staged or produced all the early plays of Havel, who had joined the theatre as dramaturg and house playwright after two years at the ABC. Working together closely, Grossman and Havel made the Balustrade home to the new Czech theatre of the absurd, whose vanguard poetics foregrounded the spontaneous, playful, and improvisational, and featured collective creation and audience rapport. Havel's landmark *Garden Party* (1963) dealt with the manipulation and corruption of language in a closed system, and *The Memorandum* (1965/6) featured the creation of a synthetic language designed to supplant the living tongue.

Although strongly influenced by Beckett, Ionesco, Pinter, and Dürrenmatt, Czech absurdism was a native product—"something in the air," Havel maintained—more concerned with social and political questions than was the Western theatre of the absurd. Absurd humor for Czechs was an actual, day-to-day response to living in a totalitarian system. In Havel's aesthetic, theatre's function was not to offer moral instruction or provide ideological solutions to problems, in the manner of Brecht's learning plays, but rather to awaken in each individual a feeling of authenticity and the need to live in truth. Drawing upon his Czech heritage, Havel takes and makes his own Čapek's fear of bureaucracy and advanced technology, Hašek's subversive humor found in *The Good Soldier Schweik*, and Kafka's metaphysical anguish in his novels and tales, whose outsider heroes are tormented by feelings of alienation, guilt, and culpability. In all Havel's works, the central theme is the threatened loss of human identity in a dehumanized world of entropic systems. Most to be dreaded is the tyranny of self-perpetuating social mechanisms that dispose of humanistic values.

During the explosion of talent during the Czech renaissance of the late 1950s and 60s many other outstanding playwrights worked in close collaboration with leading directors. One of these was Otomar Krejča, director at the National Theatre and then at the studio Theatre beyond the Gate. In 1958 Krejča staged *A Sunday in August,* by the poet František Hrubín (1919-1971), a Chekhovian drama of the everyday dilemmas of ordinary people which obliquely reflected the tensions in the larger surrounding world. It was a major break with the dogmatic and schematic formulas of socialist realism with its rigid stereotypes. Chekhov's plays—non-ideological and seemingly apolitical—offered Czech playwrights and directors artistic models of how to deal subtly and non-didactically with private life in times of transition.

Another major playwright frequently directed by Krejča was Josef Topol (born 1935), whose *Cat on the Tracks* and *Their Day* (1959) are plays of poetic sensibility dealing with familial and generational conflicts, and whose *The End of Carnival* (1963) approaches the struggle between old and new in society from a mythic perspective, using masks and ritual enactment. After the Soviet invasion, Topol was at first able to continue his literary career as a translator, chiefly of Shakespeare, but after signing Charter 77, Topol was permitted only to work at manual labor. As guest artist at the Balustrade, Krejča had directed

Havel's first play, *The Garden Party* in 1963.

Drama also flourished outside Prague in the provincial capitals. In Brno, at the small experimental studio Evening Brno, great success was enjoyed by the absurdist political parable, *King Vavra* (1964), by the Moravian playwright Milan Uhde (born 1936) who took a well-known nineteenth-century Czech verse satire directed against the Hapsburg Monarchy (based on the Irish legend of the king with donkey ears) and made it into a stinging attack on the easily recognizable neo-Stalinists currently running the regime. Audiences flocked to Brno to see the performance, but after the play was transferred to Prague, it was quickly banned. His modern version of *Antigone*, called *The Harlot of Thebes* (1967/8), shows the revolt of the Greek tragic heroine reduced to total defeat by the mechanisms of power. After the Soviet invasion of 1968 Uhde wrote a popular adaptation of Gogol's *Nose*, but since the playwright was under a ban, the play had to be credited to the director—a common ruse during the years of repression. After 1989 Uhde, like Havel, went into politics and became the Minister of Culture and Chairman of the Chamber of Deputies.

During the period of liberalization a number of reformed communist writers—most notably Ivan Klíma, Pavel Kohout, and Milan Kundera—not only recognized the abuses of the regime, but exposed the folly of their previous beliefs in the form of dark political parables and grotesque satires. In the aftermath of the 1968, they all left Czechoslovakia for careers abroad.

The well-known novelist Klíma, a survivor of the Theresienstadt concentration camp, wrote Kafka-tinged plays like *The Castle* (1964/7), a political parable exposing the moral corruption of the communist system, and then soon after the Soviet invasion, *The Jury* (1969), a parody of courtroom melodrama constructed as an analogue to the despotic regime. He gave private readings of *Bridegroom for Marcela* (1969), dealing with the Soviet invasion, until an informer filmed his living room performances with a hidden camera. Klíma's subsequent plays appeared only in samizdat in his homeland, but were published and widely performed abroad, especially in Germany.

The poet, songwriter, and prolific playwright Pavel Kohout has written works in a great variety of styles, starting with socialist realism. Then he became involved in the process of liberalization and wrote experimental plays influenced by Wilder, Pirandello, and Anouilh. In *August August, the Clown* (1967), Kohout used the traditional image of the clown as a metaphor for downtrodden humankind in an allegory about totalitarian regimes. In June 1967 Kohout was elected chairman of the Writers' Union at the Fourth Congress of Czech Writers' Union, in which the writers asserted their independence. After the Soviet invasion, his *Poor Murderer* (1971) could only be performed abroad where it reached broad audiences.

Primarily a novelist, Milan Kundera, who graduated from and then taught at the Film Faculty of the Academy of the Performing Arts, wrote several influential plays in the 1960s. A modern morality play set during the Nazi occupation, *Keeper of the Keys* (1962), dealt with love, sex, and the choice, confronting youth, of making an active social commitment or trying to stay safely on the sidelines and lead a life of material comfort. His black comedy, *Birdbrainia, or Two Ears, Two Weddings* (1968), is set in a grotesque school (presented as a microcosm of larger institutions) where spying, eavesdropping, and informing, followed by abject confession and sadistic punishment, are rampant. In defiance of all the proprieties demanded by socialist realism, the headmaster and local chairman engage in a savage struggle for power and sexual dominance within an absurd bureaucratic system.

Forbidden to teach or publish after the Soviet invasion, Kundera was allowed in 1975 to emigrate to France, where he pursued his very successful career as a novelist, eventually switching from Czech to French. Before leaving, he wrote his last play, a dramatic variation on Diderot's novel, *Jacques and His Master* (1972), which could be performed in Czechoslovakia only under cover of the director's name. When, after many years, the author finally granted permission for *Birdbrainia* to be revived, shortly after its opening at the Balustrade in Prague in 2008 Kundera became involved in a murky controversy over his alleged informing on a fellow student in 1950, documented by recently published secret police files.

The full flowering of the liberalization known as the Prague Spring lasted from January to August 1968. Prague again became the European capital of theatrical life, as it had been in the interwar years. Then in August 1968, the Soviet Union, unable to tolerate such an open display of artistic freedom in one of its satellites, led the Warsaw Pact invasion of Czechoslovakia, deposed Alexander Dubček (proponent of "socialism with a human face"), and installed the hard-liner Gustav Hušak. Purges, censorship, and strict controls over all aspects of intellectual and cultural life were only gradually instituted as power became consolidated in the hands of the harshly oppressive regime. It took several years to stifle the hopes of the Czech people, crush their re-awakened energies, and break their spirit to resist.

From 1968 to 1986 the Czech puppet rulers acting for their Soviet masters imposed on Czechoslovakia a long period of repression, called in communist jargon "normalization," but which in fact was a spiritual vacuum. The decade from 1975 to 1985 was in some ways worse than the Stalinist years when at least there were stirrings that gave hope of change. By March 1972 all major pre-invasion playwrights were either banned or abroad. Havel, Topol, and Uhde were no longer in repertory—and Havel, for daring to speak up, was imprisoned repeatedly, for a total of almost five years. The reformed communists, Kundera, Kohout, and Klíma, were also silenced, expelled from the party, reprimanded, and driven into exile.

Original drama was at low ebb. An alternative to official theatre was found in private, amateur, or semi-professional groups that performed in living rooms, halls, and barns. Artistically independent theatre often took the shape of an author's personal poetic stage. When not in jail, Havel could read aloud his Vaněk plays to friends in the privacy of his own home. A band of daring amateurs was able give a single unlicensed performance of Havel's version of John Gay's *Beggars' Opera* on November 1, 1975 in a suburb of Prague. The security police promptly arrested many professional theatre artists in the audience who in fact had nothing to do with staging the production. Havel's plays of the 1980s—*Largo Desolato* (1983), *Temptation* (1985), and *Urban Renewal* (1987)—had to receive their premieres abroad.

Besides publishing in samizdat or in the émigré press, playwrights could escape censorship by adapting lyrical prose texts or creating non-verbal theatre of movement and objects. It was not until the second half of the 1980s that a slow revival of Czech drama began to be take place. By 1988 rejuvenation had come when, as a result of glasnost and perestroika, a weakening of both official censorship and the even more insidious self-censorship became discernible. New plays now appeared dealing with the relation between artists or other exceptional individuals and the authorities in which ethical issues of choice and moral responsibility are debated, such as *Ur-Mephisto* (1988) by Jan Vedral (born 1955) about Gustaf Grundgens, the German actor who put his creative talents at the service of the Nazi regime.

Two major playwrights who came of age at the time of the Soviet invasion, Karel Steigerwald (born 1945) and Daniela Fischerová (born 1948), began playwriting in the period of "normalization" and have continued their careers after the Velvet Revolution. They are therefore representative figures of the middle generation between Havel and his contemporaries from the 1960s and the new post-Velvet Revolution writers presented in this anthology.

In plays such as *The Hour Between Dog and Wolf* (1979) about the trial of the fifteenth-century poet François Villon, and *Legend* (1987) about a medieval village during the inquisition, Fischerova theatricalizes history, myth, and fable in order to deal with contemporary abuses of power. *Princess T* (1984) is her version of Gozzi's fable *Turandot*, in which the Princess tries but fails to overthrow her despotic father and establish a system beneficial to the ruled. After 1989 Fischerová continued to write plays of fantasy dealing with issues of conscience, morality, and social responsibility; her works deal with the settling of accounts for the betrayal, informing, and collaboration during the communist years.

Karel Steigerwald graduated from the Prague Film School, where Kundera was one of his teachers, and worked as a screenwriter for six years. He began his career as a playwright in the late 1970s during the period of normalization, using metaphor and allusion at the extreme limits of what could get past the censors and be produced. Called "the bravest of the tolerated" authors, he appealed to conspiratorial spectators attuned reading between the lines. His first four plays, written before the Velvet Revolution—*Tartar Feast*

(1978), *Period Dances* (1980), *Foxtrot* (1982) and *Neapolitan Disease* (1984)— are dramas on Czech history that destroy myths about national character, portraying the average citizen as self-deluded, opportunistic, and cowardly and the infrequent idealist as naïve and foolish.

Shortly before the Velvet Revolution, Steigerwald became dramaturg of the Theatre on the Balustrade, where his *Sorrow, Sorrow, Fear, the Rope, and the Pit*—a transitional work between totalitarianism and freedom begun in 1989, but completed in early 1990—was staged in 1991 by Jan Grossman. Called by the author an "Oratorio for the Dead," the play is a collage of scenes portraying terrible abuses by tyrannical regimes in the twentieth-century, simultaneously taking place in 1930s Russia, Prague in the 1950s and 1980s, and Germany during World War II—all observed by a cynical Czech everyman, Mr. Novak. Since the fall of communism Steigerwald has continued to write political plays that caricature the new society, as in *Nobel* (1994) or make reckonings with the past, as in *Horáková vs Gottwald* (2006), about the victim of a notorious show trial in 1950.

Initiated by students and theatre workers, the Velvet Revolution—like the Prague Spring—was animated by the spirit of the playful, poetic, and absurd avant-garde of the interwar years. The peaceful rebellion that toppled communism grew out of festivals, civic activity, and street theatre and took the form of a boisterous popular carnival lasting ten days.

After 1989 with the triumphant election of Havel as president of Czechoslovakia, the restoration of social and artistic freedoms, plus the renewal of private enterprise, created unexpectedly challenging conditions for new generations of playwrights. In many cases, the older and middle generations of playwrights had lost their best years to the repressive regime and their consuming resistance to it. Many Czech writers had gone abroad, switched languages, and lost contact with rapidly shifting realities of their former land. For others, accustomed to "writing between the lines," the sudden regaining of their freedom left them at a creative impasse. Havel described the sensation as "What Sisyphus might have felt if one fine day his boulder stopped, rested on the hilltop, and failed to roll back down. [. . .] [L]ife had lost its old purpose and hadn't yet developed a new one."

Although there was a felt need for new plays that would respond to the changes in society, years with its enforced socialist realism had left a deep distaste for the topical and the political. Because of rising costs, mainstream theatres were unwilling to risk presenting new plays, and innovative directors preferred classics, adapted prose, or prestigious foreign works. Problems of funding, fights over ownership rights of theatre buildings, and the dismantling of the old repertory system in favor of commercial entertainment helped make the 1990s a barren period for new Czech drama.

Several major authors from the past were able to make striking come-backs. Milan Uhde abandoned his political career and resumed playwriting with *Miracle in the Black House* (2002)—produced at the Theatre on the Balustrade in 2007—a microcosmic family history that encapsulates Czech history from the 1930s to the 90s. Václav Havel returned to the stage with *Leaving*—begun in the late 1980s, finished between 2003 and 2007, and produced at the National Theatre)—an ironic comedy about a womanizing political leader whose misdeeds are exposed. Utilizing quotations from *King Lear* and *The Cherry Orchard*, the play treats themes of change, dispossession, and the passage of power from one generation to the next.

The present anthology is designed to introduce a new generation of writers born, for the most part, a few years before or after the Prague Spring and Soviet invasion. They came of age at the time of the Velvet Revolution. Beginning their careers after their country had regained its freedom, these playwrights have chosen their vocation and found their voices without having to fight a repressive regime or mask their vision by parable and allusion. They can say what they want to in any form they choose, and they are free to follow those traditions of Czech drama that seem fruitful to them, while disregarding others. Not obliged to carry the baggage of previous generations, they have few old accounts that must be settled. As the plays in the present volume disclose, these playwrights can tackle once tabooed subjects and confront new realities.

Daniel Gerould
New York, February 2009

Editors' Preface

As American theatre practitioners, we honor the text when approaching any script, perhaps even more so with new work. So when we began to edit these seven plays for publication, we found ourselves generating a long list of questions in order to arrive at a script which reflected only the playwrights' artistic choices, not our interpretations as directors and not the vestiges of previous Czech productions.

Our questions ran the gamut, but included everything from: did the playwright break the line of dialogue purposely, and for what reason; why are emphasized words in capital letters, something that here usually connotes shouting; should we correct seemingly inaccurate historical details, or are they meant to be inaccurate; and do these peculiar indentations exist in the original Czech or was it the translator's choice for formatting something even less conventional in the original script?

We had expected that editors in the Czech Republic would have already corrected formatting and other inconsistencies, but translator Alex Zucker explained that there is a distinctly hands-off attitude towards these scripts in the Czech Republic. This relaxed attitude toward the written text is in direct response to decades of communist censorship. Alex also suggested, in answer to a number of our other questions, that the vagaries of many of the scripts were due to the plays being produced on typewriters, with fixed margins, no italics and, of course, no logging onto the Internet for easy fact-checking. This made sense, and so we made adjustments accordingly. We believe that the scripts you will read best represent the playwrights' intention. We can make this assurance because our endless questions were met, by the playwrights, their agents, and translators, with inexhaustible patience.

In the spirit of full disclosure, we should also note the frequency with which our questions received a polite "decide for yourselves" answer. What, in another context, would sound indifferent was in fact a valuable window onto how theatre is made in the Czech Republic. It is a process defined by the playwright's openness to having a complete collaboration with the director, and it extends later to the audience as well. Playwright Ivana Růžičková wrote of the allure in making this sort of collaborative theatre: "I like the idea that by writing a play I'm giving a new 'toy' to a group of people, a 'game' that they can 'play' among themselves. And if they understand the rules correctly, those who come to watch can also get enjoyment out of it."

The scripts also benefited from having gone through rigorous phases of language editing, both in the Czech Republic and here during rehearsals for the Immigrants' Theatre Project's New York Series. As anyone working in translation knows, there are serious linguistic and cultural challenges to making a play accessible in a translated language. Nuances of grammar, context, vocabulary, and metaphor are rarely perfectly translatable, and new and unexpected meanings pop up when plays are read in English by American-trained actors. The Czech playwrights embrace these new meanings and we should as well.

Styles of presentation are, of course, also different. Czech theatre is highly "theatrical," physical, and not as focused on psychology as American theatre. Subtext is spoken, not implied. Pauses are serious, non-Pinter pauses. People wait a while before speaking, to think over what they just heard. In order to convey these differences on the page, we have kept the formatting of several of the plays where each sentence is on a separate line—representing a new thought, a breath, a pause, a glance, some kind of physical break with the line above it. According to playwright Iva Klestilová Volánková, Czech plays can vary in length from show to show because of these pauses. Her play *Minach* ran sometimes ninety minutes and sometimes three hours!

In *Opening the Drawer and Pulling out the Knife,* sentences of dialogue break across lines into smaller units with no spacing between, implying a rapid-fire delivery of sharp phrases that expect no response. *Dad Takes Goal Kicks* uses indented dialogue to denote a difference in speech pattern from what came before. Groups of indented lines of dialogue may be lines spoken simultaneously or partially overlapped. But, however the indenting of theses lines is conveyed on stage, the lines themselves should be understood as being of *that* moment and the significance of the cluster is left open by the playwright to be filled in by the production, and by you, the reader.

In editing this book we have kept our notes to a minimum. One thing to be aware of is that Czech uses nicknames in typical fashion to communicate affection, intimacy or familiarity, as in *Dad Takes Goal Kicks.* Sometimes the nicknames are close to the actual name, as with Jindra/Jenda, Blaža/Blažena, Mirek/Mirka; occasionally they are more obscure, as in Jan/Honza.

We hope that, above all, what will come through in this collection are seven unique voices enhancing our notions of what can be expressed on the stage, and how. To that end, we have tried to keep the plays relatively uncluttered by front matter, and have included only brief biographical information and some thoughts from each playwright offered during the course of putting this book together. Alex Zucker was the chief translator for this section.

There are a number of people to whom we owe special thanks for their help with this book. They include Leigh Buchanan Bienen, Irena Kovarova, Zdeněk Kříž, Branwen MacDonald, Don Nixon, Štěpán Šimek, and Alex Zucker. We also want to thank Christopher Silsby for his hard work and talent in getting the manuscript printer-ready. We are likewise thankful for Jan Stenzel's administrative and organizational skills in working with the playwrights, translators, and literary agencies in the Czech Republic. The Czech Center New York, under the direction of Marcel Sauer, has provided invaluable assistance, and we appreciate the time Radka Křížek and Jan Žahour gave to this project. We would like to acknowledge Marie Spalová of DILIA and Jitka Sloupová of Aura-Pont for their commitment to their playwrights and this book, and Sodja Zupanc Lotker for championing this project with the Arts and Theatre Institute in Prague.

Finally, we are extremely grateful to Dr. Daniel Gerould and Dr. Frank Hentschker of the Martin E. Segal Theatre Center for their support and guidance at each step in the process. Their dedication to expanding the geographical borders of theatre, while narrowing the distance between scholarship and practice, has not only enlarged our field but made this book a reality.

Gwynn MacDonald and Marcy Arlin, co-editors

Introduction

New Czech Plays in Translation

The New York Readings

We in the United States often perceive Eastern European theatre as the perfect milieu, mixing art and politics—*they* have found a way to pack intense social and political messages into a clever and entertaining art form; *they* sneak subversive messages under the noses of the somewhat stupid censors. We look at Mrożek, Witkiewicz, Havel, Čapek, Topol, and even Ionesco—these are the ones we know best. *They* were brave and taunted the Tsars, the Hapsburgs, and the Communists.

In the late twentieth century, the Czechs were particularly good at writing (sometimes banned) theatre that dared to challenge the status quo— and the Czech audience was loyal in its attendance. Theatre escaped some of the harsher censorship, perhaps because of smaller audiences and fewer venues, the censors didn't think it would have that much influence, unlike newspapers, novels, and movies. I believe they underestimated the power and tenacity of the playwrights and the connections they were able to forge with their audiences.

In 2001, in the shadow of 9/11, with the U.S. governmental swing towards the right, security clampdowns, the fear of terrorism and the fear caused by the fear of terrorism, many artists were questioning their place in American culture and wondering how much they could express without being labeled unpatriotic or getting cut off from government funding, as happened in the eighties when artists on the fringe lost funding due to supposedly "obscene" subject matter. The incipient war in Iraq was making everyone wary about free expression and protest. In other words, how much free expression in the arts did they have, could they maintain and still develop an audience, yet come in under the radar of government intrusion and censure (as opposed to censor)? How could Immigrants' Theatre Project—an Obie-winning company with a reputation of presenting new, exciting plays by and about immigrants— help solve this dilemma?

As ITP's Artistic Director, I felt that we might learn something from those who do art in stressful authoritarian times. The ascension of Havel, a playwright, to the Czech presidency of a nation was truly inspirational. Perhaps we could aspire to such a state?

I was introduced to Irena Kovarova (then Deputy Director of the Czech Center New York) by lighting designer Zdenek Kriz, an artist who left Czechoslovakia in the early eighties because of governmental censorship. I suggested to her the idea of initiating a play reading series to introduce Czech plays to the American audience. The purpose was simple—can the world and issues of these plays, developed in another country and culture, that has gone through, in the twentieth century, five occupations, one short-lived democracy, two world wars, a depression, and recently the sweetest softest revolution in history, speak to a twenty-first-century American audience? Can we Americans, with our fairly new, diverse society and love of theatrical naturalism (realism), care about and understand the theatricality of plays about the societal discomforts of a centuries-old culture?

With the assistance of the Czech Center NY (under Director Přemysl Pela) and the Theatre Institute—now known as the Arts and Theatre Institute—in Prague (with Sodja Zupanc Lotker), Immigrants' Theatre Project selected plays for our first year that would loosely represent the political phases of Czechoslovakia in the twentieth century: the Čapek Brothers' *The Insect Play* (Austro-Hungarian influence), Josef Topol's *Cat on the Tracks* (post-WWII communism), Václav Havel's *Largo Desolato* ("normalization", the clampdown in 1969 after Prague Spring), and Markéta Bláhová's *Little Pitfall* (woman writing post-Velvet Revolution). The Henry Street Settlement's Abrons Arts Center in New York City hosted these plays. Our audience consisted of curious Czechs courtesy of the Czech Center mailing list, academics working in Slavic literature, theatre artists interested in, and enamored of, Eastern Europe. ITP was hosting ArtsLink Fellow Hungarian actress Krisztina Urbanowitz, who played a butterfly in *The Insect Play.* Growing up under communism and a member of a repertory company in Budapest, she also helped us understand how these plays functioned in a censor-monitored theatre. The plays of Čapek, Havel, and Topol had some familiarity for the artists and audience. In the question and answer session after the readings, especially with *Largo Desolato,* there was a strong connection between the audience and the play's themes of paranoia, entrapment, and mistrust—themes that infused post-9/11 America.

The Bláhová play, a modern-day fairy tale about a dysfunctional family (which had a full production in 2004 produced by ITP and featured a giant Irish wolfhound puppet that now lives in the Brooklyn Puppet Library), introduced us to the real challenge of new Czech theatre, post-1989: the new writers of a new generation, familiar with communism yet not crushed by it, ready to explore those themes that had been prohibited or discouraged, hopeful for change, as we are now in this country, in 2009. The plays we saw over the next six years of the series resonated deeply with our American audience. As the energetic post-show discussions attested, these plays, while rooted in Czech culture, spoke to questions still important to us Americans, 9/11 or not: sexual identity, homosexuality, and homoeroticism; family conflicts and troubled marriages; the influence of political life on one's love life, money, and globalization; and most innovatively for Eastern Europe, women's empowerment.

One of ITP's missions, in doing American plays and plays in

translation, is to reflect on the stage what Americans look like, which means diversity in casting, which we were able to do by drawing from the multicultural actor pool in New York City. I invited directors who also are accustomed to casting across ethnic lines and were either familiar with Eastern European/American absurdism, or were open to working on very challenging plays.

Until recently, Czech theatre has been fairly ethnically homogeneous as far as casting. I believe that ITP's casting diversity enhanced the series as well as the American potential for these plays. It proved that plays from other countries can work here with our artists; it brought minority actors into roles they probably wouldn't be cast in; and it introduced Czech playwrights to the possibilities of multiculturalism. One unexpected benefit from this casting is that the actors from cultures and nations with a strong traditional theatre, or a theatre of metaphor (because of censorship, societal taboos, etc.) often instantly grasped the highly stylized rhythms of speech and situation in the Czech work.

The atmosphere for rehearsals was one of investigation, experiment, and occasional artistic stabs in the dark! But our Hungarian actress's most memorable comment to me was her astonishment at the warm support and advice given her by the other actors during the reading, which, according to her, can sometimes be lacking in the competitive state repertory company. Many of the actors and directors worked for a second and third year of the series and commented on how challenging, how intelligent, and how much fun the plays were to learn and perform.

In this first year we established conventions that continued throughout the rest of the series: 1) the need for adjustment and re-translations of some of the text from British English, complete with East End slang, to a more colloquial American English, 2) the contribution of dramaturgs Maxine Kern and Irena Kovarova, who assisted directors and actors both in "translation checks" and insight into the rapidly changing Czech society, 3) casting the plays mulitculturally, 4) question and answer sessions after the reading, which evoked a surprising divergence of reactions from the Czechs and Americans, 5) struggles with how to present the intense theatricality of Czech theatre within a reading, and 6) (when financing was possible) bringing the playwrights to the rehearsals to observe our process, meet with theatre organizations in New York, and hear their work by American actors.

Working with the playwrights, often by email before they came to New York, we learned about the extreme fluidity and flexibility with which they treat their scripts—they are accustomed to delivering a text to a theatre or director, having them work on it with a repertory company over several months, and expecting major changes to evolve during the process and the eventual production. Some of the scripts, which were—to this American eye— naturalistic psychological drama, were produced in the Czech Republic as wildly expressionistic absurdist events. A few of the scripts we read were the results of this rehearsal process. Whole sections were revised specifically for production. When these texts were read in translation, there were a few peculiar gaps that had been filled by lights and movement and stagecraft, but weren't written into the script. Another element of the Czech plays that we of course couldn't realize in a reading, was the sets, an art at which the Czechs excel—with Josef Svoboda as the great master of brilliant projections. The Czechs are incredibly skilled and talented at creating the most dazzling theatre effects on a budget: projections, puppets, magical sliding trap doors. (In Prague I saw the most ingenious eighteenth-century device for puppet theatre that created storms, floods, butterflies, all with hand-cranked machinery.)

Dramaturg Maxine Kern was enormously helpful working with directors to understand the underlying structures and thematic stylizations of Eastern European plays, outlining the political society of the first three playwrights (writing with metaphor, censorship, threat of imprisonment, a clear and present evil) versus that of the new playwrights, who were searching for new styles to express their furious rejection of and disappointment with their parents' generation. By 2004, the third year of the Series, Czech playwrights had found plenty of problems to write about. However, most of the translations were by British translators and Czechs with English as a second language. We then began working with Irena Kovarova as a dramaturg fluent in Czech and English, on such translation issues as whether or not the language was "strange" in Czech or if it was just a labored translation, how to work on class and regional differences, and getting obscene and sassy in American slang. Words and idioms would be crosschecked with the translator, if available, and eventually with the playwright, if he/she spoke English. Often the playwrights gave us carte blanche with the changes, and were pleased to have their plays worked on so diligently, occasionally incorporating our changes into their own versions of the translation.

The next six years of the Series (2003–2008) featured plays written after 1996, when the first flush of rebellion against communist censorship had ebbed and writers were finding new societal problems and quirks to write about. These plays were provided by the Theatre Institute and the Czech literary agencies, DILIA Theatrical, Literary and Audio Visual Agency; and Aura-Pont Literary Agency, selecting award winners (Alfréd Radok prize—like our Tony Awards), or those plays that are at the forefront of adventurous writing. Often, the plays were translated into English specifically for the Series.

As the series grew, so did our audiences. We then looked for a theatre venue with an interest in presenting international work as well as a built-in audience interested in new work. New York Theatre Workshop, under the Artistic Direction of Linda Chapman and James Nicola, was investigating artists' exchanges with Eastern Europe. They generously offered us the use of their lovely third-floor rehearsal studio space, which provided a warm light-flooded atmosphere for an audience of around fifty. The reputation of NYTW did much to enhance the prestige of our second year for the directors, actors, and of course the playwrights in the Czech Republic. Two plays from this year are in the anthology: *Minach* and *I Promised Freddy*.

When our audience again outstripped its venue, we looked to The Public Theater because of its historic role in presenting Czech theatre and its renown in the Czech Republic as the first American theatre to present the plays of Václav Havel. The Public's literary manager at the time, Celise Kalke, had a strong connection to the Czech Republic and Czech theatre, and facilitated our residency at The Public from 2004 through 2006, under the Artistic Directors George C. Wolfe and Oskar Eustis. For me personally as a director it was a dream come true to direct *Miriam* in the gorgeous, stark, cathedral-like Anspacher space. Here our audience doubled, attracting more students and members of the downtown theatre community.

Our three years at The Public were magical. With the additional support of the Czech Center New York under the directorship of Monika Koblerová, we presented eleven more plays and introduced many theatre artists to the wonderful developments in new Czech theatre, including the remaining five plays in this book: *Aquabelles, Opening the Drawer and Pulling out the Knife, Miriam, Theremin,* and *Dad Takes Goal Kicks.* These plays, with their humor, eroticism, mystical dialogue, and overt theatricality, started me thinking about how to bring these plays to a larger American audience.

The New York audience's understanding of Czech theatre deepened, fueling a greater interest in hearing the latest theatrical works coming out of the Czech Republic. This coincided with the plans of the Czech Center New York and Czech embassy to create an international cultural and diplomatic center at the site of the landmark Bohemian National Hall, located on New York City's Upper East Side, where thousands of nineteenth- and early twentieth-century Czech, Slovak, Hungarian, and German immigrants had settled. Newly renovated, the Hall has innovative design technology, a fine arts gallery, a state-of-the-art screening room, and an elegant theatre. What had been the erstwhile home of the Manhattan Theatre Club was, in a new millennium, creating new spaces for art and culture. ITP, in 2008, brought the sixth year of the Series to the new space with the very newest Czech plays.

The success of the Series was in many ways due to the fortuitous conjoining of talent and resources. We were fortunate to have funding for all seven years of the Series from the New York City Department of Cultural Affairs. Depending on each year's allotments, we paid actors between $75 and $125 and directors between $100 and $250. We required, for this unusually ample (by general standards) stipend, that the directors have at least one working session with our paid dramaturg, and a minimum of two rehearsals of three to five hours, which is what could best be organized given the busy, overpacked lives of NY actors. Playwrights when they visited received a per diem.

Admission to all the readings was free.

Our partner, the Czech Center New York, designed and mailed lovely postcards for each year, provided photocopying services, and paid whatever minimal house managing fees were charged by the venues, which provided us the use of their space all day for the day of the reading, use of the lights, a house manager, and access to their website. When possible, the Theatre Institute, with funding from the Czech Ministry of Culture, would help playwrights with airfare; the Czech Center helped support accommodations.

Along the way, we noticed a number of cultural differences in the practice of working on a play. Czech theatre and conversation is not averse to a long pleasant contemplative pause. An American reading, like our conversations here in New York, zips along at a bouncy pace. Though the readings sometimes topped two hours, Czechs in our audience sometimes complained that time moved too fast! We had the most contentious discussions on the roles of women in the plays—our clever playwrights managed to annoy at least a few American and Czech women in our audience. We also began to learn about an interesting cultural difference in play production. Jiří Pokorný, playwright and director of Iva Klestilová Volánková's *Minach* in Brno, was a guest speaker who initiated a lively debate about the relative merits of American versus Czech theatre. We learned, for the first time, how much Broadway is the prevailing Eastern European idea of what American theatre is and how the difficult life of most American theatre artists, especially playwrights, remains unknown to Czechs. At the same exchange, the playwright began to understand the economics of production here, especially for large casts in NYC; I think our Czech visitors were also somewhat surprised at the quantity of excellent plays that compete for production in the United States and how the market for translated international plays is much smaller than in Europe.

When the playwrights were able to attend, it was tremendously rewarding to see their reactions, and hear their explanations of what their work meant to them in the Czech Republic, and what they felt it meant to an American audience. They spoke of what they perceived as psychological readings by the actors. Very often, they saw something in their own work they had never seen before. And our project inspired staged readings of new plays in the Czech Republic, which had never existed before. Usually, new plays are given to a theatre, director, and/or dramaturg for around three to four months of rehearsal before they even see an audience. This extended development and rehearsal process is possible in state-supported theatres. But, with the new Czech economy, and a surge in new plays, some Czech theatres include this economical American system for presenting new works.

We became increasingly convinced that these plays were creating an interest among practitioners and audience, and the work played well in English. An anthology of the plays, making them more accessible, was the logical next step. In 2007 and early 2008, I approached Dr. Daniel Gerould and Dr. Frank Hentschker, friends and colleagues with whom I had collaborated over the years on various projects at the Martin E. Segal Theatre Center (MESTC), to see if they might be interested in publishing an anthology of new Czech plays, the first since the fall of communism. They had already launched an innovative series of anthologies of international plays and I hoped that one of Czech theatre might be within their purview. It was. And, with the financial support of the Czech Center, Arts and Theatre Institute, along with MESTC, we were able to make this a reality. I invited Gwynn MacDonald to be part of the editorial team. Gwynn is a director, artistic director, writer, producer, and a person with a finely tuned sense of what the anthology was aiming to do: introduce a diverse collection of new Czech plays to American theatre. Our skill sets, personalities and working methods have complemented each other beautifully.

Over a year, we re-read the more than thirty plays featured in the Series and chose the seven plays you see here. Some of these plays have won the Alfréd Radok prize. Some are runners-up. And some are just plain popular with Czech audiences. We ultimately chose these plays because they demonstrate the huge variety in style and thematic subject matter of the work being done by a new generation of Czech playwrights.

There is something wonderful in Czech culture that I, as an outsider, have identified (with some corroboration by Czech friends) as whimsical gloom, and conversely, a gloomy whimsy. This is a nation that has had plenty to get depressed about. There is ample room for political jokes and a strong sense of the absurd and also adequate space to believe in magic and the power of the word to help you survive. Some plays focus on religious mystery or the horrors of European history; some analyze changing women's roles. There's lots of sex in these plays, some down and dirty, some violent, and some, well, kinda kinky and alien. There is physical and emotional violence—murder, betrayal, self-cutting, abandonment. There is farce and pure unadulterated slapstick—and intense despair and ambition, and all the other universals that make theatre worth watching.

These plays have a deep theatricality—wonderful roles for actors, a great deal of leeway for directors and designers, and a secure understanding of how a play is made for a live, responsive, engaged, committed and socially and politically aware audience. I can't emphasize strongly enough the contributions made by the amazing group of actors and directors we worked with. A few notable highlights include Melissa Leo and Nilaja Sun dueling in *Minach*; puppeteers Michelle Beshaw and Theresa Linnihan creating some intense puppet sex in *Opening the Drawer and Pulling out the Knife*; Ching Valdes giving Tibor Feldman a hard time in *Dad Takes Goal Kicks*; *Freddy*'s director Kaipo Schwab's wacky and clever ideas on having an ensemble of young actors to read Tobiáš's space opera; and the poignancy of Lanna Joffrey and Adriana Gaviria in *Miriam*. Thom Rivera led a remarkable cast in *Theremin*, and *Aquabelles* was read by students coming to terms with their own sexual identities.

In presenting the series *Czech Plays in Translation*, and in the creation of this anthology, we hope that the plays will find new venues in classes on modern drama and that artistic directors will be interested in mounting them for main stage productions. The size of the plays makes them accessible to many production possibilities. A few have large casts, which might appeal to colleges and regional theatres; others are more intimate with small casts and simple locales. All of the plays, which range from gritty naturalism to lyrical expressionism, have undergone their American trial by fire in the readings, and have received an enthusiastic and fascinated response.

Already, the readings have inspired other reading series of international plays around New York and the United States in professional theatres and universities. Immigrants' Theatre Project is proud and honored to have introduced these remarkable plays of the post-1989 Czech theatre. We thank the hosting theatre venues, the actors, funders, and directors, who recognized the value in this work, proving that the plays are not only an important window on the international theatre scene, but work that is outstanding in its own right. We hope that this book, an outgrowth of the seven years of staged readings, will further inspire and promote productions of these original, funny, profound plays.

Marcy Arlin, Artistic Director
Immigrants' Theatre Project
March 2009

MIRIAM

Lenka Lagronová

Lenka Lagronová
Photo courtesy of Viktor Kronbauer

Lenka Lagronová, born September 22, 1963, graduated in dramaturgy from DAMU (the Theatre Faculty of the Academy of Performing Arts) in Prague, under Jaroslav Vostrý. While still a student, she wrote several plays—including *Poortown*—that were later produced at the drama school theatre DISK. As a dramaturg, she worked exclusively with director Petr Lébl at Theatre on the Balustrade in Prague. As a playwright, she writes for both stage and radio and her work has been translated into seven languages. In her early years as a writer, Lagronová dealt with the traumatic experiences of the younger generation, typically describing them with a rough humor. In *Antelope*, she focuses on a young woman's journey from adolescence to maturity. Her later work, in particular *Thérèse*, was influenced by her departure from theatrical life and her entry into a convent. In 1998 *Thérèse* won the Alfréd Radok Award for Production of the Year. In 1999 she received the Czech Radio Award for her radio debut, *Please Stand Up*, and in 2002 the play won a prize in the Grand Prix Bohemia. Her recent play, *Crying*, was shortlisted for the Alfréd Radok Playwriting Competition in 2007. She is currently at work on a play about Petr Lébl.

For a long time I thought I needed to be seen, to be famous. But now, as I come to realize how difficult it is for me to live my own life and not just fulfill the expectations of others; as I touch the emptiness that that creates inside me, I'm beginning to suspect that writing plays is a sort of compensation for me.

Miriam *is one of my most personal plays.*

—Lenka Lagronová

Gabriela Míčová (left) and Lucie Trmíková (right) in *Miriam* (2005), Pražské komorní divadlo at the Divadlo Komedie, directed by Jan Nebeský

Photo courtesy of Hynek Glos

Miriam

by

Lenka Lagronová

Translated by

Petr Onufer and Mike Baugh

CHARACTERS

VERA
MIRA

"Glorified and sanctified be God's great name throughout the world which He has created according to His will. May He establish His kingdom in your lifetime and during your days, and within the life of the entire House of Israel, speedily and soon."

from the Kaddish, the Jewish Mourner's Prayer

An old Jewish cemetery. Numerous gravestones mark the hill like shingles on a roof. No end in sight. The gravestones are really old; some are leaning, some are lying on the ground, some are half-sunk in the ground. The cemetery is old, decrepit and overgrown. High grass, lots of weeds, several large tree stumps. The cemetery is encircled by a stone wall.

After a while we notice that someone sits huddled close to one of the stumps by the wall. A female figure, leaning against a backpack. Pants, sweater. Headphones on her ears. She is listening to something. But she is anxiously looking around as if she expects an attack. She does not feel safe. She is trying to find a comfortable position so that she does not wear out the knees of her pants. Her name is VERA. Something rustles. Frightened, VERA turns around. She takes off her headphones. She stands up. She calms down. She looks around. She checks out her pants. She straightens them. After a while she sits by the stump again. She looks for something in her backpack. She takes out a packet of some pills. She looks at them and slowly starts to remove single pills. She lets each pill fall on the stump. Every now and then she anxiously looks around. She continues removing them until the last one. We hear steps approaching along the wall. VERA gets frightened. She jumps up. We can see a part of a woman's head, a part of a very beautiful head. It emerges and disappears behind the wall. VERA is both fascinated and frightened. She tries to hide the pills lying on the stump, to cover them so that the head behind the wall cannot see them. We hear a male and a female voice. A conversation.

MAN: I wonder what she is actually made of . . .

WOMAN: Well, if she fell on somebody . . .

MAN: She could really kill them.

Somebody behind the wall throws away something really heavy. Tired breathing. Steps walking away from the wall. After a while, even that sound fades and disappears. VERA stands frightened for a while. Then she straightens her pants again. She sits by the stump and carefully begins to pile the packs of pills. She rearranges the piles again and again..

VERA (*counting*): Two . . . four . . . six . . . eight . . . ten . . . twelve . . . fourteen . . . sixteen . . . eighteen . . . twenty . . . two . . . four . . . six . . . eight . . . thirty . . . two . . . four . . . six . . . eight . . . forty . . .

She touches the packs. She puts a rubber band around them. She counts them again.

VERA: Forty.

She puts the packets into her backpack. She looks at the pills. There is a heap of them on the stump. She plunges her hands into them, grabs them, holds them in her palms, cups them like water, lets them fall and cups them again. She buries her face in the pills. She looks. She sweeps them into one pile.

VERA (*counting and forming a new pile*): Two . . . four . . . six . . . eight . . . ten . . . twelve . . . (*She counts for a long time. Once in a while, a sound makes* VERA *anxiously turn around.*)

VERA: Forty two . . . four . . . eight . . . fifty . . . two . . . four . . . six . . . sixty . . . one . . . two . . . four . . . five . . . six . . . seven . . . seventy . . . two . . . (VERA *starts to nod off. She fights it.*) two . . . four . . . five . . . two . . . six . . . sixty. . . two . . . two . . . two . . . (*She falls asleep.*)

Another woman comes into the graveyard. She does not notice VERA, *who, huddled, looks almost like one of the gravestones. The woman is wearing black pants, black T-shirt and she is carrying a scythe.* MIRA. *She looks around the graveyard, a little shyly. She takes a few steps, grabs the scythe, thinks for a while, looks for the right place and begins to cut the grass. It's the first time she is doing it, so first she just cuts a few blades of grass. The high grass falls down.* MIRA *pauses after each swing, she bends to the ground as if she were searching for something, and then continues cutting. She is disturbed in her work by* VERA, *who starts making whimpering, frightened sounds in her sleep, as she tosses and turns.* MIRA *is frightened by* VERA's *presence. She stops and observes her from a distance. She tries to go on cutting the grass, but the unhappy, scared sounds disturb her.* VERA *begins to speak in her sleep.*

VERA: No . . . no . . . please . . . no . . . yes . . . I'm disgusting . . . most disgusting . . . disgusting . . . disgusting guy . . . bastard . . . bastard . . . bitch . . . disgusting . . . disgusting . . . die . . . yes . . . I deserve to die . . . nothing else . . . serves you right . . . bitch . . . die . . . die . . .

MIRA *dares to approach. She sees* VERA's *troubled sleep and the pile of pills on the stump. She stands over* VERA *with the scythe. Unsettled, she does not know what to do. She looks around as if to call someone. They are alone here. She tries to call out to her.*

MIRA: Hey . . . a

VERA: Die . . . die . . . you piece of shit . . . you little piece of shit . . . yes . . . I am the worst piece of shit . . . die . . .

MIRA *first tries to touch* VERA *with the scythe; only after that she dares to kneel beside her. She looks at the pills, touches them. She looks at* VERA.

MIRA: Are you . . . are you alright?

VERA *does not move. Helpless,* MIRA *stands up. She looks around. No one is there.* MIRA *walks around* VERA. VERA *starts to speak in her sleep again.*

VERA: Disgusting . . . bastard . . . die. I gotta die . . . for all of it . . . die . . . I wanna die. Die.

MIRA *stands over* VERA. *Then she kneels beside her and dares to touch her. Lightly.*

MIRA: Hey . . . you need to throw up . . .

VERA *keeps on sleeping. She weeps painfully.* MIRA *gets startled, she draws her hand back from* VERA. *Nothing.* VERA *makes unhappy sounds.*

VERA: Help . . . help . . . please . . . no . . . help . . . please . . .

MIRA *dares to shake* VERA.

MIRA: Miss . . . you really have to throw up.

VERA *is awoken by* MIRA'*s shaking. She gets very frightened. She jumps, she screams.* MIRA *gets frightened too. She stands up. She jumps back, holding the scythe.* VERA *begins to scream.*

VERA: Help . . . no . . . not yet . . . not yet . . . Help . . .

VERA *steps back; the pills are scattered everywhere.* VERA *wants to run away.* MIRA *is also startled by* VERA'*s reaction.*

MIRA: Don't be afraid . . . don't be afraid . . .
I was just . . . are you alright?

VERA: Fine . . . I'm just fine . . .

VERA *wants to run away. But she trips over the gravestone. She falls. Badly. She lies among the gravestones.* MIRA *stands close-by with the scythe in her hand. She is not moving.*

MIRA: Are you OK?

VERA: Yes . . . it's alright . . .

VERA *tries to stand up. It does not go very well.* MIRA *approaches.*

MIRA: Can I help?

VERA: It's alright . . .

MIRA *helps* VERA *stand up.* VERA *immediately sits down among the gravestones.*

VERA: I slipped somehow . . .

MIRA: Over the gravestones . . .

VERA: You can't even see them.

She holds onto small gravestones, half-sunk into the ground.

MIRA: It's so overgrown here.

VERA: It just looks like grass.

MIRA: Worst for the scythe. (*She looks at a tiny gravestone*)
You can't even see it and it ruins everything.
They're everywhere.
Everywhere and it just looks like grass.
Such tiny gravestones.

VERA (*looks at her torn pants*): They're ruined.

MIRA (*pays more attention to* VERA*'s injured knee*): Does it hurt?

VERA: They're done. A reminder, they were a reminder . . .

MIRA: Blood . . . there's quite a lot of blood . . . (*She tries to wipe* VERA*'s bleeding knee with her hand.*) A tissue or something would be better so that it doesn't get infected . . . (*She checks her pockets. All she can find is a piece of paper, she looks at it.*) I don't have anything . . . just this . . .

She places the paper on VERA*'s knee.* VERA *holds the paper to her knee.*

Until it stops.

They both wait a while. They sit side by side. The paper is turning red. VERA *keeps on looking at her torn pants.*

MIRA: There's a hole, huh?

VERA: It's so dumb.
All I did was fall over.
And the last piece of something nice is gone.

MIRA: The graves.
It looks like nothing but it's sharp. (MIRA *pats a small gravestone.*)

VERA: Like a knife.
It's like cutting yourself with a knife.

MIRA: Is it bleeding?

VERA: It is.
It can't take anything.
You'd think it could take falling over a grave, right?

MIRA: It should . . .

VERA: I must have fallen wrong.

MIRA: But what can you do.
Then you're falling, you're not thinking.

VERA: Well, people are usually not that clumsy . . . I always have to be the worst.

MIRA: Well, I would think that if you can't see, you just can't do it. I mean to fall well.

VERA: Some can.
Like instinctively. They aren't thinking about it. That's what I'm missing.

MIRA: Instinctively.
I don't have much instinct myself.
I am more into thinking too.

VERA: Makes people more vulnerable.

MIRA: They mostly don't know what to do.

VERA: They see too little.

MIRA: But you really cannot see the graves . . . just look . . . they're everywhere, everywhere . . . and do you see them?

VERA: No . . . well, some of them . . .

MIRA: I don't mean the ones you see . . . but the ones you can't see . . . I mean do you see them?

VERA: No.

MIRA: They're in the grass.
And you can only tell with the scythe.
But how are you supposed to know before, right?
You can't inspect everything. With your head on the ground.
You have to cut it.

VERA: Maybe somehow between . . . between the graves.

MIRA: Between!
Where?
There are graves everywhere . . . Always . . . Always.

VERA *takes the bloody paper off her knee.*

MIRA: Is it bleeding?

VERA: A little. (VERA *reads what is on the bloody paper.*)
            "Open to me, my sister, my love . . .
            My beloved put his hand to the latch,
            And my heart was thrilled within me.
            I arose to open to my beloved.
            I opened to my beloved,
            But my beloved had turned and gone!
            My soul failed me when he spoke.
            I sought him, but found him not;
            I called him, but he gave no answer!"

MIRA *snatches the bloody paper from* VERA's *hand. She crumples it and puts it in her pocket.*

MIRA: Just stupid things.
Sometimes I copy down something.

VERA: Pretty cool.

MIRA: It should be cleaned.
So that it won't get infected.

MIRA *looks at* VERA's *knee.*

VERA: You think so?
It'll get dry . . .

MIRA (*carefully inspects the knee*): It's not getting dry. This is not getting dry that easily.
What a cut.
Well I'll be . . . cut on a grave like this . . .

VERA: That's me.
For me, anything is possible.

MIRA: But so deep.
Something might easily get into the cut.

VERA: What would get there . . .
People shouldn't be so careful . . . they would die right away.

MIRA: You have lots of people dying from it . . .
Some stupid small thing you wouldn't even expect . . . Some think it's no big deal . . .
and then somebody dies from it before they know.

VERA: So what.
It's just one person less.

MIRA: Everyone would want that.
To go quickly.
But somebody has to live through it up to the end, right?

VERA: And what if they can't?
They simply can't.

MIRA: Well, exactly . . . that's when one has to go on.

VERA: But when you can't . . . you completely, absolutely can't . . . There's nothing to go on to . . . you can't imagine anything to go on to. No matter how hard you try. You just don't imagine anything anymore. You just hit the end.

MIRA: That's what it takes. To live to the end. On and on.

VERA: Till when?

MIRA: When it's different.

VERA: How?

MIRA: When it changes directions.

VERA: The end is about not changing directions.

MIRA: At the beginning.
But when you live through it on and on and on . . . One day there has to be something different.
We should put some iodine on that.

VERA: Ew!
When it's this deep . . . it'll sting my entire life.

MIRA: Getting a sting is better than losing a leg.

VERA: Don't make a big deal out of it.
I just cut myself on a gravestone.

MIRA: Badly.

VERA: But I did tell you that I always do things badly.

MIRA: Then it needs to be cleaned.

VERA: I'm not afraid of death.

MIRA: You only think so.

VERA: That I know.
That I know for sure.

MIRA: You will know when it comes. Then . . . then you can say something.
Until then one just imagines things . . .

VERA: You just see it from one angle.

MIRA: Death is death . . .

VERA: Only when you fear it.
But you can also wish for it.

MIRA: Nobody wishes for death.

VERA: They do.
There are people who do.
They can't go on, they wish for an end.

MIRA: They wish for something . . . that's true . . . but death . . . nobody knows
. . .

VERA: But what about a suicide . . . huh?

MIRA: Well . . . but how do you know that he wished for death?
How?

VERA: He died.

MIRA: Because it turned out that way . . . but what did he want?

VERA: What?

MIRA: Well . . . what?
Something. Something else.

VERA: You don't know anything.
You don't know what it feels like to be at the end . . . when you can't . . . it's just
all these words, all these . . . you just see everything from the distance . . . you
come here to cut grass . . .

VERA *waves her hand. She stands and wants to leave. She winces in pain and
sits down again.*

MIRA: Bad?

VERA (*holds her knee*): Bad.

MIRA: Bleeding?

VERA: It's opening up.
And it won't wash out either.

MIRA: It's just way too deep.
It needs a bandage.

MIRA *takes the crumpled paper out of her pocket; it's already bloody. She holds it to* VERA's *cut again.*

VERA (*reads a piece of the text*): " . . . my sister, my love."
It's almost unreadable now.

MIRA: You think you'd be able to walk like 120 feet?

VERA: Where to?

MIRA: That little house over there. It's mine. There's water there. We'll wash it and bandage it.

VERA: That's a mortuary, isn't it?

MIRA: It used to be one.
It used to be a mortuary.
They gave it to me. I am allowed to stay there. All I have to do is take care of it here.
If I hold you up somehow . . . we could make it, couldn't we?

VERA: That isn't necessary, is it?
I just need to wait. It'll go away.

MIRA: It's dirty and deep . . .
What do you want to wait for?

VERA: I just cut myself on a grave.

MIRA: Here you go.
It happens before you know.

VERA *stands up.* MIRA *holds her.*

MIRA: Don't bend your leg!
Hold it on it . . .

VERA *is slightly bent. She is holding the paper on to her knee and staggers towards the small house, being helped by* MIRA.

VERA: My sister . . . my love . . .
Stupid grave!
Stupid grave!

They are slowly leaving the stage.

VERA: My stuff . . . my stuff, please . . .

MIRA *returns to the place where* VERA *left her backpack and Walkman. The bound pill packs fall out of her backpack.* MIRA *puts them back. She returns to* VERA. *It is getting dark.*

VERA: Stupid grave!

MIRA: They're sharp . . . the graves are sharp here.

VERA: It's because of the scythe.
Like because you keep cutting the grass here.

MIRA: You think so?

VERA: Stupid grave.

It's getting darker and darker. VERA *and* MIRA *disappear. The pills are left on the stump. The scythe lies close.*

Lights go on again. We are in a small room dominated by a big wardrobe; opposite to it is a bed. Maybe a chair is here too . . . only the necessary stuff. A small window. VERA *sits on the bed with her leg bandaged and stretched. On a little stool in the corner there is a small hot plate.* MIRA *stands beside it, making tea. There are two glasses somewhere.*

VERA: And how about water?
Where do you get water from?

MIRA: I bring it in bottles.
From public restrooms or from people. It depends.
Thyme tea . . . can I get you some?

VERA: Sure . . . whatever.

MIRA: It's from here . . . from the graveyard. It has its own spot there. (*She carries a bowl of something towards the bed.*)
Raspberries. From the graveyard too. Along the wall.

MIRA *gets onto the bed beside* VERA. *They are both sitting on the bed.*

MIRA: Help yourself, please.

VERA: Thank you.

They drink tea and eat raspberries.

VERA: And that?
What is that? (VERA *points to an inscription on the wall. It is written in Hebrew.*)

MIRA: Kaddish.
The Kaddish for the dead.
It was here.
> "Glorified and sanctified be God's great name throughout the world which He has created according to His will. May He establish His kingdom in your lifetime and during your days, and within the life of the entire House of Israel, speedily and soon."
Nice, isn't it?

VERA: You understand it?

MIRA: No.
But it is nice to look at . . .

VERA: Well . . . yeah, I guess.

MIRA (*looks around*): It's tiny here.
Tiny, but cool.

VERA: Cool.

MIRA: There was no window here.

I knocked one out.

VERA: On your own?

MIRA: Yeah . . . with my hands and a hammer.
One just shouldn't think about other people living differently. It's just important to live.

VERA: You'd go completely crazy if you thought about how they live . . .
I've got this . . . (VERA *shows* MIRA *her Walkman.*)

MIRA: A gadget?

VERA: There's music in it.
When I start to think too much, I listen to it. You want to?

MIRA: Well . . .

VERA *puts the headphones on* MIRA's *ears. She turns the Walkman on. We don't hear anything. We only see* MIRA *listening. After a while* VERA *turns off the Walkman.* MIRA *takes off the headphones.* MIRA *sings.*

MIRA: Boży baranku . . .
Boży baranku . . . what is that?

VERA: I don't know.
Baranek is like Polish for lamb, I think. Some small lamb.

MIRA: Nice.

VERA: It helps.
When I don't turn it on, when I don't hear it . . . I am capable of doing a lot of things.

MIRA: Me too.
When you think about people.

VERA: I have torn a few books, broken dishes, clothes . . . that too . . . I also broke . . . In fact I broke everything. So I had to run away. Now I walk. This way I don't break anything. Only I have to pinch myself every now and then. As punishment.
Do you understand?

MIRA: Yeah.

VERA: I used to even beat myself for an hour.
As punishment.

MIRA: Me, I don't eat.
A week, a month . . . once I didn't eat for two years. I only drink.

VERA: Well, I read a bunch of books. Psychology and stuff.
Different points of view.
For nothing.
Maybe that song.
That still kinda holds me together.

MIRA: Because somewhere inside me, I have this image that when I'm completely poor, completely withered, maybe somebody will feel sorry for me. Like having mercy, pitying me or something. Dumb, isn't it? And then I don't eat for a long time.

VERA (*holds the crumpled and bloody paper*): Then you have this?

MIRA: That too.
But I also have this . . . I have this.

MIRA *carefully rises, goes to the wardrobe, and opens it. Several beautifully-colored long dresses hang there.* MIRA *leaves the wardrobe open and sits down again.*

VERA: Wow.

MIRA: Neat, right?

VERA: Dresses?

MIRA: Blue, red, green, dark blue, brown, orange and white. All of it myself.

VERA: You made it?
You made all of it yourself?

MIRA: Yeah.
A color pops into my mind and I start sewing.

VERA: May I?

VERA *gets off the bed very carefully; her leg hurts. She goes to the wardrobe and takes out dresses, one by one. They are really beautiful. Beautifully colored, beautifully ornamented, long, simple . . .* VERA *hangs them on the wardrobe's door. She looks at them, touching some.*

VERA: Do you wear them?

MIRA: No . . . Not really.
Where would I?

VERA: You have never worn them before?

MIRA: No.

VERA: You could even sell those.

MIRA: Sell?
Do you know how painful that is?
I'm not selling them.

VERA: But it would be so cool! Lots of people would die to get dresses like these.
So authentic.
I've never seen such authentic dresses.
(VERA *leans her head against one dress.*) Authentic.

MIRA: Exactly.
But where would you wear it?
You cannot wear it anywhere.

VERA *looks at the dresses. Then she goes to sit back on the bed. She looks at them from that distance.*

VERA: Well . . . there really is no place to wear them to.

MIRA: There's nowhere to go.

VERA: Nowhere to go, right?

MIRA: People.

VERA: I'm a little out of it.
Out from them.

MIRA: Me, too.

VERA *stretches her leg.*

MIRA: Does it hurt?

VERA: A little.
That was also the last piece of something nice.

MIRA: Deep . . . I told you.

VERA: Yeah, stupid grave.

MIRA: Well, a knee . . .
It's liable to . . . it's so vulnerable.

VERA: It is, isn't it?
You first fall on your knee.

MIRA: Right.

Silence.

MIRA: And where do you live?

VERA: Nowhere.
I broke everything.
I just can't comfortably . . . everything is somehow forbidden within me . . . like
from inside. Never letting me do anything. Not even live somewhere.
And I deserve it anyway.
And this too. (*She points at her bandaged leg.*)
It is like a justice thing.

MIRA: I sometimes get the feeling that there has to be some way to live on . . .
what do you think?

VERA: Maybe it's like you can't live with all of it.
That life is about something else.

MIRA: But what then?
Are we supposed to kill ourselves or what?

VERA: Well, what if that's the real thing.

When somebody is like me, maybe they're meant to kill themselves. Just like other people are meant to have kids and families . . . or do something for people, so maybe I'm meant to kill myself.

MIRA: And do you want to?

VERA: What?

MIRA: Do it?

VERA: Sometimes.
And sometimes no.
Like when I listen to music.
But in fact I do more often than I don't.

MIRA: Aren't you scared?

VERA: I am.
You never know how many pills you should take. If it's enough. If it'll do the trick. And also, when you start swallowing them . . . you never know what'll be going through your mind, and maybe you'll want to stop, and also maybe you won't take enough of them, and it'll only make you sick, and maybe it it'll screw up your brain, but you will have to keep on living with it all the same.
It takes courage to be above that.

MIRA: I'm just scared.
It's stupid but I'm scared.
Even when I imagine how nice it could be, how I would wear one of those dresses and just lay down and then it would end.

VERA: And you wouldn't have to say all those awful things to yourself . . . the beating . . .

MIRA: You wouldn't be alone anymore.

VERA: No fear . . . you see, no fear, none at all.
It's hard to even imagine.

MIRA: Only it's too bad that someone has to find you. That's bad. That person would be so shocked. You probably won't look your best . . . like pools of blood around you.

VERA: You think of that too?
If only you didn't have to be found . . . if no one even knew about it, right?
You just wouldn't be any more.

MIRA: Maybe that could work if you lay yourself right into the grave.

VERA: Swallow it all there.

MIRA: Some abandoned grave . . . a little place where no one goes . . .

VERA: And you simply disappear.
Probably no one would even look for me.

MIRA: Same with me.

They both sit silently for a while, finishing their tea.

VERA: Four hundred.
I've got four hundred pills.
Forty packs of ten.

MIRA: I've got a razor blade.
One. It was here.

They are finishing raspberries and tea.

VERA: Thyme?

MIRA: Thyme.
From such a tiny spot in the graveyard.

VERA *reaches for the Walkman. She puts the headphones on her ears. She turns it on. She listens for a while. She turns it off. She takes off the headphones.*

VERA: Do you want to also?

MIRA: A bit.

MIRA *puts on the headphones. She listens. She takes off the headphones. She turns off the Walkman.*

VERA: The end?

MIRA: The end. (*sings*)
. . . daj mi życie ukryte w twoim ciele . . .

VERA: . . . daj mi swe ciało, abyś ty żył we mnie,

MIRA: . . . daj mi swą krew, aby we mnie było twe życie . . .

VERA: Nice.

MIRA: But you have to handle the worst part all alone, anyway.

VERA: No one can follow you into that fear. (*She sings a piece of the song.*)
"Boży baranku . . . "

MIRA: Boży baranku . . .

VERA: Four hundred . . . that's a lot, isn't it?

MIRA: I don't know.

VERA: You can scoop it into your palms . . . palms full of it.

MIRA *crumples the bloody paper and throws it at the dresses.*

MIRA: Once . . . once I'd like to put them on. At least once.
I'd really love that.
To put them on and go somewhere. Like a real person.

VERA: To see people.

MIRA: To talk to them.

VERA: Lunch, maybe.

MIRA: A walk.

VERA: The movies.

MIRA: Dinner.

VERA: To talk to someone.

MIRA: Good-byes.

VERA: A smile.

MIRA: An offered hand.

VERA: And being at home somewhere.

MIRA: Closing the door.

VERA: Lit-up windows . . .

MIRA *starts pinching herself. Sometimes she slaps her face or hits her body. After a while* VERA *starts pinching herself too. They sing louder.*

VERA: "Boży baranku . . . "

MIRA: "Boży baranku . . .
            daj mi życie ukryte w twoim ciele . . . "

VERA: " . . . daj mi swe ciało, abyś ty żył we mnie,"

MIRA: "daj mi swą krew, aby we mnie było twe życie . . . "

They are both lying on the bed now, hurting themselves less and less. It even seems that they are falling asleep. MIRA *starts to cuddle with* VERA. *After a while,* VERA *starts to toss. She starts pinching herself in her sleep. She also pinches* MIRA. MIRA *wakes up and watches her.* VERA *starts to talk in her sleep.*

VERA: No . . . no . . . please no . . . I'm disgusting . . . yes, I'm disgusting . . . bastard . . . I'll die . . . I swear . . . I'll die . . .

MIRA *sits on the bed. She looks at the suffering* VERA. *She reaches for the Walkman, puts on the headphones and listens to it.* VERA *is screaming in her sleep.* MIRA *extends her hand and lets* VERA *pinch her.*

VERA: Disgusting . . . most disgusting . . . I'll die . . . bury me . . . into the grave . . . I swear . . . I'll go to the grave . . . bastard . . . I'm a dirty bastard . . . dirty bastard . . .

VERA *tosses and turns.* MIRA *listens to the melody on the walkman, hands pressed against her ears. In pain, she starts humming a new song.*

MIRA: "Pomódl się Miriam, aby Twój Syn żył we mnie . . .
. . . aby we mnie żył . . .
Gdybym umarł, on żyłby we mnie . . .
Gdybym umarł, odpocząłbym . . . "

MIRA *listens for a while, then turns off the Walkman. She looks at* VERA *pinching herself, and hums the melody.*

MIRA: "Gdybym umarł, odpocząłbym . . . gdybym umarł . . . Pomódl się Miriam
. . . "

VERA: Please . . . I'll . . . I'll die . . . I swear . . . I'll die in the grave . . .

MIRA *winces in pain, jumps off the bed. She goes towards the dresses. She feels them with her hands and starts to call.*

MIRA: Vera . . . Ms. Vera . . .

It's getting dark. We only hear the voice of MIRA.

MIRA: Vera . . .

Darkness.

Light after awhile.

We are back at the Jewish cemetery. MIRA *and* VERA *are here.* MIRA *in a red dress;* VERA *in white. Both dresses are very beautiful.* VERA *and* MIRA *stand bent at the stump, looking for something, picking things from the grass.*

VERA: Almost there, we're almost there . . .

MIRA: You said four hundred.

VERA: Forty times ten.
But we can't find all of it, I guess.

MIRA: Once it's spilled . . .

VERA *rises from the ground. With her dress she holds a handful of pills.* MIRA *rises too. She holds pills in the same way.*

VERA: This will do.

MIRA: A lot of people would die from this . . . a whole lot.
But swallowing it . . . you were right about that.
That would take a long time.

VERA: You could also get sick . . . too soon . . . before you swallow it all.
And you will only be sick. Nothing else.

MIRA: Dissolve them.

VERA: What?

MIRA: Dissolve them in something, so you don't see them. And then drink it fast.
As if it was nothing.
How about the thyme?

VERA: What?

MIRA: There's some thyme left.
Would that mix together?
Would that be ok?

VERA: Yeah . . . tea.
That won't ruin it.

MIRA *pours pills from her dress into* VERA's *dress.*

MIRA: It won't, right?

MIRA *exits.* VERA *remains alone. She stands with a great number of pills in her dress. She looks at them. She sits with them, starts counting them, and putting them on the stump.*

VERA: Two . . . four . . . six . . . eight . . . twelve . . . fourteen . . . sixteen . . . eighteen . . . twenty . . . Richard . . . twenty . . . two . . . George . . . four . . . George . . . six . . . Martin . . . eight . . . thirty . . . nobody . . . two . . . four . . . nobody . . . six . . . nobody . . . eight . . . nobody . . . forty . . . forty . . . nobody . . . two . . . four . . . I'm not . . . six . . . I'm not . . . eight . . . I'm not . . . fifty . . . I'm not . . . sixty . . . I'm not . . . seventy . . . I'm not . . . eighty . . . I'm not . . . I'm not . . . I'm not . . . I'm not.

MIRA *returns, she holds two glasses of tea. She sits next to* VERA.

MIRA: Still warm.

They warm their hands on the cups of tea.

VERA: Warm.
It'll make it dissolve faster.

VERA (*smells the tea, sips some*): Sweet.

MIRA (*drinks too*): That's the thyme.
Over there . . . it has its own spot over there. It tastes like honey.

VERA (*sips the tea one more time*): Honey.

VERA *takes a handful of pills from the stump and puts them into her glass. She starts stirring it.* MIRA *also takes some and pours them slowly into her glass. She also stirs it.*

MIRA: Will it dissolve?

VERA: It needs time.

MIRA: And to keep moving.
Keep it moving all the time.

VERA: It's good that it's warm.

MIRA: It is, isn't it?

VERA *takes another handful and puts them into the glass. She stirs, but after a while she starts pounding the pills in the glass.*

VERA: Gotta grind it somehow.

MIRA *takes another handful of pills, pours them into her glass and starts pounding too.*

MIRA: Like milk, huh?

VERA: Yeah . . .
It'll never dissolve completely, you'll always be able to see it a little . . .
Milk.

MIRA: And moving . . . it can't settle down . . .
When it's moving, it's milk.

They both put the last of the pills into their glasses. They pound, they stir. A bit of the poisoned tea spills on VERA's *dress. She tries to wipe it off.*

VERA: I'm so sorry . . .

MIRA: It's ok . . .
You don't even see it . . .

VERA: A spot?
Won't it leave a spot?

Both set down the glasses and try to clean the dress.

MIRA: You won't even notice.

VERA: This you will . . . notice.
Look!
Look!

MIRA: What?

VERA: A hole.
It ate through it.

MIRA: Show me!
It did . . . it really ate through it . . .
Well . . . stop it somehow . . .

VERA: How?
Four hundred . . . Forty times ten.

MIRA: Maybe it won't stop, maybe it'll keep eating through it . . . on and on.

VERA: You mean into my body?
That it can really go into my body?

MIRA: Don't touch it!
You'd better not touch it.

VERA *stands. There is a hole in her dress at the level of her knee.*

VERA: It's slowing down.

MIRA: It's stuffed . . .

VERA: Pretty fast, huh?

MIRA: Real quick.
Funny it's on that knee again.

They keep stirring.

VERA (*sniffs the glass*): It doesn't even stink.

MIRA (*sniffs too*): Thyme.
It's getting stronger.

VERA looks into the glass.

MIRA: I used to kinda like milk.

VERA: Warm with honey.

MIRA: When I couldn't eat anything else.

VERA: Such sweet milk would even get you through the whole day, wouldn't it?

MIRA: Even longer.
Milk, does a body good.

VERA: Healthy . . . it's always said that it's real healthy.

MIRA: Calcium. So bones don't break.

VERA: Good for the stomach too.
When you're sick.

MIRA: So you don't throw up.

VERA (*rises with her glass and looks around*): Where?

MIRA: Over there . . . that spot near the thyme.

Both go to one corner of the graveyard. They stand there.

Pretty nice, isn't it?

VERA: Nice.
And hidden.

MIRA: Nobody comes here . . . nobody has anybody here.

VERA *inspects the ground. There is a dug-up grave. The scythe is leaning against the wall.*

VERA: Right in the thyme.

VERA *puts the glass aside. She wants to kneel at the grave. It does not work. She bends over. She begins touching the soil in the grave with her hands.*

MIRA: How is it?

VERA: Good.

MIRA (*kneels beside* VERA): Will it do?

VERA: Definitely.

MIRA: I didn't know about the length.
It's hard to estimate.

VERA: Like a bed. Almost.

MIRA: That's what I thought.
Done after the bed.
I also . . .
I discovered something, but I didn't have the courage . . . If you don't mind.

VERA: What?

MIRA: It is . . . in the trash heap.
People throw everything away here . . .

MIRA *rises and using the scythe, she begins to lift something over the wall.* VERA *helps.*

MIRA: I wonder what she is actually made of . . .

First we only see a piece of something, a head with hair flying . . . then MIRA *drags an entire tall statue over the wall. She stands it on the stump. Over the dug-up grave. For a while they both look at the beautiful statue.*

MIRA: I thought it could stand here.
If you don't mind.

VERA: What is it?

MIRA: I don't know.
A statue.
Somebody wanted to get rid of it, I guess.
Can you believe that?

VERA: People.

MIRA: To throw away a statue.
They could have given it to somebody . . .

VERA: She's pregnant, right?

MIRA *and* VERA *look at the statue of a young, pregnant woman. It's the Virgin Mary of Nazareth. Her dress resembles the dresses of* MIRA *and* VERA. *They touch her belly. They stroke her.*

MIRA: Absolutely.

VERA: Sixth or seventh month.

MIRA: Maybe even fifth. It's different for everyone.
But it's going to be a boy. Girls steal a mother's beauty.

VERA (*strokes the statue again*): Tired, a bit.

MIRA: And thrown away.

VERA: You can leave her here.

MIRA: Nobody will notice her here anyway.

VERA (*looks around*): She will have a nice view.
Of everything.

MIRA: The whole cemetery . . .

VERA: And houses too . . . over there . . .

MIRA: A field . . . rye, isn't it?

VERA: And wheat beyond that . . . it has a completely different color.

MIRA: And bluebonnets and poppies in the rye . . .

VERA: Forests . . . only forests . . . all around.

MIRA: Paths . . .

VERA: A river . . .

MIRA: The sky . . .

VERA: Everywhere . . .

MIRA: Wherever you look.

VERA (*pinches herself and looks into the grave*): Maybe it would be better right in that grave.

MIRA: It would, wouldn't it?

VERA (*moves her glass to the grave*): Within reach.

VERA *starts to crawl into the shallow grave. First she kneels beside it. It seems as if she unwittingly were kneeling before the statue. She winces.*

MIRA: Your knee!
Don't kneel!

VERA: Don't kneel!
And how am I supposed to get into the grave?
It won't be cleaned anyway. (*She lies in the grave.*)

MIRA: How is it?

VERA: Good.

MIRA: Also . . . also that hole . . . (*She fixes* VERA's *dress.*)
It's on that knee again.

And it's bleeding.

VERA: Stupid grave.

MIRA: At least you'll remember it.
Cutting yourself on a grave is just stupid.

MIRA *also places her glass beside the grave. She looks around. For a while, she looks around at the landscape . . . then, also as if by accident, she kneels before the statue, and she starts crawling into the grave too. She lays herself next to* VERA.

MIRA: Good?

VERA: Good.

For a while, they both lie motionless. The statue of the Virgin Mary stands over them.

VERA: Will it really . . . ?

MIRA: In a few months, nothing will be here.
Just thyme all over. Because it is . . . it grows everywhere . . . it doesn't need anything.

MIRA *throws some soil on herself. So does* VERA. *They lie down again for a while.*

MIRA: So?

VERA: Nothing.
I was just thinking of that stuff of yours . . . it's going through my mind.

MIRA: "Open to me, my sister?"

VERA: Well . . . that "My beloved put his hand to the latch . . . "

MIRA: And my heart was thrilled within me.
I arose to open to my beloved.

VERA: I opened to my beloved,

MIRA: But my beloved had turned and gone!

VERA: My soul failed me.

Silence for a while.

VERA: How could he just leave like that, right?

MIRA: Well, exactly.
Just like that . . . fast . . .

VERA: First he calls . . . and then disappears.

MIRA: If only he left her alone, she'd be fine.

VERA: He just shows her his hand . . .

MIRA: Just so she'd suffer.

VERA: Bastard.

MIRA: Isn't he?

VERA: And how about her?

MIRA: She sought him.

VERA: After all that, she was still chasing him?

MIRA: You bet . . . it took so much time . . . she lost everything . . . they beat her . . . she didn't have anything any more . . . Tired, ruined . . .

VERA: And did she find him?

MIRA: She did.

VERA: And?

MIRA: He was like:
Who is this who looks down like the dawn,
Beautiful as the moon,
Bright as the sun,
Awesome as an army with banners.

VERA: You understand it?

MIRA: No. I still have that stuff from the wall in my mind. Right before my eyes.
I still see it.

VERA: What?

MIRA: Kaddish.
I see it all the time.
Like it's alive.
But I don't understand.

For a while, they lie in silence. They are not moving.

VERA: It occurs to me sometimes . . . that maybe . . . that you have to have a
place of your own in the . . . that there is a place for you somewhere . . .

MIRA: That you belong somewhere, right?
Like you have the right to be . . . (*She pinches herself.*)

VERA: I've already completely broken everything.
There's no place for me. (*She pinches herself.*)

MIRA: Me, I'm just bones.
Just bones.
Everything living is gone.
Since I don't eat.
Just the milk. Sometimes.

VERA: You just cannot stop feeling that you're disgusting.
That you don't have the right.

For a while, they lie in silence. They pinch themselves.

MIRA: There is still more.

VERA: What?

MIRA: Did you listen to more of it?

VERA: What?

MIRA: That gadget.
There is still one more song.

VERA: After that Boży baranku?

MIRA: "Daj mi swe ciało, daj mi swą krew . . . " and then there is some more.

VERA: Really?

VERA *produces the Walkman. She puts the headphones to her ears. She listens. At her ear,* MIRA *listens, too. They hum the song,* VERA *takes one headphone off so that both can listen; we also hear the music a little . . .*

MIRA: "Boży baranku . . . "

VERA: "Boży baranku . . . "

MIRA: "Daj mi swe życie ukryte w twym ciele . . . "

VERA: "Abym umiał pójść za tobą, abym się nielękał utracić życie . . . "

MIRA: "Abym umiał pójść za tobą, abym się nielękał utracić życie . . . "

There is silence for a while.

MIRA: And now . . . now there's more . . .

They listen. We also hear the music a bit.

MIRA (*sings a little*): "Pomódl się Miriam, aby Twój Syn żył we mnie . . .
          Pomódl się, aby On we mnie żył . . . "
          Now!
          "Gdybym umarł, On żyłby we mnie
          Gdybym umarł, odpoczałbym
          Przyspiesz, przyspiesz moją śmierć
          Pragnę umrzeć, aby żyć"

VERA *turns off the Walkman.*

Silence.

Both are lying down.

VERA: "Pomódl się Miriam, aby Twój Syn żył we mnie . . . "

MIRA: Miriam.
Some Miriam.
Nice, huh?

VERA: Nice name.

They are both lying down. MIRA *turns her head, she looks at her glass.*

VERA (*sniffs*): Thyme.
You smell it everywhere here.

MIRA: Like I told you.
It is fine everywhere. It doesn't need much. Give it anything and it starts growing.

VERA: How come it smells so strong?

MIRA: That's the way it is.

VERA: It's all rotten here and it smells so nice from it.

MIRA: It always finds something good.
A little piece of something.

VERA (*leans her head back, looking at the statue standing over their grave*):
She could easily give birth now.
Maybe she is about to.

MIRA: And they throw her away.

VERA: How beautiful it could be somewhere.

MIRA: Even a tiny spot would do.
A tiny spot and it could look beautiful for them.

VERA *and* MIRA *look at the statue for a while.*

VERA: What was it like?
Awesome as an army with banners.
Well, she goes on even if she doesn't have the right, huh?

MIRA: Even if they throw her away . . .

VERA *bows her head. She begins to hum the melody.* MIRA *adds the words after a while. They sing abruptly. They raise their voices. They sing louder and louder. It is getting dark.*

MIRA: "Pomódl się Miriam, aby Twój Syn żył we mnie . . . "

VERA: "Pomódl się, aby On we mnie żył . . .
Gdybym umarł, On żyłby we mnie
Gdybym umarł, odpocząłbym
Przyspiesz, przyspiesz moją śmierć
Pragnę umrzeć, aby żyć"

VERA/MIRA (*shouting the last two lines*):
"Przyspiesz,przyspiesz moją śmierć
Pragnę umrzeć, aby żyć"

It is getting dark. Last light remains on the statue and the glasses. The scythe leaning against the wall slowly slides onto the statue. The statue is beginning to tremble a little bit . . .

The statue of the Virgin Mary is trembling.
Shouting from VERA *and* MIRA.

Darkness.

I PROMISED FREDDY

Egon Tobiáš

Egon Tobiáš
Photo courtesy of Petra Hůlová

Egon L. Tobiáš, born April 27, 1971, graduated in stage design from DAMU (the Theatre Faculty of the Academy of Performing Arts) in Prague, after which he did a one-year postgraduate course in book illustration and printmaking at UMPRUM (the College of Applied Arts). He has written 26 plays, debuting as a dramatist in 1992 with the play *Woyzef*, directed by Petr Lébl for the Labyrinth Theatre in Prague. Since 2000 he has worked closely with the director Jan Nebeský, who has staged most of his works, including *Mal D'or* (2000), *JE SUiS* (2001), *Tempest 2* (2003), and *Solingen: Merciful Blow* (2004). His plays have been translated into eight languages, including Spanish, Croatian, Italian, and German.

As a stage designer Tobiáš has worked with Opera Mozart, the Dejvice Theatre (where his design for the 1995 production of *Sestra Úzkost* won a Radok Award), and the Theatre on the Balustrade. He illustrates comics, paints, and works as a printmaker in the print studio Hamlet. He has worked with the publishers Petrov and Argo, and currently works with the Arts and Theatre Institute and Prague Stage Publishers. In 1995 three of his plays were published in a collection titled *Woyzef*, which he designed himself.

Although originally meant for radio, this play was inspired by the world of crazy film comedies.

I once saw a performance in English in Vienna that I didn't understand much of—in fact, almost none of it—but still it was fascinating. So I wanted to try writing a play that would be almost like a dream, where the audience wouldn't understand it through words, where the words wouldn't interrupt the dream. That's what I try to do to this day.

—Egon Tobiáš

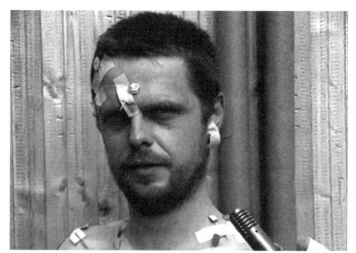

Ladislav Soukup in *I Promised Freddy* (2002), Eliadova knihovna at the Divadlo Na zábradlí Praha, directed by Jan Nebeský

Photo courtesy of Egon Tobiáš

I Promised Freddy

A Collector's Unbelievable Story

by

Egon Tobiáš

Translated by

Sodja Zupanc Lotker and Howard Lotker

CHARACTERS

COLLECTOR
FREDDY
SHEPHERD
JAPANESE TOURISTS' FEMALE GUIDE
MINER
AIR OPERATIONS INSPECTOR
GLENN, *an astronaut*
DIRECTOR OF THE INSTITUTE OF COSMIC RESEARCH
ARMSTRONG, *an astronaut*
VENUSIAN LADY
CNN ANNOUNCER
AIR OPERATIONS SECURITY CHIEF
CHILDHOOD FRIEND
PSYCHOANALYST
FBI AGENT

EARTH
The original countdown of the launch of Apollo 13, including flashes, roars of motors, whistling, and yells of excitement.

COLLECTOR: It was pitch black, but I was decided. I am not going to give up, I will keep my promise! I climbed to the top of the mountain and had been walking for a while on the ridge when I caught a glimpse of a shaggy shadow and the undulating bodies of sheep.

Wind, bleating of sheep.

SHEPHERD: We exchanged a few words. He was offering me something. Stamps or pins, I don't know anymore. I don't care about that stuff, I don't collect it. Then he pointed a gun at me or at least that's what it looked like, and so I took the miniature sheet with the monkeys.

COLLECTOR: I wasn't thinking; the ball was already rolling. As soon as I forced the Shepherd to take that darn miniature sheet with the monkeys, I broke free of his weariness and ran like crazy down the bear path to Snake Hollow.

Bus starting up, yodeling in Japanese.

JAPANESE TOURISTS' FEMALE GUIDE: I had just finished my talk about Snake Hollow with that funny comparison as usual and we were on our way back to the parking lot when that lunatic came and started shouting all that dirty stuff. The Japanese are very sensitive about that kind of thing, so I snapped at him and he threw himself right into the abyss. I don't feel guilty.

COLLECTOR: When I realized they weren't Collectors I had no choice but to jump. I was flying for about thirteen seconds, I lit a cigarette. I was decided, there's no turning back. I will keep my promise no matter what. There were just a few meters left. I quickly oriented myself at the bottom—I was running off toward the veiny rocks when . . .

In the background the sound of a pneumatic drill, in the foreground the click of a Zippo.

MINER: I admit the guy scared the heck outta me, but when I looked him over a bit I found those albums. I said to myself, this guy must be some kind of artist, and I dug a bit deeper. I didn't hardly have to do nothin' to get that miniature paper with the astronauts. Good deal, all in all . . .

The sound of a pneumatic drill is getting stronger; it echoes as if in a cave.

COLLECTOR: I gave a gift to the mole, though he bit a bit—but so what—forward, onward, there was still a chance. I ran up to the ramp completely wet with sweat. The engines were starting to glow, that's what they do. I was thinking, this is it, nothing is going to stop me now, but . . .

The sound of footsteps spreading over a big concrete stretch, echoing in the distance.

AIR OPERATIONS INSPECTOR: That guy had no business there. They should really figure out how he got there in the first place. He could have easily been a spy, God knows whose . . . (*laughter*) maybe from Mars. You couldn't get a word in edgewise with him, he just went on blabbing that he made a promise to someone—I kept on talking to him and the boys from security were already on their way. I know what I know and nobody without clearance has any business getting anywhere near that ramp. Well, then he took out those nails or pins and stabbed them into my overalls . . .

Very strong roar of engines, countdown in the background.

COLLECTOR: That nerd was still picking the pins from out of his uniform while I was hopping up the stairs, and bang—I was in the space suit. It all came together . . . I didn't even need a weapon. Freddy would probably not be too thrilled about it, but my plan was working out incredibly well . . . the only thing left . . .

The muffled sound of engines as if heard from the cockpit of a rocket.

GLENN: He broke in through the door and he was pushing himself into the cockpit, his receiver wasn't on or something. He just sat right down on Armstrong and put the seat belt on. It was irritating me, that camera of his kept banging against the visor, something easily could have happened. After a few hours I got used to it. Anyway, he was showing me his albums and I have to admit that it was a very decent collection, except for those Chinese cats—they were really kitschy.

Clicking of cameras, shuffling of papers, simply: sounds of a press conference.

DIRECTOR OF THE INSTITUTE OF COSMIC RESEARCH: Of course, not even during a simulated flight can one exclude certain dangers. Let's take the presence of an, to a certain extent, unauthorized person—a Collector for instance—that could, to a certain extent, get into the cockpit of the training machine.

Cosmic silence and cosmic roar, a weird rumble.

COLLECTOR: I wanted to get off, I also wanted to call Freddy and tell him what happened, but at that point we were going around and around on this orange road and there was no way to get off.

VENUS
A deafening bang, similar to a small explosion.

GLENN: We were not at all prepared for something like that. It was a bit like Christmas, I mean like getting presents and all. Me and Armstrong, we thought we belonged on the scrap heap. Even the flight was simulated. Who would have thought we would land on Venus? The first thing that came to my mind was: shit, how am I gonna explain this? Of course at the time I didn't connect it to the Collector.

COLLECTOR: I jumped out first. The Michelin men were stunned, but the footprints of my sneakers were already in the soil of Venus and I was off looking for a phone when . . .

The sound of Venus, weird voice of a female Venusian.

VENUSIAN LADY: Of course, he was not exactly what you'd call my "Little Prince," but he would have to do. He was unusually red and he kept on covering my body with sticky little papers with little teeth.

Dialing of the phone, phone beeps.

COLLECTOR: She was totally naked!!! I did find the phone, but there was no way I could remember the area code of our planet in that mess anyway.

EARTH
The radio news is on in the background, the whistling of a boiling kettle, sipping.

FREDDY: Yes, I remember the little blurb about it on TV very clearly. There was some kind of view from a telescope. They noticed what looked like a wedding on Venus.

Crackling sound of TV, crackling sound of the CNN ANNOUNCER.

CNN ANNOUNCER: And now, back to the accident at the Center for Cosmic Research in Tennessee Williams Snake Cave. Test pilots Armstrong and Glenn and some kind of . . . Collector . . . have disappeared together in a cloud of antimatter. And now we return you to . . .

Marbles falling from a height onto concrete, in the background the sound of a forklift.

AIR OPERATIONS SECURITY CHIEF: I was picking out the pins from my overalls and, when I took out the last one, I think it was some kind of a hammer and sickle emblem, I heard a weird roar and I saw a lot of light and then whoops, the flight simulator was gone. It threw me on that railing and since then I am here in this wonderful corner painting colorful pictures. The mole also came, he was smiling, he is my friend, he was very nice, we played . . .

VENUS
Weird Venusian music, in the distance weird Venusian laughter.

VENUSIAN LADY: Yes, I kept lending him to my girlfriends. How could I have known they would bruise him so much?

A clock ticking unbearably loudly.

COLLECTOR: I still don't understand it, I planned everything perfectly and then—boom—it was over. It felt like I was suddenly locked in a clock and I had to jump over the little hand every minute. Then a big one started coming closer, long like the little hand, but much fatter.

ARMSTRONG: No, I don't really mind it, what happened, happened. But that bit with the simulator was too much. Research is research.

GLENN: No comment.

EARTH
The radio news is on in the background, the whistling of a boiling kettle, sipping.

FREDDY: Actually, I didn't believe him from the start. If you ask me he is a lunatic, well, he's a weirdo . . . but he does have these special abilities. I told him that nobody collects those things nowadays, and that he won't get a dollar for it . . . I told him that here, on Earth, he simply won't sell it.

Hoarse sound of TV, hoarse sound of the ANNOUNCER.

CNN ANNOUNCER: Scientists from the Center for Cosmic Research now believe that there is not only water, air and life on Venus but also two astronauts and some kind of a . . . Collector.

The jabbering of hundreds of little children.

CHILDHOOD FRIEND: He was always weird, I am not saying he was a deviant, but he was weird, that's all, I can't tell you any more!

Hoarse sound of TV, hoarse sound of the CNN ANNOUNCER.

CNN ANNOUNCER: Cosmic fever is spreading; for some reason people have come to believe that these stamps and pins are redeemable for cosmic flights like some kind of intergalactic tickets. The story of the Collector is on the front page of all major newspapers all over the world—he is a real American hero— he has opened the eyes of the human race and fulfilled the dreams of many generations of, er, astronauts.

VENUS
A thousand balloons pop.

COLLECTOR: The big hand rammed into me and I thought it was all over . . . and then I heard the bang. One of those Venusian beauties was playing with my pins and . . . well, who would have thought that such a huge planet was inflatable.

Whistle of falling.

ARMSTRONG: Well, everything fell into pieces in a second. I felt like Baron Munchhausen.

Muffled whistle of a fall.

COLLECTOR: While you are flying through space it feels like you are falling from one embrace into another, but not all of the embraces are, let's say, pleasant. I don't know exactly what you'd call a Black Hole, but this one was definitely white. I flew into it like a fleck of ash into a vacuum cleaner.

EARTH
Tinkle of therapeutic balls.

PSYCHOANALYST: In 2030 his subconscious started showing what we call "acrobatic deviations." During these sessions it felt like I was in a flea circus. Later, during my own psychoanalysis, I found out that for a few years I had been analyzing a fictitious patient.

In the background we hear shooting at paper targets, a dot matrix printer, twenty phones ringing.

FBI AGENT: His portrait gave us little information. Was he human? Hard to say. This question can't be answered with certainty until we get the results of all the tests, which won't be for another three or four years.

COLLECTOR: And then it spit me out in the other world, into my wife's bed. She asked me if I would like some coffee or tea and I said radio. I took the rest of the albums from the table and I drank my radio and went off to meditate in the mountains. Before all that I phoned Freddy of course, I did promise I would call him in the morning.

Sound of alarm clock.

THE END

DAD TAKES GOAL KICKS

Jiří Pokorný

Jiří Pokorný
Photo courtesy of Martin Špelda

Jiří Pokorný, born April 4, 1967, began his career in the theatre studying directing at DAMU (the Theatre Faculty of the Academy of Performing Arts) in Prague. After completing his studies, he moved to the Drama Studio in Ústí nad Labem, where from 1993 to 1997 he served as the Artistic Director. During this time, Pokorný went to Antwerp to take part in the Tempus Educational Exchange Program in 1993, and later in 1995 was accepted to the playwriting program at the Royal Court Summer School in London. Considered part of the first wave of "cool" in the Czech Republic, Pokorný led HaDivadlo in Brno from 1998 to 2002, and then was one of the artistic directors of the Theatre on the Balustrade in Prague till 2006. His plays *Daddy Shoots Goals,* also known as *Dad Takes Goal Kicks*, and *Rest in Peace* were honored with the Alfréd Radok Award for Best Original Czech Play in 1997 and 1998, respectively.

Pokorný is currently working on a play called *Shackling*, which is his response to Havel's latest play *Leaving*; an adaptation of *The Taming of the Shrew* for Lucie Bílá; and a collaboration with Tomáš Meze, Kristina Cibulková, and others on a new version of *Othello* for the Aréna Theatre in Bratislava which he will direct.

I was sitting in a dive and I said to myself: All these broken men need a catharsis, and a story began to emerge . . .

—Jiří Pokorný

From left to right: Tomáš Krejčíř, Marie Spurná, Veronika Rašťáková, and Matúš Bukovčan, in *Dad Takes Goal Kicks* (1999), Činoherní studio Ústí nad Labem, directed by Jiří Pokorný

Photo courtesy of Martin Špelda

Dad Takes Goal Kicks

by

Jiří Pokorný

Translated by

David Short

This play is—with a blush and a promise of some embarrassment—dedicated to the torch of the torch-bearer of contemporary Czech drama, J.A. Pitinský. I hope he'll be forgiving.

CHARACTERS

JENDA (*pronounced YEN-da*)
MIREK (*pronounced MI-rek*)
RENATA
BLÁŽA (*pronounced BLAH-zha—as in "measure"*)
SLÁVEK (*pronounced SLAH-vek*)
DUŠÁN (*pronounced DOO-shan*)
BRONĚK (*pronounced BROH-nyek*)
VELEBORSKÝ
BLIZZARD, *an Alsatian dog*
POLICEMAN 1, *a policeman*
POLICEMAN 2, *a policeman*
EMT 1, *a paramedic*
EMT 2, *a paramedic*
DOCTOR

(Editors' Note: Much of the play is written in working-class Czech slang. We are using Standard American English, and suggest messing up the grammar every now and then.)

THE SCENE
A refreshment stall lit by a streetlight. On the left some scruffy shrubbery, a chestnut in bloom; on the right an entrance path disappearing deeper into the park. Further away a set of goalposts, of the size used in park games. In front of the stall, standing ideally on gravel, three tables and nine chairs.

The action takes place roughly between 2 and 4 a.m. in and around the Blažena 24-hour refreshment kiosk on June 22.

The text is riddled with punctuational ambiguity, which is a consequence of the situation's relativity.

SLÁVEK: You have to be gentle
look
like this and it'll go by itself
see

BLÁŽA: Ha ha stop messing will you
what good is it to me

SLÁVEK: Once more look
and there it is
but there are special coins for it

BLÁŽA: A twenty came up today
these Petra Lights burn away like paper

SLÁVEK: You don't know what to do with your hands
try it
honest it'll help
and I know various other ones
watch

BLÁŽA: Tricks from prison

SLÁVEK: You got a rubber-band?

BLÁŽA (*lighting up*): No. And please stop it

SLÁVEK: I know another trick with a rubber-band
a condom'll do
you got any?

BLÁŽA: You're crazy for God's sake no I haven't taken a walk through the trees
here you might find some

SLÁVEK: What if someone jumps me

BLÁŽA: It's quite fun with you

SLÁVEK: Or lend me your boxers for a moment

BLÁŽA: You're as nutty as a fruitcake

SLÁVEK: I'll let you have them back

BLÁŽA (*enjoying the conversation*): I'm well you can't have em
I'd catch a chill and what then
who'll take over for me here, any ideas

SLÁVEK: Me

BLÁŽA: Joker

SLÁVEK: Look they're here honest he really has brought him along the striker
I wonder what we're in for
hold on to your hat
the fun's about to start
wait for it

BLÁŽA: Really
good God
so Jenda's kept his word
are they smashed?

SLÁVEK: Don't look like it
they've got some chick with them
good looker
here they come

BLÁŽA: You owe me a bottle

SLÁVEK: Don't worry

Enter JENDA *in polyester trousers and a white freshly ironed shirt, carrying a backpack. Behind him, arms round each others' shoulders,* MIREK *and* RENATA, *tanned and casually dressed.*

JENDA: Hi

SLÁVEK: Hi

BLÁŽA: Hi Honza
fancy seeing you

JENDA: Ah
son Mirek and me are celebrating my name-day
so we've come out with his fiancée Renata
for a pint
so here we are

SLÁVEK Hello
I'm Slávek

RENATA: Hello
Renata

SLÁVEK: That's a nice seaside tan you've got

RENATA: We're just back from Greece Mirek had about a week off it's actually cheaper before the holiday season gets into full swing

JENDA: What'll you have
my treat
Mirek a beer?
What are you having Renata?

MIREK: I'll have a coke with ice
        JENDA: Won't you have just one?
        MIREK: I'm training later
        JENDA: Okay obviously not even a short
        RENATA: I'd like a spritzer it's terribly hot suddenly it's like high summer
        BLÁŽA: How d'you like it
        RENATA: In a big glass
        normal mix
        with ice as well

BLÁŽA: Sorry no ice left

RENATA: Hmmm
never mind
I'll have it without

MIREK: Is the beer cold?

JENDA Yeah
beer's good here

MIREK: Okay a small one

JENDA: Great
make mine a pint
and
yes and a rum

BLÁŽA: Double?

JENDA: Hell it's my day ha ha
          SLÁVEK: So it is
          There you have it
          it's St. John's Day
          JENDA: What'll you have
          You will have something?

SLÁVEK: Not now

RENATA: Mike it's great
there's no one here, mmh
I'd never have thought of coming here
the air's fabulous

MIREK: Don't call me Mike here
          RENATA: Why not you're weird okay
          JENDA (*tossing down a double rum at the counter*): Pour me another,
          Bláža
          BLÁŽA: I'll bring it to the table
          SLÁVEK: I'll take it to him
          BLÁŽA: That's all right just go and sit down
          JENDA: Okay
          I'll join the youngsters

JENDA: So
What do you think?

RENATA: I like it here
I was afraid we'd bump into bums
yet it's great
isn't it Mike

MIREK: Told you not to call me that
          JENDA: It's your nickname at the club now
          MIREK: Yeah, but on the field
          RENATA: At home as well though
          Mike just gets a bit embarrassed

MIREK: Cut it out will you

JENDA: What you said about bums it's right

but 'cause it's in the park you get tough cops here
real tough
then Bláža keeps a grip on things she does
    BLÁŽA: Here you are
    RENATA: Thanks
    JENDA: I come here at night 'cause it's quiet
    always have a chat with Slávek here or someone
    your health

RENATA: Good health all round
    JENDA: I'd rather drink to Mirek's here
    MIREK: My health's okay what about drinking to your liver
    JENDA: Since you're thinking
    of my
    all right
    long live my liver

RENATA: I've never ever come across anything like this father and son who
haven't seen each other for five years it's fantastic you've made up
isn't it Mike
stop scowling (*giggles*)

JENDA: You see Renata
sometimes life
well it's difficult
just as long as you two get along
and Mirek scores goals
that's the main thing now
grab each other
while you've got the chance and hold on to it
'cause not everyone gets a chance
and if you let it slip there might never be another

RENATA: That's right
    JENDA: Mirek's made me very happy that you've both come
    SLÁVEK *brings a tray with 4 shots of Becherovka.*
    RENATA: Those for us?
    SLÁVEK: Well Jenda's celebrating
    MIREK: Not for me
    BLÁŽA (*coming over*): Yes
    that's what we thought
    so Slávek ordered
    just the four

RENATA: Goodness I can't this spritzer's quite enough for me thanks honest

SLÁVEK: Just one
since it's Jenda's birthday

JENDA: It's my name-day
but I don't think one'll do you any harm

BLÁŽA: He talked me around too
I don't drink normally
      RENATA: What do you think Mike
      SLÁVEK: Your name Mike?
      Mine's Slávek

MIREK: Do what you want

SLÁVEK: Right
down the hatch

He empties the glass, lurches into MIREK. *They stagger and* SLÁVEK *filches* MIREK*'s wallet without anyone noticing.*

MIREK: Oops didn't mean to do that
"sorry".
Never mind
never mind
it'll wash out
that's okay, don't worry

BLÁŽA: Mmmm that was good
      JENDA: Bit sweet but all right
      SLÁVEK: Becherovka's not Fernet
      so what about it
      how about Fernet?

JENDA: Don't mind if I do
      RENATA (*giggles*): But leave me out this time really
      MIREK: Shall we go then?
      SLÁVEK: Okay two Fernets and two Becherovkas
      BLÁŽA: Only one
      I'm on till six then all night again tomorrow

MIREK: Renata
Jenda

right thanks Slávek
maybe later

RENATA: Won't you join us?
    SLÁVEK: I'd love to sit and chat but I'd have thought you'd rather be
    alone
    MIREK: I think we ought to be going
    RENATA: Already?
    SLÁVEK: Thank you young lady perhaps I'll come back later
    RENATA: Thanks listen Mike
    perhaps we should get him a Becherovka as well

MIREK: Get him a barrelful for all I care
alright
how on earth can you drink spritzer on top of Becherovka
beats me
honest
I'll never be able to understand

RENATA: I haven't got anything else to drink so what's your problem up to now
it's been great
Miss
two more Becherovkas
for Dad here and for that gentleman
just chalk it up on the board for now would you
and have you got anything to nibble?

BLÁŽA: Chips nuts pistachios cookies pretzel sticks chocolate wafers
    RENATA: I'd like what shall I have Mike
    MIREK: You got anything hot?
    BLÁŽA: I can make you a hot dog or a slice of meat loaf?
    RENATA: What's the meat loaf like?
    JENDA: Good I sometimes have it
    I'll have another beer Bláža

RENATA: I don't know perhaps I'll have some
what are you having

MIREK: I'd prefer a nice steak
    SLÁVEK: Me too
    RENATA: But Mike I'd really like something to eat don't I
    MIREK: Have some nuts
    RENATA: They're too salty

JENDA: The meat loaf really is good
BLÁŽA: Some bread with it or a roll?
RENATA: Or perhaps I'll have chips
MIREK: But they're just as salty
RENATA: All right no but then I don't know what
JENDA Don't know why I didn't think
I could've brought something from home
Sorry

MIREK: Sheesh!!! For goodness sake have something . . . if you wouldn't mind
Miss bring me some chips pretzel sticks pistachios
chocolate

BLÁŽA: What sort?
MIREK: Doesn't matter.
RENATA: What's up with you?
MIREK: You having something
or not
you can always throw it away
or take it with you or I dunno if you can't hurry up and choose
something
honestly it's driving me nuts or have a hot dog

JENDA: The meat loaf really is excellent
MIREK: And a slice of the meat loaf for my dad here
JENDA: You needn't have
BLÁŽA: Not the meat loaf
thanks
really

SLÁVEK: Hey there's sardines as well so if you've got an onion Bláža
I can make a sardine spread
you do have bread don't you

BLÁŽA: Where would I get that from you sure you don't want a jet plane? . . .
So come and get it I don't normally waitress
just that they were drinking a toast for Jenda's name-day so I came out
otherwise I don't see? . . . Here you are

RENATA: And get me another spritzer while you're at it

BLÁŽA: So here's the beer
shall I put it on your tab too

JENDA: No not the beer
    MIREK: Go on no harm done
    RENATA: So I'll try the meat loaf some other time
    when we all meet up again (*giggles*)

JENDA: Okay by me
    RENATA: What have you got in that backpack
    JENDA: Oh I was cleaning out the house
    so I've brought some of Mirek's old things
    from when he was a kid
    thought he might be really glad
    and one surprise for him

RENATA: I'm truly sorry we didn't have a present for you Mirek never said anything so I'm a bit annoyed with him aren't I
Mirek God they're a bit spicey these fries pity to waste them

JENDA: I don't need anything the main thing is you and Mirek here found the time
here
(*Unpacking the backpack and pulling out a shoebox.*)
some of your old papers letters odd postcards
and here
(*Taking out a slingshot.*)
look (*laughing*) your slingshot

MIREK (*absently accepts the box*): Hmm

RENATA: Wow can I borrow it you used to shoot things with it did you this is fun let me see that's the surprise?
    JENDA: No that's still in the backpack
    RENATA *aims the loaded slingshot at* MIREK.
    MIREK: Stop it stop that (*Sticks the shoebox in the garbage can.*)

JENDA: I thought
you might find a use for it

MIREK: No It's just old stuff I'd completely forgotten about
    JENDA (*taking a ball from the backpack*): Here
    MIREK: What's that?
    JENDA: A present take it
    it's for you

MIREK: You've got the name-day and I get the present
You should've given it to me when I was ten not now
it's like if I gave you a bottle

JENDA: Take it
it would make me happy
go on

RENATA: Go on Mirek
     JENDA: I also meant it as sort of a joke
     MIREK: A joker
     If I bought you a bottle would that be for a joke?

RENATA: Dad what Mirek meant by the bottle thing . . .
     MIREK: Why'd you call him Dad?
     JENDA: Give it a rest
     MIREK: You're not her dad
     RENATA (*laughing*): You're being clever again
     JENDA: Are you going to take it?
     SLÁVEK: We could have a game of penalties
     MIREK: Put it back in the pack
     RENATA: Mirek your dad's being nice to you
     MIREK: I don't want being nice to
     I'm tired
     let's go home
     Where'd the ball come from?

JENDA: It's a soccer ball
Not new I know
bit worn here and re-stitched
but I got it just so I could give it to you
and so we could even have a kick-around today
inflated it this morning
so?

SLÁVEK: I wouldn't mind a game
     MIREK: Where d'you get it
     JENDA: Bought and paid for
     Mirek . . .

MIREK: When?
     JENDA: 'Bout a week back
     MIREK: Where?

RENATA (*long giggles*): I like it it's a really nice one I'll go in goal.

She dribbles and passes it to SLÁVEK, *who starts showing off, then passes to* MIREK.

MIREK: So this is your present for me . . . so . . . a ball . . . football
mmm thanks . . . so what now
Another beer?
What do you want?
Me to have a kick-around with your guys?
(*To* RENATA.) You keep quiet

JENDA: I wanted to see you and give you something as well
      MIREK: You don't say
      JENDA (*tears gushing from his eyes with the strain, he goes to the kiosk counter*): Rum!
      (*Briefly gets a grip on himself, then bursts into tears; repeats this several times.*)
RENATA *bursts into tears.*

MIREK: Bitch!

RENATA: Wash your mouth out will you!!!
Keep your hands off me!!
(*Goes to the counter.*) A Becherovka (*Puts her arms around* JENDA.)

MIREK: What's going on now
bitch
what's this
hell
(*He goes to the counter, takes the empty glass from* RENATA's *hand and smashes it.*)

      BLÁŽA: Young man you wouldn't like to smash up my stall as well would you I don't care much for the awful way you're treating your father and fiancée you must be some sportsman if that's the way you live that's fifteen crowns I'm putting on your bill
      MIREK: How much for the stall?
      RENATA: Mirek stop it and
      let go of my arm do you hear

MIREK: How much then?
      BLÁŽA: Millions

MIREK: How many
BLÁŽA: Do you know what
take your young lady and go
you can have your drinks on me
but I'll be sending the bill for the glass to your club
Here Jenda take this hankie

MIREK: What? . . . Father?!!
JENDA I told her you play for Sparta
MIREK: For God's sake how did you know
the transfer isn't sewed up yet
you shouldn't go about blabbing they're still negotiating
God it makes me insane
Bill please Christ did you see where I put my wallet

RENATA: Calm down first
MIREK: This is ridiculous haven't you got it it was here in this pocket
hell have you got it?
RENATA: I haven't got anything
MIREK: Don't be so dramatic you're drunk
see if you haven't got a thousand at least
BLÁŽA: Hundred and eighty-two fifty
JENDA: Put it on my tab
I get my pension next week
you'll get it all then Bláža

BLÁŽA: Let your son pay for himself
throwing his weight around all the time
wanted to buy my stall and God knows what
so he can pay up
he can go home
I'll wait here for him let him go home
he must have got plenty of cash there like you said Jenda and he's so uncivil

JENDA: Please don't talk like that don't you go pissing me off
MIREK: What did he say??
JENDA: Didn't say a thing
just Bláža here
stay out of it Bláža

MIREK: What did he say?

BLÁŽA: That you're fantastically rich

that clubs all over Europe are fighting over you
that you'd easily save him from poverty
but Jenda says he doesn't want you to even if you begged him and damn right
too

JENDA: But I never said that

BLÁŽA: Yes you did
I always know very well what you'll say

JENDA: I didn't and give it a rest will you?
   BLÁŽA: You did
   MIREK: Whaddaya mean clubs are fighting what clubs are fighting
   Where do you get that from you dare to bullshit with me like that here
   you know damn well that
   they're still talking
   I don't want you fussing about me
   or even talking about me it's my affair and my life
   is no business of yours

JENDA (*showing him a newspaper clipping*): Stop shouting
Mirek look
it's here in black and white
I cut it out and keep it with me wherever I go

BLÁŽA: Bought up all my stock to give away to the guys

SLÁVEK (*showing his own cutting*): I've got one too
I want it autographed

MIREK: Journalists do more harm than good
you've no idea of the problems I have to cope with
(*Giving* SLÁVEK *his autograph.*)
all the denying this and confirming that
and still nothing's certain
and here's you taking the credit for me yourself!
Come on Renata we're leaving
I'll drop by with the money tomorrow
I've got a training session in the morning come on then
My next training's tomorrow morning
Okay I'll go and get the money
I still had my wallet an hour ago
ah well must have lost it

four thousand down the tubes . . .
we're off stop standing there with your mouth open we're going come on
shake hands and give them a kiss Sweetie we're off
I might've guessed it was all a con!

JENDA: For God's sake Mirek what do you mean a con
I'm glad to see you

RENATA: I'll wait for you here
I'm going to chat to your dad
and I'm no Sweetie of yours today

SLÁVEK (to BLÁŽA): Has Jindra been around?
        BLÁŽA: Not that I've seen
        SLÁVEK: Get me a coffee
        This ain't no good
        no one about
        no fucking party
        you said we were going to have a ball Jenda
        Jenda Benda's gone to sea da-dee da-dee da-dee-dee
        Ah well

MIREK: You coming?
Get moving

RENATA: No
        MIREK: So you're not coming?
        RENATA: No
        MIREK: Meaning you want to stay?
        RENATA: Yeah
        MIREK: Fuck all, why'd I bother coming
        Coach's going to kick the shit out of me
        I hate booze

BLÁŽA: Hundred and eighty-two fifty for just you two and a hundred and twenty
for your socially disadvantaged father
it's his day but even if it isn't
I'll make an exception and he can have it on the house
I don't play for her team but I don't mind treating an old friend

JENDA: Don't worry Bláža I'll make it all up to you one day

BLÁŽA: Oh go on
and stop sniveling

MIREK: Renata I'm telling you come on
    RENATA: Let go of me I'll have bruises
    MIREK: All right, ok
    all right
    I'll get a cab back

RENATA: Just go will you still standing here babbling
    MIREK: Do you mean that?
    RENATA: What?
    MIREK: Me babbling

RENATA: You're in a foul mood and you've been saying such stupid things that my heart's been ready to break from the start of the evening I can't take much more of this

MIREK: No
You accused me of babbling

RENATA: You've been behaving awfully

MIREK: You say that as if I've never told you
about my childhood

JENDA: Go with him Renata I'll pay it out of my pension I get it next week

RENATA: No just let him pay himself
His table's covered in fries and stuff
I dunno . . .

MIREK: That'll do madam
    BLÁŽA: Mirek's such a terrific guy they say
    big spender
    sensitive and generous

MIREK: Excuse me nobody's talking to you
    BLÁŽA: I wouldn't say that right Slávek
    SLÁVEK (*to* JENDA): Well I dunno should I go in to work shouldn't I . . .
    MIREK: You coming then Renata?
    RENATA: Could you give me a tea Miss I'm feeling a little cold
    SLÁVEK: And a rum for me can't do me any harm
    RENATA: All right (*giggles*)
    MIREK: I'm off
    RENATA: Get back soon shall we sit down Mr. Vracel?

MIREK: Kiss
RENATA: Another time maybe
MIREK: I think we'll be having words about this (*exit*)
SLÁVEK: I'll join you
BLÁŽA: Might as well get out there now
treat myself to a bit of fresh air
SLÁVEK: You should've pounded on him
JENDA: Do you mind he's my son for Christ's sake
BLÁŽA: All you can think of is pounding on people
very nice
really
I reckon they pounded on you a bit much

SLÁVEK: I gave as good as I got

BLÁŽA: Oh yeah oh yeah you
ha ha I bet you did

SLÁVEK (*offers her his flexed biceps and looks towards* RENATA):
Have a feel
go on feel it
and that's not the hardest muscle
I've got either

BLÁŽA (*laughing*): I've got an Alsatian indoors trained for
you know what you know what
. . . just watch it

SLÁVEK: He's always dopey
JENDA: Hic probably eats too much hic
RENATA: What's he trained for?
BLÁŽA: Slávek's a dirty bastard
so I have to frighten him a bit now and again

SLÁVEK: I'll tame him
Want to see me tame him?
Just let him out
Go on let him out
I think I'll show him something he won't get his jaws around
(*Undoes his fly.*)

JENDA: Whadda you . . . whadda you . . . whadda you . . . whadda you
. . . whadda you

thinking of you skunk . . . let's have none of that
. . . skunk

BLÁŽA: Leave him Jenda
and you're crazy Slávek a raving lunatic

RENATA: So have you really got an Alsatian in there or not?

BLÁŽA: Course I have
I wouldn't be doing this job without my Blizzard
Come and have a look at him

RENATA: I love dogs but I'm also a bit afraid of them

SLÁVEK: Blizzard's an old sucker
'cause women don't have nothing to bite off

JENDA: Just go will you
go before you really piss me off
go will you
fuck off you old bastard
I'll kill you I'm telling you
I'll kill the shit outta you

BLÁŽA: Break it up or I'll stop serving you
come and have a look
(*Opening the door.*)
Blizzard
Blizzard good boy you dopey old thing
come inside so there'll be just the two of us for a change
dopey old thing

They disappear inside.

    SLÁVEK: Nice tits
    JENDA: Hmm
    SLÁVEK: Not too bad-looking, huh?
    must give her the once over it being
    Midsummer's Night and all that
    Don't worry
    I might feel her up a bit
    but I won't screw with her
    but only 'cause you're my buddy

JENDA: You're pissing me off

SLÁVEK (*laughing*): She'd go for it, old man
I'd give it to her here in the bushes
you wouldn't even notice
she wouldn't either
right now her memory's shrunk smaller than her cunt

JENDA (*as if suddenly sober*): I'm warning you

SLÁVEK: Your son's turned out bad but her
what about her?
When they get a house
tell me
the boy's away at a match
she's by the stove in her panties and says
what'll you have Dad what d'you like
huh? what will you say?

JENDA *bends down slowly to reach for the slingshot under the table and gropes for a stone.*

SLÁVEK: She'll sit on the table
open her legs wide
her cunt smelling better than the stew
so take yer pick Jenda get an eyeful
had enough huh? . . . (JENDA *stands erect over the table, takes a few steps back and aims.*)
I left my apple at home
Dad William ha ha Tell you stupid twit give it here
you'll hurt yerself
stop aiming at me or
I'll hit you come on don't try anything
I'll give you what for you lousy jerk you promise
your son that plays for Sparta will give us a game
he's a conceited creep
we're nothing to him couldn't give a shit about us
and you threaten me with a slingshot
d'you know what would happen to you inside?
You know what'd happen to you?
Look I did everything I could to keep him here
unlike you so I'm going to enjoy myself
(*Takes* MIREK*'s wallet out of his pocket.*)
you fucking cunt

JENDA *fires and shoots* SLÁVEK *in the eye,* SLÁVEK *staggers with pain but silently, then collapses to his knees and hisses:* "ohfuckohfuckohfuckohfuck." JENDA *leaps on his back, grabs him by the forehead, strains both arms until there's a crack and* SLÁVEK *is dead.* JENDA *drags him into the bushes and finishes his beer. After a moment he notices that* SLÁVEK *'s legs are poking out of the scraggy bushes, goes back to him in a matter-of-fact manner and drags him further in. Enter two grinning young men* DUŠAN *and* BRONĚK *in cheap suits and with attaché cases; at the same moment a slightly tipsy* RENATA *comes out of the kiosk.*

RENATA: Hello.

She goes and sits at a table, opens a packet of peanuts and tips them into her mouth. Smiling uncertainly at the two men she munches on the nuts.

DUŠAN: You alone?

RENATA: Just for a moment.

BRONĚK: Any chance of being served, Miss?

He taps on the window, silence.

DUŠAN: It's like a submarine with the engines turned off

BRONĚK: Is there no one there, Miss?

RENATA: There was.

BRONĚK: And who . . .
just like a fairy-tale, don't you think?
The sixteen ravens?

DUŠAN: Seven . . . seven, somewhere hereabouts

RENATA: Blažena's there, and Blizzard.

BRONĚK (*to* DUŠAN): Blažena's mobile brothel with an alpine theme, except this fucking chalet hasn't got any wheels
too bad, we'll have to fuck outside

DUŠAN: Blizzard?

RENATA: Uh-huh

DUŠAN: Now there's a thing and how are you feeling

BRONĚK: Hello there (*Knocks on the window.*) hello hello hello

BLÁŽA: What'll you have?

BRONĚK: Mmm . . . what've you got and what does what you've got cost

BLÁŽA: What exactly do you want?

BRONĚK: I'll have a drink first
how about some bubbly . . .

BLÁŽA: Tea's out, I'm out of water

BRONĚK: Dušan, come here and stop staring
the young lady's eating can't you see?
Somebody's bullshitting me
come on don't stand there like an asshole, are you listening . . .

DUŠAN: I can hear you

BRONĚK: The lady here claims to be out of tea
That's an odd thing. I wonder what she was like *in* tea.

DUŠAN: It's June and four in the morning, ain't it . . .

BRONĚK: Okay, but I don't know what she means

DUŠAN: So ask her

BRONĚK: I wanted champagne, can you figure it out?
there's rules ain't there
market mechanisms and stuff and she's
screwing around with me

BLÁŽA: Don't get nervous sir just tell me what you want
and either I'll tell you that
I've got it
or that I
haven't
that's all

BRONĚK: I'll have . . . smoked snake

BLÁŽA: Haven't got any

DUŠAN: So gimme the same as what this young lady's drinking
I guess that's simple enough

BLÁŽA: I told you I'm out of tea

DUŠAN (*slurring his speech*): Buy a bottle and let's sit down my feet are killing
me

BRONĚK: What've you got that's more expensive?

BLÁŽA: Antonín Dvořák vodka for 480 crowns

BRONĚK: Say that again?

BLÁŽA: Antonín Dvořák vodka for 480 crowns

BRONĚK: Is this the ministry of music?

BLÁŽA: Aren't you the joker

BRONĚK: Just checking, in case you're trying to confuse me . . .

BLÁŽA: I said four hundredandeighty crowns and if you've got no money don't
go asking for expensive items, sir
that means that if you ask for cotton socks instead of nylon
better ones you might feel better
but don't go trying that kinda thing on me
in short
if you haven't got 500 quit showing off

BRONĚK: That's no way to speak to a customer!

BLÁŽA: Look here, sir I always try to be as obliging as possible to my customers
in my somewhat confined circumstances

BRONĚK (*shouts over to* DUŠAN): Got any cash?

DUŠAN: Mmm . . .

BRONĚK: Come and kill this woman so I don't have to . . .

BLÁŽA: Fourhundredandeighty crowns please, and I recommend no lemon ice or anything

BRONĚK (*nudging the sleeping* RENATA): What do you do during the day, miss
I don't suppose you sleep all day and now
Wakey, wakey, rise and shine
Fat chance
(*To* DUŠAN.) Dammit, the bitch is smashed out of her mind
hell Dušan
I tell you
she's out of it
you following me?
I'll just have a quick look round to check if anyone's watchin'
see
the old cow's got doughnuts for eyes
I'm going to take a leak, I'll be right back . . .

DUŠAN (*jogging* RENATA*'s legs*): Miss, miss

BLÁŽA (*comes out of the shack and almost wakes* RENATA):
Come on, come inside
you can lie down

DUŠAN: I expect she's worn out . . . yeah?
. . . it's been pretty hot

BLÁŽA: She's had more than enough today

DUŠAN: She's past it, no? She's good-looking . . .

BLÁŽA: See here, mister if you're contemplating any impropriety
you'd be better off avoiding trouble and going home . . .

DUŠAN: What d'you mean, trouble?

BLÁŽA: I mean what I mean the cops are around here every five minutes and
and I've got a dog inside
(*She shows him her mobile.*)
you're a disgusting bunch
you and your friend
she's not one of your . . . she's going out with Mirek Vracel, the guy who plays

for Sparta
you horny bastard
we've had a bit of a problem but that's just people for you
. . . Renata
come and wait for Mirek inside . . .

DUŠAN: Okay sorry . . . I didn't know . . . sorry
. . . . will you have a glass with me . . .

BLÁŽA: No thanks

DUŠAN: I *am* sorry, honest

BLÁŽA: . . . Come on Renata . . . there . . . gimme your hand . . . and don't go
puking . . .

DUŠAN: You really won't have a drink with me?
That vodka's really something

BLÁŽA: Don't talk to me I don't like you and your friend and that's the end of it

RENATA: Where's Mirek . . . ?

DUŠAN: You give short measures like hired staff, that's what I think . . . I wonder
what'd happen
if an inspector turned up

BLÁŽA: I'd be shot

Dawn begins to break.

Enter the fisherman VELEBORSKÝ *in camouflage outfit, with all his fishing
tackle and a backpack.*

VELEBORSKÝ: Morning Blaženka Tea

BLÁŽA (*dragging* RENATA): Mirek'll be back soon
You have a little lie-down,
Blizzard will keep an eye on you girl

JENDA (*returning*): Where are you hauling her off to
What's happened . . .

BLÁŽA: Where've you been all this time?

JENDA: Went for a bit of a stroll

VELEBORSKÝ: Someone's been having a whale of a time by the looks of it

JENDA: You had a good time?

BLÁŽA: Tea

VELEBORSKÝ: One tea and two bottles of beer to go I dreamed about are you listening to me?
Rockets with teeth, Blažena and then these two rabbis were explaining how they put their socks on in the trenches you just lie on your back and pull them on

BLÁŽA: Has Slávek gone?

JENDA: Yeah, gimme a shot of rum darling if I'd met you earlier

BLÁŽA: What would you have done with me?

JENDA: Who cares

BLÁŽA: So rum was it?

JENDA: It's all on me (*Takes out his son's wallet.*) That guy I saw off stole my boy's wallet

BLÁŽA: How'd you find out?

JENDA: He dropped it, Granny

BLÁŽA: Don't push your luck, ok? How did he drop it?

JENDA (*crying*): I helped him and today we'll push the boat out

BLÁŽA: Jenda, this is serious . . . how come you didn't figure it out sooner before Mirek went home for some money I wanted to punish him for being rude to his dad, who might like a drink or two, but otherwise he's a good man, then he goes and lets me down 'cause for one thing I've got Renata asleep in my shack, then I purposely bumped up the price of fries because of the way he was swaggering and you're mad you've no idea what's going on (*furtively*) Some guys we've never seen are after Renata

JENDA: Guys we've never seen?

BLÁŽA: I'll call a cab now you've Mirek's money home and dry

JENDA: Don't
Mirek's bound to come
He's bound to pop back for a moment
don't call that cab
let the little lady sleep . . .

VELEBORSKÝ: I'd like that tea

BLÁŽA: Hang on, I'm not a machine

BRONĚK (*coming back, to* DUŠAN): It's all wet everywhere must be dew or something
She'll be no good standing up
I'm not going to get my jacket dirty today
where is she
did you let her go?

DUŠAN: I was petting her
then her royal highness here took her inside
Have the vodka

BRONĚK: She's a fucking slut
boozes
sleeps
she don't fuck
what does she live on, huh, think about it

JENDA: Did I hear right?

BRONĚK: What

JENDA: Something about prostitutes or . . .

BRONĚK: Who's that prick?

DUŠAN: Dunno, he's only just turned up

BLÁŽA: Where's Slávek, Jenda?

You disappear for a sec to feed the dog
how clever of you
So where's Slávek now
silly ass that he is
I'm sorry but I understand why he pounded on your boy
he was going to rip *him* open
I saw it
coming
didn't I?
he was watching him from the start

JENDA: If you could suspend your eloquence Blaženka and gimme another shot of rum . . .

VELEBORSKÝ: Tea for me
is it boiling yet

BLÁŽA: Here your bottles o' beer

JENDA (*pause*): Some party this has been
dunno why I bother to celebrate
this is great
I wasn't expecting this
Something about prostitutes or . . .

BRONĚK: No
we're talking about whores
thanks for asking
good night
kindly wizard

JENDA: I don't care about anything today

BRONĚK: Thanks for the information

JENDA: Anything at all

DUŠAN: Good night

JENDA: What'd you mean jerk
stop staring at me

BRONĚK: Did I hear right?

DUŠAN: Don't let him get to you don't let him get to you here, have a drink

BRONĚK (*to* DUŠAN): He makes me mad dammit mad mad

BLÁŽA: Jenda, would you like some meat loaf . . . ?

VELEBORSKÝ: That tea's a bit
won't it brew or something look at it.

JENDA: Look woman I've just started a lifetime fast so keep your meat loaf and food to yourself, ok?!!

BLÁŽA: It's ordinary PG tea.

BRONĚK: Crazy

DUŠAN (*to* VELEBORSKÝ): I like your tackle
Shakespeare's?

VELEBORSKÝ: Aha

DUŠAN: Can I see?
I fish myself sometimes . . .

VELEBORSKÝ: No

DUŠAN: Why not?

VELEBORSKÝ: I won't let them out of my hand

DUŠAN: Sure . . . principles . . . all I want's a quick peek . . .

VELEBORSKÝ: No

DUŠAN: There's no need to get excited pal

BRONĚK (*standing up with his pistol drawn and utterly composed*):
Gimme them rods . . .

DUŠAN: Ha ha Broněk put that thing away
(*To the others.*) He doesn't mean any harm
All I wanted was to have
a chat about fishing

BRONĚK (*to* VELEBORSKÝ): Give him them rods right now
and you
(*To* DUŠAN.) you
you show me how you cast for sander

DUŠAN: Sit down, Broněk
have a shot of vodka
stupid idiot, what's got into you

JENDA *sneaks across for his slingshot, which is still lying by the table.*

BRONĚK: You sit here on the ground
kindly wizard
you woman stub that butt out
right now
if there's anything I can't stand it's smokers
put yer hands above yer head that's right just like in a film

DUŠAN: I'm going home

He tries and fails to grapple BRONĚK *from behind.*

Broněk . . .
. . . I haven't been fishing for ages
I've no idea how to catch a sander
Put the cannon away stop acting crazy

BRONĚK: Then we'll get the bitch

DUŠAN: Okay . . . So excuse me Mister . . .

VELEBORSKÝ: Veleborský

DUŠAN: Mr. Veleborský
so I'll try and show my partner here
how you cast to catch a sander it's just a game
that thing isn't loaded

BRONĚK: Oh yes it is

VELEBORSKÝ: That telescopic rod is an ordinary one you've got weights and
hooks there too

BRONĚK: And no tricks Dušan
I'm warning you don't go near that
backpack

VELEBORSKÝ: It's only a blanket . . . Blaženka I've come to tell you I love you it's
sheer hell at home and . . .

BRONĚK: Button it
our kindly wizard is going to stay put

DUŠAN: I'm ready now . . .
. . . come on home Broněk
it's morning

BRONĚK: Now tell me this kindly wizard
who called me a jerk just now
I'll have him for breakfast . . .

DUŠAN (*wielding the rod*): With your permission kindly wizard

As he casts the line, the hook sinks into BRONĚK's *head,* BRONĚK *fires
spontaneously hitting* VELEBORSKÝ *in the leg; the gun falls from his hand.*

VELEBORSKÝ: Owww

BRONĚK: What's up you bastard have you shit in your pants

DUŠAN: Sorry Broněk
didn't mean that to happen (*Pulls the hook out of him.*)

BLÁŽA (*calling from the shack*): Mr. Veleborský, speak to me
speak to me
Are you alive Véna?

VELEBORSKÝ: I'm not quite done for yet

MIREK (*running in*): Dad . . .
. . . what's happened to Renata?

DUŠAN *kicks* BRONĚK's *gun towards* JENDA *and runs away.*

JENDA: Get away!
Mirek . . .

MIREK: Where's Renata?

JENDA (*grabs the gun and aims at* BRONĚK): You're under arrest sir

BRONĚK (*with his hands above his head*): This looks serious

JENDA: You bet

MIREK: Dad please where's Renata?

JENDA: In there son

BRONĚK *makes a break.*

Stand still you

MIREK *bursts into the kiosk. Then a strange sound is heard followed by a harrowing shriek from* MIREK *that seems never-ending, joined after a moment by* RENATA*'s hysterical screaming against the background of* BLÁŽA*'s shouting* "Blizzard Blizzard" *in a tone of growing resignation.* BLÁŽA *comes staggering out.*

BLÁŽA: Oh Christ Jenda Blizzard's got his teeth
into your boy's
balls
I can't drag him off
do something

JENDA (*to* BRONĚK *with icy calm*): You got a mobile?

BRONĚK: Here in this pocket

JENDA: Nice and slow reach into your pocket so I can see everything
and phone
for an am-

BLÁŽA: I've already called the cops

BRONĚK: Oooo

VELEBORSKÝ: Owww
fucking fishhooks
my leg
call all the

BRONĚK: Yes hello
there's been an accident
it's like
a dog's kicked it

A noise from the kiosk. RENATA *comes out.*

RENATA: I'm really sorry Blaženka I've killed Blizzard (*Wipes the blood from her mouth.*)
Mirek mirek mirek mirek (*Staggers off back inside.*)

BRONĚK: There's a kinda
oh dammit
wood or something
and I've shot this guy
a fisherman
in the leg

JENDA: Gimme that
careful though
Vřesanský Park near the stadium that's right and bring along a wooden
sleeping-bag
the police are on their way the dog Blizzard has bitten off my boy's . . . he's
injured him bastard no not you get here quick my boy's bleeding and I can't
comfort him 'cause I've got to keep my eyes on this other bastard (*To* BRONĚK.)
I've already taken one down today
Renata Renata
Renata Renata
Renata speak to me
Renata how's Mirek
Renata is he alive?!!!!!
Renata please answer me

RENATA (*peeping out of the kiosk*): He's alive
He's still alive
I wish they'd get here quick

JENDA: Shit
LifesabitchohMirekwhatthehellshappened

Long pause. The sound of crying.
The wailing of a police siren.

JENDA *points the gun at* BRONĚK*'s groin.*

BRONĚK: No please no

JENDA *moves the gun-barrel to point-blank range, takes aim, and squeezes the trigger.*

BLÁŽA: Oh Christ Jendaaaaaa

BRONĚK: Help

POLICEMAN 1 *and* POLICEMAN 2 *run in with pistols drawn.*

POLICEMAN 1 (*shoots* JENDA *in the shoulder*): Drop it!!!!!!

JENDA (*eventually drops the pistol*): So that's that

POLICEMAN 1 *and* POLICEMAN 2 *aim nervously first at one then at the other.*

POLICEMAN 2: Call for reinforcements for chrissake! (*Aims several kicks at* JENDA.)

JENDA: Officer
I need to tell my son something he's inside
plays soccer
he's good ow
plays for Sparta (*Receives a kick.*)
he's bleeding
I just want to cheer him up a bit
you didn't have to shoot at me
next time aim at my head
my head

BRONĚK: You swine you swine

JENDA: He's there in the hut and he must be worried

POLICEMAN 1 *traps* JENDA *on the ground with his foot and handcuffs him.*

VELEBORSKÝ: I don't believe it
I go out fishing
and my leg's fucked

JENDA: As ever was

VELEBORSKÝ: The minute I'm back on my feet
I'll kick your ass off with this leg (*Gets a kick from* POLICEMAN 2.)
Excuse me

JENDA: You'll have to dig up my coffin and kick my corpse
Fish-murderer
(*Indicating* BRONĚK.) This bastard started the shooting

BRONĚK (*groaning aloud*): I didn't mean to fire

VELEBORSKÝ: For no reason at all
he fired at me

POLICEMAN 2 *handcuffs* BRONĚK.

POLICEMAN 1: Okay, I'm on my way
the men'll be here soon
If you have to
shoot (*Disappears into the bushes.*)

Two PARAMEDICS *and a* DOCTOR *run in with a stretcher; they freeze.*

JENDA: There
inside
there in the kiosk

VELEBORSKÝ: Here
here
it stings like mad
ow it stings

JENDA: There's a seriously injured man inside
It's not his fault
Mirek Vracel of Sparta

EMT 2 (*glancing inside*): Oh hell

The paramedics go inside.

The silence is broken by the women's sobs.

The paramedics bring the stretcher out with MIREK *on it.*

DOCTOR (*examines the injured, speaking into his mobile*): Two more emergency ambulances

JENDA: Mirek!

MIREK: Dad!

JENDA: Mirek!

RENATA (*with blood on her face, stops the paramedics*): Leave them alone!

DOCTOR: Do you want him to bleed to death?
Let's go!

JENDA: Forgive me Mirek!!!

POLICEMAN 1 (*rushing in*): In the bushes
I've found
a fresh corpse
use your tear-gas
give them all some I tell you
use your tear-gas
Do it!!!!!

The two adrenalin-charged policemen start furiously squirting tear-gas in everybody's faces, then accidentally in their own, then join the rest of the wretched company, a bunch of groaning, crying, kneeling riff-raff.

With all the strength he can muster JENDA *picks himself up, gets the soccer ball ready and prepares painfully to kick the ball towards the goal nearby.*

JENDA: Here's one for you
Mirek

He kicks and misses.

Daybreak ends. It's daytime.

MINACH

Iva Klestilová Volánková

Iva Klestilová Volánková
Photo courtesy of Aura-Pont

Iva Klestilová Volánková was born October 4, 1964 and began her career in theatre as an actress. In the 1980s, Klestilová was a member of the Children's Studio of Theatre on a String, in Brno, and the amateur group Unroadworthy Caterpillar. From 1984 on, she was an actress with the HaDivadlo company in Brno, and until 1989 she worked on the scripts of all of HaDivadlo's original productions. After returning from maternity leave, she found few opportunities for actresses and so began to devote herself more to playwriting. Her early work was highly influenced by Arnošt Goldflam, the driving creative force behind HaDivadlo. After his departure, she became known for her own, independent, feminist-oriented plays. She has been shortlisted for the Alfréd Radok Playwriting Competition multiple times and won several awards: in 1997, fourth prize for *All Saints*; in 2000, third prize for *Minach*, a trilogy; in 2003, second prize for *Encroachment*; and in 2003, third prize for *3sisters2002.cz*. Since September 2004 she has lectured in dramaturgy at the National Theatre in Prague.

In 2006 Volánková returned to her maiden name, Klestilová; the same year she had her biggest success to date with *My Country*. This satirical take on the absurdity of contemporary Czech politics, produced by the Rokoko Theatre, took first place in a survey of critics at *World and Theatre* magazine, and won the 2006 Alfréd Radok Award for Best New Play. Also that year, she wrote a script for the special summer project *The Shed* at the National Theatre in Prague. Her play *Heroes* served as the basis for a production by the directing team nicknamed Skutr. Klestilová is currently at work on a political puppet play.

For twenty years I worked as an actress for HaDivadlo. During that time, there was a Czech playwright and director at HaDivadlo who went through a phase of doing performances made up of actors' personal statements. He said, "Write a play and be God." And I fell in love with that empty sheet of paper that slowly fills with words. I still enjoy the solitude, those intimate moments I spend with my characters as I bring them to life. Even when they break free of me, tell me to go to hell, and begin to live their own lives.

As a playwright, what's influenced me most of all has been my acting career. That is, not only freeing the text of ballast, since it often trips actors up when they have to pick through it in detail to get to the essence of the text, but also the detours that happen in the process of rehearsing. Sometimes, without even being aware of it, the actors start to act on some other theme that maybe isn't connected with the play you're working on but is brilliant. Seeing that, those little mistakes? That's the most inspiring thing for me, to this day.

With Minach, I wanted to write a great part for a fine actress. The biggest challenge was finding my own style. I'd been searching for it for ten years. After writing Minach for more than a year, I think I found it, and I finally started to feel at home with my own voice.

—Iva Klestilová Volánková

Mariana Chmelařová and Marek Daniel in *Minach* (2002),
HaDivadlo, Brno, directed by Arnošt Goldflam

Photo courtesy of HaDivadlo Archives

Minach

A Triolgy "about" and for Women

by

Iva Klestilová Volánková

Translated by

Alex Zucker

Love and hate are not instincts, but expressions of the ego. Instincts are largely unconscious, which is not the case for love and hate.—Sigmund Freud

CHARACTERS

Minach the First
SISTER
BROTHER
LOUIS

Minach Number Two: Narcissistic
WOMAN
MAN

Minach Number Three
WOMAN 1
WOMAN 2

MINACH
The First

June 22 and 26, 2000

for Mína

FIRST CONVERSATION: SISTER AND BROTHER

A room. BROTHER *sits in an armchair, almost completely still. Only a few, very small, nearly undetectable movements of his fingers reveal that he is conscious. He slowly crumbles a bread roll onto the ground, as if he were feeding pigeons. This scene plays out slowly as the lights come up onstage. His* SISTER *appears. She engages in activity throughout their conversation, being the type of person who is "always in motion."*

SISTER: The air in here is awful! Mornings it's always so stuffy . . . (*Walks to the window and opens it.*) Ah, there we go! Now for a nice, deep breath, that's it . . . (*Breathes in deeply.*) Whoa, my head was totally spinning. (*Sits down.*)

It's supposed to be beautiful out today. Just look out the window and see for yourself. This summer is the warmest I've seen in years. Nice and hot. Forget summer—it was already hot this spring! Nothing bad about that. Hot is hot . . . You sure you're not cold? I could get you a blanket . . . Yesterday on the news they said there might be thunderstorms. God, there it goes again. Rain. Talk about bad luck. God. I can't even stand to look.

BROTHER: I could go for a cup of hot cocoa . . .

SISTER: You know what I heard on the radio? They were asking people on the street what they would take with them from their house if one day they had to just suddenly pick up and leave. It was fascinating, the answers they got. One man said his sweater. Can you believe it? His sweater. Someone else said the Bible. There was a man who said his photos. Oh, and then there was this one woman who just said "nothing." Can you believe it? "Nothing."

And the reporter, she was so surprised she asked the woman again. And the woman goes: "Nothing." But it was the *way* she said it, you know? It was amazing. I mean it wasn't just like "nothing," like when somebody asks you a question and you're like, "Buzz off, I don't have the time." She said it all quiet and sad, like she had just totally given up. Like she was looking at something, some picture, like some *thing* that she was looking at, as if *nothing* were a tangible thing . . . *nothing*. I just can't stop thinking about it.

SISTER (*walks out of the room, then calls in from the kitchen*): You sure you don't want a glass of milk instead?

BROTHER *sits without answering, crumbling the roll.* SISTER *re-enters the room with a box of hot cocoa mix in her hand.*

SISTER: You know you shouldn't drink so much hot cocoa. It isn't good for you . . . Did you see that? He flew right up to the window. Those crazy birds, I've never seen them act so bizarre. One morning—you were still asleep—I got woken up by this dull thud. Like somebody running into something? So I got up and went to see what it was, and just then this bird came zooming in and—*bam!*—it smacked right into the window. And then another one right after him. Isn't that weird?

So I opened the window and put a mirror there, thinking maybe then they'd be able to see their reflection . . . but it didn't work. Those crazy birds. It was like they *wanted* to bash their heads in. I had to sit out on the ledge with a flyswatter to keep them away . . .

I'll make you that cocoa a little on the weak side . . .

SISTER (*leaves room, continuing to speak from the kitchen*): Louis is coming by today. This afternoon. I hope you'll be nicer to him today than you were last time. Last week you didn't say a single word to him. (*Re-enters the room holding a mug of hot cocoa.*) I'm not going to bake anything. Who would eat it in this heat anyway? I'll go and pick up some apple strudel and cookies. Those chocolate ones that you like. Louis is a good man, I'll have you know. I don't see what you have against him. He comes once a week, we have a chat, he fixes what needs fixing . . .
What do you know about it, anyway? *Nothing.* There are things a woman can't do without help. For some things you need a man. And Louis does it without my even having to ask—fixes the faucets, tightens the hinges, adjusts the blinds. Sometimes I think he must be from another planet. The way he just sits there. Listens. Gets up. Fixes something. Sits back down.

BROTHER *sits silently. After a while,* SISTER *continues.*

SISTER: You're right. It's not all *that* innocent. But you're far too critical about these things, little brother. I know you don't like him . . . Don't forget to stir, or the sugar will stick to the bottom and then it's hard to scrub off . . . But he's the only person who ever comes over to see us.

You see? (*Refers to birds.*) There goes another one. Louis came and took what

he needed. He could sense it intuitively. On the other hand, it stands to reason
. . .

Anyway, so what? What's wrong with that? *Nothing*. He comes over, helps out
. . . Louis cares about me. And he's always so patient, too. He drilled patience
into me and I'm grateful to him for that. And he doesn't want a thing from me.
No decisions, nothing. He never asks what comes next . . . Isn't that strange?
What do you think? I don't know. I just can't tell anymore. I sit there, looking at
him, waiting for some kind of sign . . . and nothing. Not a thing. Not one single
thing. I guess that's just how it is. But I ought to be feeling something, right?
Don't you think?

I probably shouldn't be asking you. The last time he was here . . . we were all
just sitting here, talking. And all of a sudden I got the urge to ask him . . . to ask
him something personal. You know what I mean? So at least I'd *know*
something about him. You know what I'm saying? But then I chickened out. It
just seemed stupid. I mean, after all these years he's been coming to see us
. . . to just suddenly ask one day, out of the blue: "So, Louis? How's life?" It's
ridiculous.

I really enjoy these mornings of ours together. The way we sit here, just the two
of us, pondering the state of the universe . . .

Come on now, snap out of it. Don't worry, little brother. You're not alone. I'm
here with you, aren't I? Did I do something wrong? Why won't you answer me?
Come on. Say something, please? You won't even look me in the eye anymore.
Why don't you try standing up? Go ahead, sit there, see if I care. You don't want
to walk, don't walk. For God's sake, though, at least say something . . .
So that's it. Nothing.
I think I'll close the window. Those birds are getting on my nerves.

SISTER *goes to the window.* BROTHER *sits silently, crumbling the roll. After a
while,* SISTER *continues.*

SISTER: You're like a slug, that's what you are. All closed up in your little shell
. . . I could never be like that. I can't. Stay active, I say to myself every day. Get
some air in your lungs and all that. But even just saying it now makes me tired.
A miracle. It's a miracle. Just the two of us here alone. Us two. Mother and
father . . . gone.

SISTER *stops, realizing what she's said.*

SISTER: Why can't I say it? "Dead." Somebody asks, "How are your parents?"

And I, for no good reason at all, I say, "They're gone." Instead of: "They're dead."
I told myself I'd get over the pain. The pain. The loss. "Get over it." That's what they say, right? Time heals all. But *nothing* has changed. *Nothing.* I can't get rid of it.
Are you done with that yet?

SISTER *takes his mug and goes into the kitchen.*

SISTER (*from the kitchen*): How about another roll? No? Don't tell me you decided to stop eating again?

SISTER *re-enters the room.*

SISTER: It's been so long since we were out together, just the two of us . . . why don't we go see a play? Come on . . . please? How about *Dance of Death*? Doesn't that sound great? Just the title: "*Dance of Death . . .* "

The sound of wings.

SISTER: Those birds are going to kill themselves . . . I was going to read it, you know, *Dance of Death*. But I'm not really much of a reader, and then . . .

I think I'd like to take a walk. Get out and go for a stroll . . . that's what I want to do. Put on my brown dress and . . . we could go together. I'll polish your shoes, how about it? You don't have to talk to me. Not a single word, I swear . . . You don't have to decide just yet. Maybe later. Whenever you feel like it.

I saw some photos of the performance . . . it looked wonderful . . . "*Dance of Death*" . . .

Want to wash up? No? All right then. Just sit there, I'll do it myself. I'll give you a bath like a little baby . . .

SISTER *leaves, then returns with a T-shirt, a wash basin, and soap and water. She undresses* BROTHER, *examining his body.*

SISTER: You should have played the piano. Yes. You should have listened to Mom and taken up the piano . . . All you needed was a little bit more patience . . . You've got wonderful hands. And such long fingers. You could have played like a god.

Your skin is so white . . . it's like marble . . . my sweet little marble-white brother . . . like ice . . .

And you've got Daddy's shoulders . . .

BROTHER *reacts, or* SISTER *gets frightened . . . some sort of reaction.*

SISTER: I won't say it again . . . not ever, I swear. I'll never say that word again . . . *"Daddy."*

My dear little brother. I'm getting old, you know. And you're all I have left. Do something, won't you, please? I don't know what . . . But I definitely feel something . . . here. (*Touches her heart.*) Please . . .

BROTHER *remains silent.*

SISTER: Please . . . Ask me, at least, what I would take with me if I had to . . . *nothing.* We don't even have any photos. You ate them all up. With these sweet little hands right here, you tore them up into pieces, stuffed them into your mouth, and devoured them . . .

White as marble . . . and cold as ice . . .

Are you sure you don't want something to eat? I'll go out in a while and pick something up . . . wouldn't want to run into anyone . . .

(*Combing* BROTHER*'s hair.*) Remember that picture? From when we were little? The one where we're in the bathtub, playing? Wait . . . what was it . . . oh, I know: You had that steamboat. Yes . . . that little blue steamboat, and you used to make that tooting sound . . . Can you still do it? Oh, come on. Please? Do the steamboat . . .

BROTHER *sits silently.*

SISTER: And I was just sitting there, right? Yes, I think that's how it was. I was just sitting there, looking at Father . . . and then he pushed the button—*click*—and that was it. What a nice picture . . . the two of us, and the steamboat . . . toot, toot!

You sure you don't want a bath?

BROTHER *sits silently.*

SISTER: We could fill the tub with hot water . . . put in some bubblebath . . . You'll turn all red and be nice and warm . . . I can scrub my hands till they're spick and span . . . and then I can wash you all over with that sweet-smelling herbal soap . . . just like a baby . . . cut your nails . . . rub you with lotion . . .

BROTHER *sits silently.*

BROTHER: I could go for a cup of hot cocoa.

SISTER (*under her breath*): Stick your hand down my pants . . . (*Out loud.*) You shouldn't drink so much cocoa, it isn't good for you. You're totally drunk on the stuff . . . in this heat . . . day in, day out . . . Cocoa, cocoa, cocoa, cocoa . . . I can't *stand* it . . . I think I'll puke if I even so much as smell the stuff again . . .

Fine, I'll make you some cocoa then, if you really love it so much.

SISTER *enters the kitchen.*

SISTER (*from the kitchen*): Louis likes the Moravian Highlands. We were sitting here one day . . . and all of a sudden he says, "I like the Moravian Highlands." I mean it was like he was saying "I like Highland Foods bacon" or something. But no: "I like the Moravian Highlands," he said.

SISTER *re-enters room, carrying a mug of hot cocoa.*

SISTER: He said he would take us there sometime . . . how does that sound? We could take our bikes and ride around . . . We should go. Come on, let's go. Please? You can't just sit around here forever.

And don't forget to stir. The sugar sticks to the bottom, and then it's hard to wash off.

BROTHER *sits silently.* SISTER *watches him.*

SISTER: Nothing . . . nothing . . . nothing. My God . . . nothing.

SISTER *finishes washing* BROTHER.

SISTER: You know what I saw on TV? It was *awful.* There was this story about the floods, and there was this son who went after his father who had gone out to rescue his dog . . . and the son took his video camera with him . . . and taped the whole thing . . . his own commentary and everything . . . and he was describing the scene . . . and then all of a sudden he starts screaming and crying . . . and right there, on camera, is his dad, and his dad is dead . . . My God . . . what did I . . .

BROTHER *reacts, or* SISTER *reacts.*

SISTER: Dead . . . His father was . . . dead. Terrible. He goes out with a video camera . . .

Do you think it's all just a lost cause? You know that feeling you used to get when you knew something bad was going to happen, and it did? I remember. You must remember, too. You do, don't you? That fear deep down inside. That feeling of premonition . . . what is that?

SISTER *clears things away into the kitchen.*

SISTER (*from the kitchen*): And that man with the camera, just walking along, not expecting anything . . . and all of a sudden, full on, right in his face . . . his dad lying there in the water, all puffy and bloated . . . You should have seen it . . . And him standing there, just sobbing . . . God, there's so many bad things going on in the world these days . . .

SISTER *re-enters the room.*

SISTER: Nothing to say? Trying to see how long I can hold out, huh? Well, guess what? I've had enough. Talk, talk, talk, talk, talk . . . but that's the end of it. Do you enjoy tormenting me?

I'd like to go on that trip with you and Louis.
I'm scared. You've got me scared now, understand?
Nothing.
Hold me, please.
Won't you at least come to the theater with me?
Nothing.
Just like Father. He hated the theater too. Mother loved it. I guess we got it from them.

Going to the theater's so nice . . . the way you sit there, watching them acting . . . getting all *involved* in it . . . And yet the whole time you keep telling yourself, "Careful—it isn't for real. It's just make-believe."

Don't forget to stir your cocoa.
Remember that time . . . up in the Tatras with Mom and Dad . . . that time we met that actress? The one Mom recognized from that movie. Don't you remember?

BROTHER *sits silently.*

SISTER: There she was . . . sitting there . . . in the middle of the Tatra mountains

... taking in the fresh air ... talking to herself ... and she was totally drunk. I mean, *totally*. And the next day it was the same thing. What a shocker. Monday, Tuesday, Wednesday, Thursday, Friday, Saturday, Sunday ... same table, every time ... all by herself ... totally drunk ...
She was a really famous actress ... What was her name, though? I should have been an actress. And you should have played the piano. The two of us could have performed together. You would have played like a god. I would have dressed up in fancy costumes ...

Don't look at me that way. You know that I drink. What's the big deal? Anyway, what about you? How come you don't drink? Nothing but that cocoa of yours ... cocoa, cocoa, cocoa.
I drink because I'm bored. I don't even get drunk anymore. Mother used to drink when she was cleaning the house. First the wine ... then the vacuum. She used to sing dirty songs while she was dusting ...

Do something ... please. At least ask me what I'd take if ...
Nothing.

BROTHER *sits silently.*

SISTER: Totally drunk. Just a drunk ... washed-up ... actress ...

Both are silent. After a while, SISTER *continues.*

SISTER: I'm going to pour that goddamn cocoa down your throat until you puke ... till you choke to death on that disgusting cocoa of yours. So I'm not even worth a full sentence, huh? Lift your fat ass out of that chair! Come on: Up!

Tell me that someday at least ... that someday you'll do it. Someday you'll go somewhere with me. That's all that I'm asking ... just someday ...

Do you love me? You don't know, do you?
Nothing.

Both sit silently. After a while, SISTER *continues.*

SISTER: I drink in the kitchen, on the sly. Did you know that? You cocoa, me vodka. Out of boredom. Don't look at me like that ...

Louis is a good man, and he likes me ... We're going to have our portrait taken together. And if you lay a hand on that picture ... if you so much as touch it ... not to mention if you go and eat it, like all the rest ... I will *kick ... your ... ass.* Understand?

Let me tell you something. Yesterday I went out . . . and I got this strange intuition all of a sudden . . . this sort of shiver down my back. Like something was telling me, "Turn around. Turn around." So I turned around . . . and saw you in the window. Looking out. You were watching to see if I was gone yet. Just looking out the window . . . there were crumbs there afterward . . . I saw you.

Nothing to say to that? Fine. Silence gives consent. So I waited. I went and hid in the underpass
. . . and I waited. And I saw what I was waiting for. A little while later, you left the house.

Still nothing to say? I couldn't care less where you went or who you were with
. . . it doesn't matter to me.

She's hysterical. That's what you're thinking, right? She's a snoop and she's hysterical. Don't worry. I didn't follow you.
It wouldn't have killed you . . . to tell me you were going somewhere . . . or you wanted to be alone . . . or you were seeing somebody. I mean, what does it matter? But no. Not you. You lie. You're a liar. And not only that, you lie about things that don't even matter . . .

Your moods change like the weather. And when you do talk to me . . . once in a blue moon, when you deign to talk to me . . . you always complain that you're sick . . . practically incapacitated . . . it's blackmail, that's what it is . . . you're just plain blackmailing me . . . all those crazy games of yours . . . acting like you're dying . . . sobbing and moaning . . . going on and on about your health . . . Why do you do that to me?

You said I couldn't leave you, not even for a minute, or you'd die. That's nonsense. Just plain nonsense. A thousand times I've said it's ridiculous. And it is. In the end, I fell for it, though. You're the healthiest person I know . . . you're tough . . . you won't die that easy . . .
Like a torture machine . . . just sitting there, silently, torturing me . . .

And then all of those questions about Louis: What, when, where . . . What do you want from me, anyway? When I told you the truth, you laughed in my face. But that wasn't enough for you. You wanted to know it all. You always did want it all. Eat it all . . . Take, take, take, always taking and never giving . . .

You wanted to know what happened? I told you. I told you everything. But you wanted scandal, you wanted dirt. You want to know what he's like, huh? You're a miserable wretch. That's it. I'm finished with you.

SISTER *starts to pack her things.* BROTHER *sits silently.*

SISTER: And you know what? I don't want anything. You can keep it all. I'm not going to sit here and fight over some stupid shirts . . .

SISTER *goes into the kitchen. Comes back with a bottle in hand.*

SISTER: And it was true love, what a shame . . . True love, between siblings, and the kind you don't see everyday . . .

Aren't you going to ask where I'm going?
Nothing.

BROTHER: I could go for a cup of hot cocoa.

SISTER *stops in the doorway.*

SISTER: Fuck your cocoa.

BROTHER *stands and walks toward her.*

BROTHER: A nice, hot cup of cocoa . . .

SISTER: Never . . .

BROTHER *grips her hands firmly.*

BROTHER: Cocoa.

SISTER: No . . .

BROTHER: Cocoa . . .

BROTHER *hits her.*

SISTER: Are you going to kill me? Are you going to kill me too?

BROTHER *hits her again.*

BROTHER: Cocoa . . .

SISTER: Kiss my ass . . .

Hits her.

SISTER: For God's sake, what is this, an encore performance? You know what I'm talking about.
Dad saw you that day.

BROTHER *tries to hold her mouth shut.*

SISTER: He saw you . . . trying to kiss me. And he knew what he was seeing. That was why he beat you. Like a dog. Do you remember? You had to get ten stitches on your back. He beat you till his belt fell apart.

SISTER *slips out of his grasp.* BROTHER *chases her around the apartment.*

SISTER: He broke your nose and split your upper lip. You had to get three stitches there. Tore your ear . . . fractured his little finger while he was doing it, too. Then the doctor came, someone called him . . . Father was white as death . . . He was ready to kill you . . . he would've killed you . . . he was that close . . .

Then the doctor came, and Father said . . .

BROTHER *grabs her and hits her again.*

SISTER: He said, "My God, so crazy all of a sudden. He just went wild, out of the blue." You told everyone he was beating you for no reason. The doctor examined you. You squeezed out those little-boy tears . . . exaggerating your suffering . . . planting the seeds of sympathy . . . and everyone felt sorry for you . . . but you know very well why he beat you.

BROTHER *tilts* SISTER*'s head back and pours the rest of the bottle of vodka down her throat.* SISTER *sits on the ground,* BROTHER *stands over her.*

SISTER: Remember that photograph? You remember . . . the first one you ate. It was a picture of you marching around . . . the little soldier. When Father took it, you were furious . . . like a child . . . absolutely furious.

You hated that picture. You always asked him to give it to you. But he wouldn't. He just laughed. Laughed at you with that photo in his hand . . . that was the beginning of the war between you two . . . it started so innocently . . .

BROTHER: Shhhh.

SISTER: Let me finish.

You killed them. Mother and Father . . . you killed them both, that Sunday night . . .

BROTHER *stares at her, long and hard.*

BROTHER: Shhhh.

SISTER: It's the truth. You poisoned them like rats.

BROTHER: Shhhh.

SISTER: Like rats . . .

BROTHER: Shhhh.

SISTER: Do the steamboat . . .

BROTHER: Shhh . . .

SISTER: March, my little soldier.

BROTHER: Shhh.

BROTHER *helps* SISTER *up from the floor. She stands and looks him in the eye.*

SISTER: Ask me . . . what I'd take with me if I had to . . .

BROTHER: Shhh.

SISTER: Nothing.

BROTHER *gives* SISTER *a long kiss, lifts her into his arms, and carries her into the bathroom. Sound of running water and the tooting of a steamboat.*

SECOND CONVERSATION: SISTER AND LOUIS
THREE PIECES WITH LOUIS
Louis as a Honeybee on a Flower

SISTER *and* LOUIS *sit on the floor by the doorway, late at night, in the dark, drinking cognac and talking. They both have had a lot to drink. Sitting in an armchair, unnoticed, is* BROTHER.

SISTER: We should be a little more quiet. My brother is sleeping and I don't want to wake him up . . . Wait—did you hear something?

They both listen.

SISTER: Thank God . . . *nothing.*
Today was wonderful, Louis. One of the best in my life . . . If we finish the rest of this bottle, we'll be drunk, and we wouldn't want that, would we?

Open the window a little, would you? . . . The birds will be starting up again soon . . . The air is so bad in here.

LOUIS *gets up and goes to open the window. He then returns to* SISTER *and starts insistently hugging and kissing her.*

SISTER: What would you take with you if all of a sudden you had to leave your house? Quick, don't think about it, just give me an answer . . .

LOUIS: Is this important?

SISTER: Don't analyze it, just answer . . . quick, what would you take?

LOUIS: Can't it wait a minute? This is important too. Maybe even more important.

SISTER: Don't you want to tell me?

LOUIS: Do you want to talk?

SISTER: Come on, hurry . . .

LOUIS: My trunk. I'd take my trunk, I guess.

SISTER: Why?

LOUIS: Because it's sitting right by the door.

SISTER: Your trunk . . .

LOUIS: It depends where I was when I heard the news. If I was in the kitchen, I'd probably just take whatever I was holding, my coffee mug or whatever. If I was in bed, I'd probably take my pajamas. In the foyer, I'd grab my trunk.

SISTER: And what do you have in there?

LOUIS: My tools: drill, screwdriver . . . everything. Everything I need.

SISTER: I don't know anyone else like you. Such a practical, handy man . . . You're so kind . . . Tell me, what do you think, Lou: are all actresses sluts?

LOUIS: What do you want me to say? That they are, or that they aren't?

SISTER: I wanted to be an actress so bad . . . My father used to say that all actresses were sluts. So I was afraid . . . I'd be one too . . . when I grew up . . . and no one would try to stop me . . . from being a slut . . .

They both continue to drink slowly throughout.

SISTER: If we drink all of this, we'll be drunk. Is that what we want? Louie, you randy tomcat . . . my little pussyhound . . . you've got your hand in my panties . . .

LOUIS: Does that bother you?

SISTER: Do you know how to drink with your left hand?

LOUIS: Why?

SISTER: Quiet, shh, we don't want to wake him up . . .

You'd take your trunk, I'd take *nothing.* Nothing.

LOUIS, *ever the practical, capable lover . . .*

SISTER: Is that your way of saying goodbye, putting your hand down there? Is this your last time here? Are you going to pick up your trunk and go fix someone else's stuff now?

Lou . . . can you do a steamboat?

LOUIS *toots like a steamboat.*

SISTER: You're so handsome . . . and kind . . . and such an able lover . . . I love you . . . Louis . . .

(*Speaking slowly and forcefully.*) Now take your hands off me, my sweet, or they'll end up turning black. When something is dark, there's nothing you can do about it. And inside me, Louis, it's very dark. Pitch black . . . So take your head off my lap and look at me . . .

SISTER *lifts* LOUIS's *head, teasing him.*

SISTER: Louis . . . I've got something to tell you . . . Do you . . . ?
Shh, be quiet . . . (*Continuing to tease him.*) Instincts, urges . . . what a mess. Get an urge in your head and next thing you know, you're acting like an idiot. But there are some things fucking can't help. You can do whatever you want: stand on your head, be kind and able and considerate . . . you could be the best person ever, and still . . . nothing.

A finger from above . . . that finger is pointing down at you, and it won't leave you in peace. Isn't that awful?

Vanity, Louis, my dear. Sheer vanity . . .

Listen, Lou . . . get up and run . . . run away, while there's still time. You're not a total fool, are you? How could it happen so fast? How can a person change so quickly into an idiot?

Urges . . . instincts . . . my God . . .

All right then, Lou, you irresistible, indefatigable conqueror . . . Go ahead, you whiner, have it your way . . . Fuck me all you want, maybe it'll make you feel better . . .

After a while . . .

SISTER (*refers to the birds*): Have they started yet? Strange . . . (*Walks to the table carrying a tray of cookies.*) Are you asleep?

LOUIS: No . . .

SISTER: Are you leaving now?

LOUIS: No . . .

SISTER: What about life, Louis?

After a while . . .

LOUIS: Don't you enjoy it anymore?

SISTER: Why do you ask?

LOUIS: Well, it just occurred to me . . . that maybe actually . . . you don't enjoy it . . . maybe it's just a question of coordination . . . or maybe the problem is . . . I don't know, something else entirely . . . we could talk about it, if you want . . . maybe there's some other way you'd rather do it . . .

SISTER: Are you going to give me back my panties?

LOUIS: No.

LOUIS *sits, drinking.*

SISTER: What do you think, Louis? Do I like attentive men? That's what you're trying to figure out, isn't it? Where did you go wrong? What mistake did you make? *Nothing.* You do everything just fine. You . . . do . . . everything . . . absolutely perfectly . . . Louis . . . my sweet . . .

(*Continuing to tease him.*) Now you're confused, aren't you? I'm warning you, Louie. Get up and run while you can . . .

(*Takes a drink.*) Tell me, Louis: Do you think . . . do you think you could ever . . . would you ever be able to kill me?

LOUIS (*startled*): What?

SISTER: Now wait a second, don't interrupt. Think about it now, carefully. Could you kill me?
Does that frighten you? Is it too awful to imagine? Really? Is it so bad? The whole world is killing itself—over nothing, for no good reason at all—and you're frightened . . . Now hold on, Louie, don't interrupt . . . Do you think we could do it so that . . . so that it would seem like . . . so that it would feel like you actually wanted to kill me?

Oh, Louis, you stud, you . . . with your hand back in my panties again . . . my cute little stud horse, you don't understand a thing, do you? It's no problem to fuck all night . . . even two or three times in a row . . . no problem at all. It's not a question of how you do it. You're great, don't worry. It's great, it feels good to be with you . . . even better than . . . even better than when I do it myself . . .

(*Pushes* LOUIS *away, teasing him.*) Kill me . . . and everything'll be different. Louis, please. Please kill me. Because if you don't, if you don't do it, I'll just have to do it myself. And I'm afraid. I'm afraid I won't have the strength. Just like I don't have the strength to stop doing "it" . . . because some things are perfect . . . because he was created perfect . . . because he did more for me . . . more than anyone else . . . He did a terrible thing . . . Louis . . .

Fine then . . . have it your way. We'll have another go at it and afterwards it'll be better.

After a while . . .

LOUIS: Why don't we live a normal life? I mean, for fuck's sake, I don't want to spend the rest of my life doing it under the coat rack. We could at least try . . .

SISTER: But this *is* normal life for me. For me, this is the most normal life that I know how to live. I can't imagine anything more normal than this . . .
(*Drinks, thinking out loud.*) You're the most normal man I know. Everything about you is normal. With you, everything is so nice. So nice and . . . ordinary. Ordinary as could be. How could it possibly be more normal?

LOUIS: I want us to live a normal life. Like regular people . . . you and me . . . just the two of us . . . maybe have children . . .

SISTER: A normal life? What do you mean "normal?" What's that?
Are you going to give me back my panties?

(*Takes a drink.*) ". . . sitting in the Tatras, talking to herself, and she was totally drunk . . ."

LOUIS: What?

SISTER: Nothing.

LOUIS: So that's enough for you?

SISTER: Now, honey . . . you have no idea what you're saying . . .

LOUIS: Should I go now?

SISTER: Do you want to?

LOUIS: Have I offended you?

SISTER: This is bullshit.

LOUIS: Why?

SISTER: Because you enjoy it. (*Again teasing him.*) Are you going to leave your hand there forever? It's nice, actually. I could just cut it off and leave it there . . . I'm not kidding.

Fine then. Have it your way. We'll have another go at it and afterwards things'll be better.

After a while . . .

SISTER: Here they come . . . shut the window.

LOUIS *shuts the window. Sound of wings banging into windowpanes.*

SISTER: You can keep the panties . . .

LOUIS: I'll kill him one of these days . . .

SISTER: Over my dead body . . .

LOUIS *leaves the room and is gone.* BROTHER *sits in his armchair, motionless except for a few, small, nearly undetectable movements of his fingers, which reveal that he is waking up. He slowly crumbles a bread roll onto the ground, as if he were feeding pigeons. This scene plays out slowly as the lights come up onstage.* SISTER *speaks to* BROTHER . . .

SISTER: Ask me . . . what I'd take with me . . . if I had to . . . leave my house: Nothing. Not a thing.

End of First Minach

MINACH
Number Two: Narcissistic

for Arnošt Goldflam

MAN *and* WOMAN *in a room. They sit on the bed, not speaking.*
After a while . . .

WOMAN: Those two hills over there remind me of butt cheeks—like the butt cheeks on somebody's big, fat ass.

They sit without speaking. After a while . . .

WOMAN: Do you think it's the climate, or maybe the shifting of tectonic plates, or maybe . . . what do you think it is that made it look like that?

They sit without speaking. After a while . . .

WOMAN: I rule out human influence. No human being could have such a sense of humor and authenticity . . . such a remarkable sense of esthetics . . . No human has that. Maybe somewhere out there is someone who could stand to be ridiculed by the people over on the other side of the hill, but she wouldn't be able to stand the thought that everyone else would assume that it was *her* ass on display.

Man is a great actor . . .

They sit without speaking. After a while . . .

WOMAN: . . . and yet he can't resist. He has to look. And what he sees, he develops, he builds on. Getting all tangled up in thoughts and ideas—some perverted, some just outright boring. As boring as this view that I'm looking at right now.

They sit without speaking. After a while . . .

WOMAN: They should take a picture of that and put it on a postcard. They should put a trail in there.

They sit without speaking. After a while . . .

WOMAN: The Moravian Highlands . . . (*pause*) the Hana Highlands . . . Pálava . . . Šumava . . . Brdy . . . A brick in the backpack, to build up the legs . . . and an egg in a loaf of bread, to satisfy the stomach . . .

They sit without speaking. After a while . . .

WOMAN: Nothing stinks worse than eggs . . .

MAN *lies back, folding his arms behind his head.* WOMAN *sits, looking at* MAN. *After a while . . .*

WOMAN: This morning I went for a routine exam at the gynecologist, and the doctor told me I was a virgin. He looked up from between my thighs, with this funny grin on his face, and said "virgin." At my age, the polite thing to say would have been "old maid." At my age, it isn't polite to talk about things like that.

After a while . . .

WOMAN: I hate altruists. I swear to God. Nothing disgusts me more.

MAN *sits up again. After a while . . .*

MAN: I'm not an altruist.

WOMAN *takes* MAN'*s hand in hers and shakes it, as if trying to wake him up. After a while . . .*

WOMAN: Incompetence as a category . . . incompetence as such-uch-uch-uch . . . "old maid" . . .

MAN *lies there.* WOMAN *gets up.*

WOMAN: You're incompetent, all of you . . . and yet you all want it. Even the doctor would if he could
. . . "virgin" . . . with that stupid grin on his face . . .

"July 5, in the office, on the examination table: old maid. July 5, two minutes later: deflowered, without so much as a squeal . . . "

They say that women are more competent than men . . . as the years go by, they say, they learn how to get by in life . . . that's what they say, anyway . . .

WOMAN *stands over* MAN, *as a victor stands over his defeated enemy. After a while . . .*

WOMAN: Isn't it ridiculous? Reducing an entire life down to two words?

WOMAN *sits on top of* MAN.

WOMAN: At a skiing course once, in the mountains, I threw up for two days straight. "It's from the air," said the instructor. She made me some herbal tea. Then she took me into the bedroom where all of the students slept and started to kiss me.

Sex is ridiculous.
Categorical incomprehensibility? Bullshit!
Firmly established incomprehensibility? Bullshit!

Play by the rules and you'll never get any unpleasant surprises.

After a while . . .

WOMAN: I can't stand men who don't talk.

WOMAN *sits down next to* MAN. *After a while . . .*

MAN: I talk.

MAN *sits up. Shrugs his shoulders. Lies back down.*

WOMAN (*under her breath, aside*): Woman, alone with man . . .

WOMAN *leans over* MAN *and kisses him.*

WOMAN: Comedy. Tragedy. Farce. Men are so transparent. Their physicality is so transparent. They're all filled with transparent desire. And that gives them away.

WOMAN *aggressively kisses* MAN. *He remains lying down. After a while . . .*

WOMAN: So. What shall I call you today? Harold? Fine. Harold it is. That's a good name.

Rarely does a woman meet such a laughable yet attractive man as Harold Lloyd . . . When you make those Harold Lloyd eyes, no woman can resist you.

MAN: No . . . Harold.

WOMAN *kisses* MAN. *After a while . . .*

WOMAN: My magic man, my sweet . . . All it takes is a name to make somebody real. All of a sudden they're more believable. Just a minute ago, you were a nameless, unspecific man. A nothing. And now? Now you're a somebody! Now you exist! Now you are a human being!
I'll never remind you that it was all thanks to me.

WOMAN *tries to kiss* MAN, *but he moves his head.* WOMAN *grasps his head firmly with both hands and stares into his face.* MAN *remains unruffled.*

WOMAN: What are you hiding? What secret are you keeping from me? Where should I look to find it?

Do I have to share you with somebody else? I don't mind. In fact, I couldn't care less. Just as long as I know I'm the only one.

Pride, you say? Say what you want. I don't care. I don't care what you think.

MAN *sits up and prepares to stand.*

MAN: No . . . Harold . . .

WOMAN *tosses a cookie to* MAN *as if he were a dog. He reacts automatically, catching it.*

WOMAN: A cookie! Have I offended your vanity? I'm sorry. I said it out of ignorance. I'll never mention your smallness again. And I won't talk about my hatred for the Moravian Highlands either . . .

If you want, I'll be quiet. You don't even know what you want.

MAN *starts to stand again.*

WOMAN: I'll take away your cookie!

MAN *sits, cookie in hand, arm raised high, like a child who doesn't want anyone to take away his toy.*

WOMAN: Don't make those eyes at me . . . you know I can't resist . . . Why do you torture me? You want it? Here? Right now? Gross! Are you making fun of me? My God, what are you doing . . . what in God's name are you doing to me?

WOMAN *surveys* MAN, *who sits, arm raised in the air. After a while . . .*

WOMAN: I surrender—but put your arm down. Put it back there, nice and snug against your body. We're not getting any younger. We're not used to kinky stuff in our sex lives. For that matter, I don't think that holding your hand in the air is all that much of a turn-on.

WOMAN *surveys* MAN, *who sits, arm raised in the air. After a while . . .*

WOMAN: As soon as you make those eyes, I know right away what you're up to. All right. That's all right. What's not all right is that hand. Put it down.

MAN *sits, arm in the air, holding the cookie. After a while . . .*

WOMAN: It's asymmetrical. Absolutely asymmetrical. Arms belong alongside the body.
No! Don't tell me it's logical when it's not! Arms belong alongside the body! One arm up and the other one down is a sign of a bodily lack of symmetry. In other words, asymmetry!

WOMAN *stares intently at* MAN, *who sits, arm in the air, holding the cookie. After a while . . .*

WOMAN: My God, don't you know anything?! Are you really that dumb? How could your parents do that to you? You poor, neglected child . . .

MAN *sits, arm in the air, holding the cookie. After a while . . .*

WOMAN: I'm sorry . . .

So what *do* you think? Don't you have any desire to get to the root of things? Analyze them, dissect them . . . discover, decipher—it's fascinating! It's an integral part of the male arsenal: Columbus! Einstein! Mendeleyev! Gagarin! Armstrong! Freud! Moses!

WOMAN *stares intently at* MAN, *who sits, arm in the air, holding the cookie. After a while . . .*

WOMAN: Are you trying to send me a signal? Is there something you'd like to say? I always fall for that . . .

I'm the fool, not you . . . I didn't understand your game. A child's soul is so pure. And your thoughts are only pure . . . as pure as pure can be . . . That's why I love you.

I often dream of opening up your ribcage . . . lifting out that beautiful heart of yours . . . your heart . . . your soul . . . and holding it against my chest . . . so you could slowly beat and beat and beat . . .

What do you say to *that*? Well?! Come on! Hurry up! You want me to take back your cookie?

WOMAN *grabs for his hand.* MAN *raises it even higher. After a while* . . .

WOMAN: You're a fool. You know nothing about life or symmetry. It isn't just a question of bodily asymmetry. It's about the asymmetry of . . . our relationship. Our love. Everything moves toward symmetry. Symmetry is logical. Symmetry is beautiful. Once we find symmetry in our relationship, we'll be happy. Trust me. Happy . . .

You poor thing. You don't know what it is to be happy, do you? You always have to upset things . . . Well, you're upsetting the symmetry of our relationship. You're upsetting the symmetrical order.

Are you doing it consciously? Well then, you deserve credit for that. But I'm not just anyone, you know. I'm a fierce opponent. You don't want to do battle with me . . .

MAN *sits, arm in the air. After a while* . . .

WOMAN: Hah!!! Your eyes don't mean a thing! Now that hurts, doesn't it? All of a sudden, after all these years, the bait doesn't work anymore. Just one huge, great-big nothing!
Listen: "The Moravian Highlands are nothing but one big fat ass after the next." Just one after the other . . .

MAN *tries to get up but* WOMAN *pushes him back to the ground. She kisses him. After a while* . . .

WOMAN: You don't know anything about women . . . how magnificent they are, how amazing . . . adaptive . . . crafty . . . beautiful . . . stupid . . .

Nothing. You don't know a thing.

WOMAN *tries to take away* MAN*'s cookie.* MAN *straightens arm back into the air. After a while* . . .

WOMAN: I walk around in my underwear in front of your best friend. Hurts to hear, doesn't it? Just imagine: in those yellow . . . lace . . . panties of mine. That's right, *those* . . . the ones where you can see *everything*. They're awful, those panties. They cut into me all over. To wear them is true torture. But it's a small price to pay . . . to have your best friend . . . your only friend . . . the only person in the world who still likes you . . . except for me, of course . . . drooling with desire . . . when he sees me in my panties. Just picture it! Ridiculous, huh? Drooling over a pair of underwear . . .

WOMAN *kisses* MAN. *After a while . . .*

WOMAN: You disgust me . . . cold as stone . . .

WOMAN *kisses* MAN. *After a while . . .*

WOMAN: You don't exist anymore . . . you're nothing. You've vanished from my heart. Dissolved away. You couldn't free me of my anguish. My pain. My suffering. You left a weight on my chest. You could never father my kids. This is the end. The end of love, and of platonic love-making.

WOMAN *kisses* MAN. *After a while . . .*

WOMAN: What do you think? How many pairs of yellow panties do I own?

WOMAN *kisses* MAN. *After a while . . .*

WOMAN: I'll put on my brown dress to show that I'm in mourning. Go ahead and eat your cookie. This is the end. Do you hear me? The end. I don't give a damn about the Moravian Highlands.

I'm crying . . . you see? Crying . . . because you're not mine anymore. Crying over a squandered life.
Here's another cookie . . . here you go . . .
You don't exist . . . You're dead . . . You're . . . nothing . . .
Open your mouth . . . how're those cookies? Good, huh?
Are you scared? Are you frightened of death? Don't be afraid, honey. That funny man Harold is dead and gone now . . . he won't haunt us anymore. He's gone away and taken everything from the past with him. All of it . . . gone . . .
And you were born. You're here. Right here. For me. With me. Mine. Edgar?

MAN *sits, cookie in hand. After a while . . .*

WOMAN: That man is dead now, unfortunately. That asymmetrical man . . . is dead and gone. But don't worry . . . by the time he died, he meant nothing to me. He was a simple soul. Life with him seemed to drag on forever.

He was sick. He suffered from a serious case of asymmetrical melancholy. You know what that's like? He didn't like himself. He didn't like anyone. Anyone except me, that is. Me he loved. More than anything else in the world. He lived for me. And I for him. But only for a while. Till I realized . . . until I realized what a treacherous disease it was . . . until I realized what the cause of his hatred was, his hatred of everything: Life. Animals. The Moravian Highlands. His body, his own physical presence. Everything. Everything except me, that is. He didn't hate me. Me, he loved.

WOMAN *takes off* MAN*'s shirt. After a while . . .*

WOMAN: Don't look at me that way. There were days, months, years when he was everything to me. Yes, it's true. But there were also days and months when he was nothing to me. Nothing at all.

WOMAN *tosses* MAN*'s shirt aside.*

WOMAN: Farewell, you, over there . . . on the other side. Farewell . . .

MAN *sits without shirt, holding a cookie.* WOMAN *sits down in his lap.*

WOMAN: You should wear your hair differently. Are your eyes blue? Brown eyes would look so much better on you. Think about it.

WOMAN *caresses* MAN*'s face, as if sculpting it. After a while . . .*

WOMAN: There's no point in demonizing, or idealizing, the life I had with Harold. I don't mean to moralize. I blame only myself. My puritanical nature . . . which of course he planted in me, preparing the soil for my moral catastrophe.

Is it hard to understand? Yes? But it's really so simple. He demonized love and took away the magic of sex. He put a spell on me . . . like Sleeping Beauty. I want to wake up. I want to wake up from this cruel dream. I want to find solid ground . . . and sit on it and stay where I am with the knowledge that that's what I want.

What do you think? Do I want it?
But of course I want it, honeybunch. Otherwise I wouldn't ask.
I'm suffering, truly suffering. You can't imagine the pain. Too big to measure,

too heavy to weigh. Believe me. When it comes to my pain, all you have is my subjective testimony.
Please, I beg you. Help me wake up.

WOMAN *stands. After a while . . .*

WOMAN: Another cookie, hon? Don't worry that I'm not eating. I'm suffering, you know? If I ate anything . . . I'd throw up.

WOMAN *begins taking off* MAN*'s pants.*

WOMAN: Your silence used to hurt me, but now I'm grateful for it. Grateful for the fact that you don't inundate me with questions. You wouldn't get answers anyway.

I feel abandoned . . . abandoned. I feel wounded and deceived. I feel all of the world's injustices and excesses from above. I feel wronged.

MAN *sits, half naked, holding his cookie.* WOMAN *carefully folds his clothes. After a while . . .*

WOMAN: Sweetie . . . Honeybun . . . My little studmuffin . . . What do your eyes remind me of? No, don't move them. There's nothing to be afraid of. You haven't done anything wrong. It's just me. It's me who makes choices. Look at me! Edgar. I've got a nice tummy.
Think about those eyes of yours. It's just a color. No big deal.

After a while . . .

WOMAN: Harold's best friend sticks his hands down my panties. Don't act like such a moralist. Men do it to women all the time . . .

MAN *shifts position uncomfortably.*

WOMAN: Tell me: Is it because you're ashamed? Excited? Or are you embarrassed? Why is it that men always close their eyes . . . when they do that?

I think they only *pretend* to want us. They're just trying to convince themselves that I want it.
What do you think: Do I?
Me, my eyes are wide open. Biology handles the rest. It's got no deeper meaning for me. Emotionally, I mean. In terms of love, that is. Love.

I'm not the one who engineers those panty plunges. I'm a passive observer. What am I supposed to do? Tell me, what should I do? When it comes to male desire, a woman is defenseless.

WOMAN *undresses* MAN. *After a while . . .*

WOMAN: Enough of this silence already! Your lack of facial expression is getting on my nerves. I don't know how to respond to silence with silence.

You're making me into nothing but an outline. A shadow of your shadow. The depth of your silence overwhelms me. I've got vertigo. I'm choking on my own vomit.

Are you trying to kill me?
Here, have a cookie.

MAN *raises hand in the air.*

WOMAN: Everything in the world has already been before.

After a while . . .

WOMAN: You look like a corpse . . .
Facial expressions . . . are caused by the action of striated muscle. So take control! I don't want to look at a mask! I want to see a real live face! Forget about your internal organs. Listen . . . I'm your first aid . . . Concentrate your thoughts on your striated muscle. Let your duodenum and your urethra go to sleep. They'll go on functioning even without you. Without your intervention. Without your will.

Now . . . focus your will on me. On me, do you hear? It'll be a big relief.

MAN *gets to his feet, arm held high, then stands, unmoving. After a while . . .*

WOMAN: Fine then. Run along. I'm not going to scold you. Don't worry. I don't blame you for anything. I'm going to be broad-minded and brave.

You wretched . . . laughable . . . talk about an inferiority complex. Poor thing. You're an emotional cripple. A psychopath . . . not a pleasant sight.

MAN *bends over* WOMAN, *cookie in hand. After a while . . .*

WOMAN: Are you scared of me? Scared to touch me? Are you afraid our coupling could lead to something more horrible? It's all purely by chance . . . cruel coincidence. Fear's got nothing to do with it.

Listen now. Listen carefully: You're going to be miserable till the day you die. You'll never know the warmth of a woman. You'll leave nothing behind when you're gone—nothing. That's it, the end.

You were afraid to admit it, but it crept across the Moravian Highlands like a bad smell. And now it's right behind you.

So what'll it be? What's your decision? Will you stay? Or will you go? Are you thinking?
The empty head can't think a thing. The empty head is full of shit.

MAN *slowly brings hand down, eating the cookie, then leans over* WOMAN, *and slowly, calmly, begins to strangle her. After a while . . .*

WOMAN: Honey . . . What you're trying to do . . . is a terrible thing. A demon has gotten into you. It's controlling you. But soon it will fly away . . . and leave you at the mercy of the awful realization of your cruelty. Your sweet blue eyes will swell with tears . . . and you'll sit next to my cold body and weep . . . but it will be too late. Trust me. That's how it'll be.

Let me go! Listen to me! I have an idea!
Stop controlling your striated muscle and focus instead on your urethra! Then repeat three times, nice and loud, "I gotta pee, I gotta pee, I gotta pee!"
Let me go! Murder is senseless! Murder is always senseless! Let me go and I'll let you into my yellow panties! We'll have a great time!

MAN *continues to strangle* WOMAN.

WOMAN: Let me go! Everyone's going to hate you and point the finger at you! The Moravian Highlands will ring with the cry of "Murder! Murder!" Even the meat on your plate will cry for me!!!

MAN *lets her go. Stands, looking at her. After a while . . .*

WOMAN: You piece of shit.

MAN *sits back down. After a while . . .*

WOMAN: Unfortunately . . .
Nothing? Nothing at all? As usual . . . And you were so beautiful . . . so beautiful . . . But those eyes of yours . . . those eyes . . .

It's all over, this is the end. Are you dying? Or are you already dead?

WOMAN *lies down on top of* MAN, *covering him with her body.*

WOMAN: I'll cry for you, honey, believe me . . . tears and tears and tears . . .

Do you feel how warm it is? My urethra works even without me. Your striated muscle has gone to sleep, you could hear it loud and clear: "Good night." What? You didn't hear? Then listen again, and repeat: Edgar is dead. Edgar should have been dead ages ago . . . twenty years ago . . . He doesn't exist anymore.

What's wrong? Are you scared? There's nothing to be afraid of. I'm right here . . . and I'll be here till your dying day . . .

Sweet dreams . . . sleep sweetly in my embrace . . . and remember . . . write it on the back of your hand, honey . . . Edgar doesn't exist anymore. Now there's only . . . Louis . . . ? My manly, beautiful . . .

WOMAN *kisses* MAN *on cheek.*

WOMAN: Welcome . . . My sweet, lovely, little doggy . . . Thank you for coming . . .

End of Second Minach

MINACH
Number Three

December 15, 2000

For Jiří Pokorný

The carousel mentioned in the text should start to spin at certain moments throughout the play. I have indicated one point in the text where it could take place, but it could also be elsewhere. I think it should spin more than once, but the director should feel free to decide for him or herself.

A room. In the room, WOMAN 1 *gazes out the window into the distance. In the background, among the shadows, stands* WOMAN 2, *watching* WOMAN 1. WOMAN 1 *pays her no attention.* WOMAN 2 *remains in the shadows, waiting and watching* WOMAN 1 *as she stares into the distance. After a while,* WOMAN 1 *speaks, but continues to stare off into space, as if speaking not to* WOMAN 2 *but to the room around her.*

WOMAN 1: You . . . ?

WOMAN 1*'s words break the silence—as if she had ripped a postcard in two while we were looking at it. The scene comes to life.*

WOMAN 1: By yourself . . . ?

WOMAN 2: My name is . . .

WOMAN 1, *still staring off into the distance, interrupts.*

WOMAN 1: A window is a window. A plate is a plate. A bed is a bed. Things . . . have a life of their own, even without us. Only man dies . . . and his name along with him.

Photographs? Perhaps. (*Speaking to the window.*) A week ago they put in a carousel here. Now it just sits there . . . totally useless . . . revoltingly still . . . completely nonfunctional . . . It's terrifying.

WOMAN 2, *standing in the shadows, listening to* WOMAN 1, *will be known as* KAREN *from this point on.* KAREN *now becomes active, setting the table.*

WOMAN 1: I told them to turn it on. "Give it a spin," I said. And they did, they turned it on, and it spun around all afternoon . . . alone . . . abandoned . . . useless . . .

KAREN *walks over to* WOMAN 1 *and stands behind her, shifting her weight back and forth. Finally, she turns* WOMAN 1 *around and leads her to the table.* WOMAN 1 *sits down, hands on the tabletop.* KAREN *looks at her;* WOMAN 1 *looks at the food.*

WOMAN 1: Chicken . . . So, they told you. What else did they say about me?

KAREN *stands up again and takes a few steps back from the table, watching* WOMAN 1.

KAREN: Nothing.

WOMAN 1 *sits at the table, looking at the food in front of her. She speaks in a matter-of-fact tone of voice.*

WOMAN 1: Nothing . . . I can believe that. Sure. Did they tell you what I like to eat and drink? Did they tell you about my mood swings? Did they tell you I'm a freak?

KAREN *stands, looking at* WOMAN 1 *as if she were an animal.* KAREN*'s eyes shine like coral.* WOMAN 1 *looks at* KAREN *for the first time, staring long and hard, then speaks, with a smile.*

WOMAN 1: Yesterday, a carousel; today, you. (*She slowly begins to eat, concentrating on her food.*) Did you cook this chicken yourself?

KAREN: Yes.

WOMAN 1: What are you just standing there like an idiot for?

KAREN: I just thought . . .

WOMAN 1: Look at that, she even thinks! Oo, a smart one! Are they paying you lots of money?

KAREN *walks slowly toward* WOMAN 1.

KAREN: Shall I sit down with you?

WOMAN 1: Go ahead.

KAREN *sits down at the table.* WOMAN 1 *continues to eat slowly, concentrating. Both women are silent. After a while . . .*

WOMAN 1: Yesterday a carousel; today, you . . .

KAREN: Shall I eat with you?

WOMAN 1: Yesterday a thing; today, a person.

KAREN: Actually, I'm not hungry . . .

WOMAN 1: I guess they're not paying you *that* much. A carousel that doesn't spin; a companion who bores you to tears . . . What else did they tell you?

KAREN: Do you mind if I have some?

WOMAN 1: Wine is all I drink . . . white wine. So. What did they tell you?

KAREN *pours herself a glass of white wine but says nothing.*

WOMAN 1: So boring, she couldn't bore you if she tried.

WOMAN 1 *eats her chicken slowly, with great concentration, while* KAREN *watches, sipping her glass of wine. Both women are silent. After a while,* WOMAN 1 *speaks, again in a matter-of- fact voice.*

WOMAN 1: I wanted company; I got it. I wanted distraction, I got a carousel.

How did they find you?

KAREN: Through an ad.

WOMAN 1: Who did you talk to? Was it a man, or a woman?

KAREN *sits, sipping her wine, answering with the same matter-of-fact tone.*

KAREN: A man.

WOMAN 1: I thought so. Men always pick the lookers. A woman would have picked someone who knew how to be a good companion.
What did he tell you?

KAREN: "Sick, lonesome woman seeks female companion to share her final days. Knowledge of cooking required."

WOMAN 1 *pushes away her plate and pours herself some more wine.* KAREN *says nothing, slowly sipping from her glass.*

WOMAN 1: He told you right: "Sick, lonesome woman" . . . body and mind in just two words. Everything can be crammed into two words . . . "sick and lonesome"—clever! "Knowledge of cooking required."

KAREN: I know how to cook . . .

WOMAN 1: . . . and so boring, she couldn't bore you if she tried . . .

WOMAN 1 *sips her wine, rolling it around in her mouth. She smiles.*

WOMAN 1: . . . "seeks female companion to share final days" . . . "Companion" . . . do you know what that means?

KAREN: A maid?

WOMAN 1: Like in an old-fashioned novel . . . Final days and first days . . . happy days and unhappy days . . . holidays and everydays . . .

Did he say for how long?

KAREN: A month?

WOMAN 1: Did he tell you the diagnosis?

KAREN: He said it was a noninfectious deadly disease.

WOMAN 1: A *well-informed* companion.

KAREN: He said I had to stay to the end.

WOMAN 1: He told you right . . . Did he give you the money?

KAREN: Just part of it.

WOMAN 1: You should've asked for the whole thing up front.

KAREN: He didn't want to give it to me all . . . right away.

WOMAN 1: Will you get more if it takes longer than a month?

KAREN: Yes.

WOMAN 1: Ah, the market economy . . . There, there now, no reason to be offended. You're here to endure my dying days . . .

KAREN *sits, slowly sipping her wine.*

WOMAN 1: I suppose, after all, a woman *is* better.

KAREN: Why?

WOMAN 1: For this sort of thing, it's better.

KAREN: I don't understand . . .

WOMAN 1: Men are too nervous . . . that god-awful, irritating nervousness. That's what's so . . . nice about them.

KAREN: Is there anything I can bring you?

WOMAN 1: Round and round, on the carousel . . . bring me another carousel . . .

The body is a shameless whore. Even when it's at its worst, our base instincts remain.

WOMAN 1 *sits, forehead resting on table, breathing slowly and deeply.* KAREN *sits across from her, slowly drinking her wine. She speaks in a detached, matter-of-fact tone.*

KAREN: Are you in pain?

WOMAN 1 (*smiling to herself*): Terrible pain. Even as a child I was in pain. There's always something that hurts . . .

KAREN: It'll pass in a while.

WOMAN 1 *remains sitting with her forehead on the table.*

KAREN: Do you take any medication?

WOMAN 1 *stands, lets out a deep sigh, and goes to get another bottle of white wine. She opens it nimbly, pouring a glass for* KAREN *and herself. The two women sit, facing each other silently.* WOMAN 1 *lets out a deep sigh as* KAREN *watches her.*

WOMAN 1: I should have gotten a dog . . . to eat the leftovers.

WOMAN 1 *takes a clean plate and slowly fills it with food for* KAREN.

WOMAN 1: There you go . . .

WOMAN 1 *sets the plate down in front of* KAREN *and slowly goes back to sit down. The two women sit facing each other, silently sipping their wine. After a while . . .*

KAREN: I could get you a man . . .

WOMAN 1 *sits impassively, sipping her wine.*

KAREN: What do you like? Blond? Tall? Black?

WOMAN 1 *sits silently, drinking her wine.* KAREN *begins to eat.* WOMAN 1 *stands up and pours some more wine for* KAREN *and herself.*

WOMAN 1: He made the right choice. I couldn't have picked better myself.

KAREN *gives* WOMAN 1 *a puzzled look.*

WOMAN 1: Eat.

KAREN *goes on eating, while* WOMAN 1 *goes back to the window and looks out it again. After a while . . .*

WOMAN 1: What could be appealing about making love with a person who's dying? How much does it cost to screw a corpse?

KAREN: Not a whole lot . . .

WOMAN 1 *starts to unbutton her shirt.*

WOMAN 1: My body is fading away . . . every day, another pound. Every day you can see my bones just that much more . . .

WOMAN 1 *takes out a new glass, making a show of wiping and inspecting it to make sure it's clean.*

WOMAN 1: There you go . . .

She hands KAREN *the clean glass.* KAREN *shows no reaction.*

WOMAN 1: My best friend was a ballerina . . . a really good one, too. The critics said someone as good as her came along only once every hundred years . . . She had her breasts cut off. Said they got in the way when she did pirouettes. What do I know? Maybe it was true. Afterwards, all she had on her chest was the scars. She was so thin . . . When I saw her in the shower, it made me sick to my stomach. Five years she was number one. Five years—in ballet, that's a long time. Then she got married. To another ballet dancer. When he got drunk, he used to say that he had the tenderest little boy of all . . .

WOMAN 1 *hands* KAREN *the clean glass, pours her some wine, sits down across from her.* KAREN *sits, concentrating on eating and drinking.*

WOMAN 1: Do you have children?

KAREN: I'm waiting until I have enough money.

WOMAN 1: That isn't quite right. What you should have said was: "When the lady across from me croaks, *then* I can have children."

KAREN: When the lady across from me croaks, then I can have children.

WOMAN 1: He made the right choice . . .

The women sit silently, drinking their wine. WOMAN 1 *discovers that the table is wobbly and tries to steady it with her hands. After a while . . .*

WOMAN 1: Why are you here?

KAREN: For the money.

WOMAN 1: Doesn't that bother you?

KAREN: No.

WOMAN 1: Death doesn't bother you?

KAREN *sits, drinking her wine, not reacting.* WOMAN 1 *folds up a piece of paper or a napkin or something and puts it under one of the table legs.*

KAREN: Who was that man?

WOMAN 1: Which man?

KAREN: The one I talked to.

WOMAN 1: That was my husband.

KAREN: He seemed very nice.

WOMAN 1: He is.

KAREN: Does he ever come out here?

WOMAN 1: No.

KAREN: Are you rich?

WOMAN 1: The money is his.

The table no longer wobbly, WOMAN 1 *settles back into her seat and continues sipping her wine.*

WOMAN 1: He sent me here. Gave me the carousel. Paid for you. What more could I want? From my loving patron . . .
In a month, he'll be available. Think about it. You two would make a good match.

KAREN: Does he ever call?

WOMAN 1: He's thinking of me.

Are you going to see him?

KAREN: He gave me an address.

WOMAN 1: He said for you to go there?

KAREN: He said to send a telegram.

WOMAN 1: So he didn't give you a number?

KAREN: When it's over, he said to send a telegram.

WOMAN 1: Uh-huh.

WOMAN 1 *leans her head on the table again.* KAREN *sits silently, drinking her wine.*

WOMAN 1: What would you do if it didn't happen?

KAREN: What?

WOMAN 1: If I didn't die.

KAREN: That's impossible.

WOMAN 1: Now that would stink, wouldn't it?

KAREN: He said it was a sure thing.

WOMAN 1: You wouldn't be happy for me?

WOMAN 1 *straightens up again, a look of calm on her face. She takes a drink.*

KAREN: He was very clear: He said "within a month."

WOMAN 1: "Within a month," he said . . .

KAREN: I don't care!

WOMAN 1: I didn't say anything! Do you hear me? I said nothing!

KAREN: I wouldn't advise you to try to cheat me.

WOMAN 1 *stands and goes to get a new glass. Holds it up to the light to check whether it's clean.*

KAREN: No worming out of it, understand?! The terms were clear: a month and that's it.

WOMAN 1: Don't threaten me . . .

KAREN: Quiet!!! The terms were clear, crystal-clear: a month—that's it. Or else . . .

WOMAN 1: Or else you'll get angry, huh? You'll get pissed off, and then the sparks will fly, is that it? Lightning will flash across the sky, lava will come pouring down from the mountains! What else? What else can you think of? Shit. You can't think of shit, you little bitch. Repeat it to yourself every night before you go to sleep: shit, shit, shit.

WOMAN 1 *pours herself some wine in the new glass.* KAREN, *now quiet again, pours what's left in her glass out on the ground and pours herself a new glass. After a while . . .*

KAREN: So nobody comes to see you, huh?

WOMAN 1: What're you going to buy with the money?

KAREN: Not even your mother?

WOMAN 1: How much are you getting, huh? Come on, spill it! How much am I worth to him?

KAREN *stands and walks to the window that* WOMAN 1 *always looks out of.* WOMAN 1 *sits, drinking her wine.* KAREN *breathes onto the misty window and starts to draw pictures on it, the way children do. After a while . . .*

WOMAN 1: . . . couldn't be boring even if she tried . . .

You know what I think? You aren't going to get anything. Not a cent. Just one big *nothing*.

KAREN *remains standing at the window, drawing on the glass.*

WOMAN 1: Oh, pardon me. Maybe you'll get the carousel . . . that heap of metal . . . you can sell it for scrap . . .

After a while . . .

KAREN: What should I make for tomorrow? How about dill sauce?

WOMAN 1: The sight of dill sauce makes me puke.

KAREN: Eggs in dill sauce . . .

WOMAN 1: I'll puke right onto your plate.

KAREN: Maybe with dumplings?

WOMAN 1: I'll puke until your plate's full and dump it over your head.

KAREN: Hmm . . . Dill sauce is pretty quick . . .

KAREN *pulls herself away from the window and absentmindedly crosses the room. Maybe she is trying, again like a child, to see pictures in the floor.*

WOMAN 1: Pour me a drink!

KAREN *goes to* WOMAN 1 *and pours her some wine. Then she breaks off a piece of chicken that is on the table and starts to eat it. She walks around the room, eating.*

WOMAN 1: Drop dead!

KAREN: You drop dead!

WOMAN 1: Silly goose!

KAREN: Up yours, dead feet

WOMAN 1 *stares in disbelief.*

WOMAN 1: Did you say "dead feet?"

KAREN: No, I . . .

WOMAN 1: "Dead feet?"

KAREN: Umm . . .

WOMAN 1: Are you really that dumb, or are you just pretending?

KAREN *walks around, drinking her wine and eating.*

WOMAN 1: You are a total, and I mean absolute, total idiot! . . . "dead feet" . . . where did you hear that? Where in the world did you hear such a stupid thing like that? Or did you read it somewhere? Are you listening to me? No, you didn't read it. You're too dumb to read. You are the prototypical idiot. You're a recipe for idiocy. Take three drops of you daily and become an instant idiot. A top-notch retard. You are a . . .

KAREN *stops walking around and asks calmly, eyes shining.*

KAREN: Why are you so mean?

After a while . . .

WOMAN 1: Mean? Who, me? I'm not mean at all.

KAREN: Yes, you are. You're mean and nasty.

WOMAN 1: Is calling things by their true name mean?

KAREN: You aren't calling things by their true name. You're insulting me.

WOMAN 1: No, I'm not.

KAREN: Yes, you are.

WOMAN 1: No, I'm not.

KAREN *sits back down at the table, across from* WOMAN 1.

KAREN: All right, then. Let's get this clear: So you don't want any sauce or gravy?

They sit looking at each other.

WOMAN 1: What do you want? Just name it! What do you want?

KAREN: I want to finish up here and go away.

WOMAN 1: Where to?

KAREN: The sea.

WOMAN 1: By yourself?

KAREN: I don't know.

WOMAN 1: Which sea do you want to go to?

KAREN: I don't know . . . any sea . . . just as long as there's water.

WOMAN 1: Do you know how to swim?

KAREN: Yes, yes . . . yes, I know how to swim.

WOMAN 1 *stands, gets a new glass, and repeats the ritual of cleaning it. After a while . . .*

WOMAN 1: When I was little, one of my classmates died. She was sort of a homely type . . . always pale . . . always cold, even in summer. I guess that's why she never went swimming with us. Before she died, she asked for cherries.

KAREN: You've got some pretty weird friends . . .

WOMAN 1: What was that?

KAREN: I said, what was that? A fairy tale?

WOMAN 1: Fuck off . . .

WOMAN 1 *pours wine into the new glass. The carousel begins to spin. The empty seats of the carousel appear on the walls. The women notice, watching them.*

KAREN: How much can you drink?

WOMAN 1: A lot . . . what do you think? Do you hear? I'm asking your opinion. I'd like to know.

KAREN *watches the carousel spin.*

KAREN: In my opinion, you drink too much. Way too much.

WOMAN 1: You're not exactly a picture of moderation . . .

KAREN *walks to the window and looks out at the carousel.* WOMAN 1 *does the same.*

WOMAN 1: The Moravian Highlands . . . You know what they are, don't you?

KAREN: Be quiet!!!

WOMAN 1: Excuse me . . . the Moravian Highlands: the cure for every pain. The Moravian Highlands: health itself. Rest assured, I'm not making this up. The Moravian Highlands: one big fat ass after another.

Carousel slowly comes to a standstill. WOMAN 1 *fills* KAREN*'s glass with wine.*

KAREN: The city is better . . .

WOMAN 1: Yes, isn't it?

KAREN: It's anonymous there. Anything goes.

WOMAN 1: Yes, tell me more.

KAREN: You can sit by the window and just look out and . . . think, without anyone bothering you.

WOMAN 1: You sure can.

KAREN: And it's got a life of its own, its own energy, that gives people the drive to go forward.

WOMAN 1: They're always walking somewhere . . .

KAREN: Yeah, always walking somewhere . . .

WOMAN 1: And if they're not walking, they're driving.

KAREN: Yep. That too.

WOMAN 1: But did you ever get the feeling that life in the city is meaningless? I mean, here, when you look outside and you see someone, you can tell by looking at them what their goal is.
Do you understand? You see a tractor, and right next to it is a field. You see children, and right there a river. Do you get my drift?

KAREN: Be quiet.

WOMAN 1: In the city, there are only waves. Waves rolling in, one after the next. I love the city. I want to go home.

Hold me . . .

KAREN *obediently holds* WOMAN 1.

WOMAN 1: Take me home, please?

KAREN: I can't.

WOMAN 1: Then send him a telegram.

KAREN: I can't.

KAREN *goes back to the table.* WOMAN 1 *follows her.*

WOMAN 1: Ask him to come get me . . .

KAREN: That's your business, not mine. It has nothing to do with me.

WOMAN 1: My sweet little child. If I decide to practice yoga, that is truly my business. But not this. This is a wish. This is a request. And I am asking you: Take me home.

KAREN: All right. How about a compromise? I won't make dill sauce; I'll make stuffed peppers instead, okay? Stuffed peppers with rice.

WOMAN 1: Do you not understand, or do you not *want* to understand? Tell me, truthfully, I'm begging you. Do you not understand, or do you not want to?

KAREN: I don't understand.

WOMAN 1: All right then. Once again: This is my final wish. Consider it my final wish. You know that one from books, right? You've read about that before, haven't you?
Now wait—I'm not trying to insult you. I just want you to remember . . . There's this thing people call their final wish. Right? Remember? There. You see. So that's what I want. I want to go home.

KAREN: I understand. I'll do all I can for you, anything you want. I'll cook for you, take care of you, you've got nothing to worry about . . .

WOMAN 1: Oh God . . . Hold me . . .

KAREN *takes* WOMAN 1 *on her lap and holds her.*

KAREN: I'll take care of it, don't worry . . . I'll even do yoga with you . . .

WOMAN 1: Take me home . . .

KAREN: How about if I brought you a man? That would take your mind off things. Don't worry. These guys are professionals. They know what they're doing. They're psychologists, too. Trust me. Sex works wonders. It'll clear out your head. How about it? . . . Yes? No?

WOMAN 1 *looks at* KAREN.

WOMAN 1: You know what? Listen good, you little cunt. I want to go home.

KAREN: Uh-uh.

WOMAN 1: Listen and try to understand: There are illnesses of the body, and illnesses of the soul. My soul is sick, and probably my body, too. Is that clear? Now look . . . here, inside, by my heart, that's where my soul is.

Sometimes I feel really good, and sometimes I feel really bad. Sometimes I just laugh at myself. And other times I don't know what to do. I've got a horrible life, don't I? Take me home . . . Please, take me home.

KAREN *rocks* WOMAN 1 *on her lap.*

WOMAN 1: Until you came, I had only a hunch—no certainty, nothing. Do you understand? I didn't know how close I was. I didn't know I had a month. You're the first one who told me . . .

KAREN: Why are you doing this? Why are you saying these things?

WOMAN 1: He brought me here so I'd feel better. "It'll give you a chance to relax," he said. I remember it plain as day: "It'll give you a chance to relax." He put in that carousel. To make me happy . . .

KAREN *rocks* WOMAN 1 *on her lap.*

WOMAN 1: I was alone. I've always been alone. But here I was desperately alone. Sometimes I would imagine . . . standing there by the window . . . that I'd run away and escape . . . home . . . I could do that, right? Couldn't I?

KAREN: Shhh . . .

WOMAN 1: If it's true . . . if I'm really dying . . . if you're telling me the truth . . . then, please, I beg you, take me home. He'll still pay you. Trust me, he will.

KAREN: Try and go to sleep. Just go to sleep and don't think about it. I'll sing you a lullaby if you want.

WOMAN 1: There's not that much left anyway, right? You said you already got part up front . . .

KAREN: Silly, this isn't about money; it's about the principle of the thing. It's about character. And promises. Giving your word. Trust. It's a lot more complicated than you think. You want an answer to everything right away. Well, I prefer to wait.

WOMAN 1: Send him a telegram, please. Tell him I'm begging . . . Don't forget to tell him that I beg him with all my might to come here and stay a while . . . so he can hold me . . .

KAREN: Shhh . . . sleep . . .

KAREN *rocks* WOMAN 1 *on her lap, singing her a lullaby.*

WOMAN 1: I can't sleep! I can't walk! I peed my pants! I'm scared! I'm sick! Everything hurts!

KAREN: I'm supposed to put down all that? That's what you want? After all that?

WOMAN 1: I'm scared, don't you understand?

KAREN: Of what? Of what, for Christ's sake? What do you know what it's like? Why are you so stuck-up? Why can't you accept things the way they are? Why can't you accept people the way they are?

You think I don't get scared? Well, think again, I do. It's all about you . . . the only thing you ever talk about is you . . .

KAREN *sits, rocking* WOMAN 1 *on her lap, singing her a lullaby.*

WOMAN 1: So many types of death to choose from. And in the end . . . it's almost always some dumb thing.

KAREN: I forgive you for everything . . . all of it . . .

KAREN *smiles at* WOMAN 1, *who is still in her arms.*

KAREN: Don't get mad, okay? Don't try to blackmail me. My word is my word. You have your word and I have mine. But the main thing is not to be afraid. I'm right here, and I'll be here to the end. I promise.

WOMAN 1: Take me home . . . I beg you . . .

KAREN: Stop begging.

End of Third Minach

End of Play

AQUABELLES

David Drábek

David Drábek
Photo courtesy of Hynek Glos

David Drábek, born June 18, 1970, received his degree in film and theatre studies from the Philosophical Faculty of Palacký University in Olomouc. While an undergraduate, he co-founded, with Darek Král, the Burning Giraffe Studio, specializing in modern cabaret. There, Drábek wrote and directed all the studio productions. From 1996 to 2001 he was dramaturg for the Moravian Theatre in Olomouc; and from 2001 to 2003, he led the alternative company Burning House. In 1995 Drábek received the Alfréd Radok Award for Best Play in the Drama Competition for *Joan of the Park* and again in 2003 for *Aquabelles*. Two years later, *Aquabelles* received the Alfréd Radok Award for the best Czech Play Produced. His *Mašín Brothers Square* won second prize in the Alfréd Radok Playwriting Competition of 2007.

Currently, Drábek works as author, director, and dramaturg with The Theatre Company of Petr Bezruč in Ostrava, the Minor Theatre in Prague, and the Klicpera Theatre in Hradec Králové, where he is now the Artistic Director. His latest play, *Unisex,* is about the end of violence in Europe, and features wizards, European commissioners, seal people, and birthmarks. He is collaborating with the director Vladimír Morávek on a film adaptation of *Aquabelles*, and writing a screenplay for the film *Chocolate Eaters*. Movies, TV, kitsch, the media, and pop culture are all fertile source material for his comedies, cabarets, and dramas. A collection of seven of his plays was published in 2005 by Větrné Mlýny Publishers.

Woody Allen writes, in a story called "My Apology" set in ancient Greece, that being a philosopher beats picking olives. And that's how I feel about being a playwright. Yes, I get up every morning and slave at a machine. But what a machine, with a glowing logo of a bitten apple! Maybe I thought I could pick up girls with my comic texts. But no, you probably just can't help it. Your surroundings lack the words, action, and images that hatch in your head and race through your mind. And so you write them down. And in my case the urge is so strong, I'm also forced to put them on stage.

My inspiration for this play is best captured by the title of the Erich Maria Remarque novel Three Comrades: David, Petr, and Jan. Joined by our involvement in the "Velvet Revolution," as well as our studies in Olomouc, we were "Havelists," that is, supporters of Václav Havel; in other words, great romantics and idealists. So the play, whose characters are a mix of fact and fiction, confronts this idealistic experience with the actual course of events in the Czech lands after the revolution. The disenchantment, the anger, the fears, but also the enormous power of friendship.

Aquabelles got me two prestigious Radok awards, it won a competition for European plays in Berlin, and the very first production of it in Hradec Králové was, without exaggeration, a cult hit. At this point it's been translated into at least eight languages and even my enemies admit, gnashing their teeth, that it's not bad. Although many "experts" also use it as a stick to attack my other plays, saying, "We want another Aquabelles," I couldn't care less. I constantly need to try new forms and new themes. I don't make clones.

—David Drábek

Front to back: David Steigerwald, Ondřej Malý, Jan Sklenář, and Filip Richtermoc, in *Aquabelles* (2005), Klicperovo divadlo, Hradec Králové, directed by Vladimír Morávek

Photo courtesy of Josef Ptáček

Aquabelles

by

David Drábek

Translated by
Don Nixon

Language editing by
Pavla Matásková

CHARACTERS

PHILIP
KAJETÁN
PAVEL
EDITH
IVAN
RADEK
MARKÉTA
SIMON
MRS. MAGDA PROSPER
HER SON
FIRST (female)
SECOND (female)
OLD WOMAN
VOICE OF THE STOMACH SPIRIT
ASSISTANT DIRECTOR
KAJETÁN'S ASSISTANT (female)
DIRECTOR'S VOICE
MAGDA'S SON
SOCCER FANS
VILLAGER, an elderly man

With regards to Cher and Celine Dion, the references in the original Czech version were to Czech pop singers. Other pop divas, along with the relevant details of their lives, can be substituted as necessary.

ACT ONE

THE OLD WOMAN

A room well preserved in an art-nouveau style, contaminated with figurines made of plastic—obviously gifts from children and grandchildren. An old woman sits in an armchair and concentrates as she polishes the knee of her stockings with her ring finger. A pendulum clock indicates it is late in the afternoon. The OLD WOMAN*'s eyes become flooded in defiance, and she suddenly jumps out of the chair, straining: "*No way! Not like this anymore . . .*" and leaves the room in determination.*

PHILIP's VOICE: One day my Grandmother decided to start her life anew. She took her raincoat, her hiking boots, a couple of books, her bamboo snorkel, and her knapsack. Then she left. We never saw her again. I carry a picture of her in my wallet—taken when she was a little girl at the girl's high school. She told me: "That's me—second from the left. I love water."

DRAGONFLIES FROM THE ABATOIR

An indoor pool. We can hear music. Three hairy masculine legs surface above the water in time to the refrain. They circle around above the water in a "flamingo" position. We are reminded of three dragonflies. What follows is a somewhat disharmonic "barracuda," then a completely disjointed "albatross," and finally three heads break the surface of the water, ending the sequence in a "tub position." KAJETÁN, PAVEL, *and* PHILIP, *wearing nose clips and protective goggles, breathe heavily.*

PAVEL: What are you laughing at?

KAJETÁN: You kicked me in the back. During the turn. And what's more, those new goggles make you look like something from Star Wars!

PAVEL: I completely lost the rhythm . . . You got too close to me! It should just be like this: leg, leg, this, this, leg, leg, this and that!

KAJETÁN: Aha. So, that's why you were glaring at me. Hey just like right now! Like that galactic little creature!

PHILIP: Other than that, we're fantastic! I can feel it! Really! I know it! I'm gonna go swim for a while.

KAJETÁN: I'll open the slivovitz. Want some?

PHILIP: Leave it for me on the steps. I'm just gonna . . . dive for a bit.

PAVEL: It's fucking cold in here today! Aren't they heating the place?

KAJETÁN (*feeling the radiator*): It's hot. You're just cold, 'cause you're so scrawny. Look at my love handles! Now that's insulation! I'm not that bad, am I? How I keep it a meter away from my spine, it's fine. (*beat*) I've got some great peppers.

KAJETÁN *unpacks a huge shopping bag.* PAVEL *undresses, timidly with his back toward the audience.*

KAJETÁN: Why'd you turn your back on me? Why are you showing me your pitiful, pimpled butt!

PAVEL: I don't have a pimpled butt.

KAJETÁN: It's so pockmarked. Why don't you show me your extraordinary penis? That magical witch-killing wand! Such a rarity!!

PAVEL: What are you babbling on about?

KAJETÁN: Someone stole my car. Assholes. Man, today, I could just stuff myself! I'm so fucking depressed.

PAVEL: You mean your snobby Jetta?

KAJETÁN: Hey. I'm not crying anymore. See. I'm strong. I'm fine. (*He jumps up.*) Just give me a knife and let me at that asshole! To hell with the courts! How can anyone who has an ID and a mother just run off with somebody else's stuff? (*He sits down.*) Tomorrow, I'm gonna buy a new one.

PAVEL: Do you have any idea what to do with all your dough?

KAJETÁN: Is this my towel?

PAVEL: It's Philip's.

KAJETÁN: Did he drown?

PAVEL: There's some bubbles down there. I can hear him.

KAJETÁN: This one?

PAVEL: Mine.

KAJETÁN: Then it's this one. (*The Hotel Europa insignia can be seen on the towel.*) Hey, look at this—she packed a hotel towel for me . . . this is how a man should feel at home?

PAVEL: Lucy would never have done anything like that. What's that new one . . . ?

KAJETÁN: Just leave it, okay? Lucy once packed her swimming suit in with my stuff. Remember? Then, I put them on, just for a joke, and ripped them apart. I'm with Edith now.

PAVEL: With that . . . ?

KAJETÁN: Yeah.

PAVEL: Do you love her?

KAJETÁN: Hey. Do you want my job on the game show? Don't ask such tricky questions. (*He knocks on the poolside.*) Hey! Shall I pour the slivovitz into the water for you, my little gold fish?

PHILIP *surfaces. He rubs his red eyes.*

PHILIP: Hey, guys! Imagine two piranhas, you know, swimming up to each other. One piranha is just as strong as the other, right? They're exactly the same. And they start attacking each other, just tearing each other to shreds and eating each other up. Munch, munch, munch. Just gnawing each other's flesh, and swallowing it whole. And because they have exactly the same strength, they could actually eat each other up entirely—right to the bone, until, there'd be nothing left. Not even the tiniest bit of skin.

They howl with laughter at PHILIP. KAJETÁN stabs *a corkscrew into the cork.* PAVEL *takes the wrapper off some hard goat cheese and slices it, together with some sausage.* PHILIP *lifts his skinny, blue arm out of the water, and nibbles on the pieces of food.*

PAVEL: How much should I cut up?

KAJETÁN: All of it! (*He lights a cigar.*) Ah! This is the life!

Fade to black, except for a cloud of smoke from the cigar.

PHILIP´S VOICE: When I was a kid, I was always terrified of water. Today, maybe I kind of idealize that moment, but I think that one particular dream drove away my fear of water. I saw myself fall out of a little rickety boat into the night ocean. I flapped around hysterically in the foamy waves and saw miles of dark water under me. I felt as though some horrible indescribable monsters were coming to the surface toward me. Hundreds of creatures with poisonous tentacles and thorns, with their deadly, white, protruding eyes . . . And then all of a sudden, my grandmother appeared in the water next to me. But she had such smooth skin, and she looked so young. Then she took my hand, and I immediately calmed down . . . then I woke up.

Light. Time has passed on the Aquabelles' picnic.

PAVEL: You didn't smoke in school, did you?

KAJETÁN: Just the pipe, remember? We were unconventional, weren't we? Now, we only have these vulgar and dull cigarettes!

PAVEL: We really believed in something back then. I'm horrified now how my students know absolutely nothing about the regime and the stench that we actually lived in. They don't care about Bolsheviks at all. They're so far removed from it, that in a couple of years when the next Big Brother comes along and snatches their things out from under them, those idiots will still be so calm, so "cool," that they won't know what's happened until it's too late . . .

PHILIP: It's easy to control brothers who are drugged up, isn't it? (*He reaches for the bag of potato chips.*)

PAVEL: But I'm not gonna give up. I'm not gonna just sit back and watch how the Communist keeps on being manager and everyone in the underground movement is still a night watchman! Fuck! I'm not forgetting!

KAJETÁN: That's just old controversy, now, believe me. Show business swallowed up all of those old atheist assholes a long time ago, pal. (*He stubs out his cigarette and lights another.*)

PHILIP: You're smoking one right after the other.

KAJETÁN: This guy from Karvina was also addicted to nicotine. One day, he went over to his neighbor's. And just when he was peeking over the guy's fence, this dog's head just all of a sudden flew out at him. Some Rottweiler or something, and the bitch bit the bottom lip right off the guy's mouth.

PHILIP: Jesus!

KAJETÁN: I'm not kidding! And that champion, with his mouth flapping like a widowed labia runs home, and the first thing he has to solve is how to get his nicotine fix, right. But without his lip, he can't take a drag, right? So, the fool orders his wife—a non-smoker—to cut the top off one of those plastic water bottles. Then he stuffs it into his mouth and inhales the smoke that his poor wretched wife puffs out. (*He turns to PAVEL and howls with laughter.*) Don't be such a sour puss! People are so incorrigible! Fuck them!

PAVEL: The words of an entertainer. It's always just words with no meaning. A nursery rhyme. Background. Every morning, instead of a warm up: Israelis killed this many Palestinians, Palestinians killed this many Israelis . . .

KAJETÁN: It's a sport. It's back and forth all the time. Like soccer, Sparta and Baník.

PAVEL: What are you talking about, you overstuffed Central European pigs? Why are you so cynical?

KAJETÁN: Hey, you've had a little too much! You're annoying when you're wasted. You always get aggressive.

PHILIP: Guys, I'm just gonna dive for a while, okay? (*He goes underwater.*)

PAVEL: Actually, I brought you something. Markéta picked it up. I chewed her out, and told her not to bring that shit into the house. But then, she opened it up to page 22. (*He gives the magazine to* KAJETÁN.)

KAJETÁN: Shit! . . . No fucking way! . . .

Black.

ON THE FRONT PAGE (COVER BOY)

KAJETÁN*'s apartment. Ikea standards. Several framed pictures of* KAJETÁN *with celebrities on his dresser. One is with* EDITH *at the sea. Frowning,* KAJETÁN *angrily smacks the magazine down on the polished table.* EDITH *enters.*

EDITH (*endearingly*): Kajetán, I . . .

KAJETÁN: What?

EDITH (*even more endearingly*): Kajetán, I swallowed my SIM card.

KAJETÁN: What?!

EDITH: I can't talk very well. I swallowed my SIM card.

KAJETÁN: Why?

EDITH: You never called, never sent any text messages . . . I just wanted to somehow get revenge.

KAJETÁN: Open your mouth.

EDITH (*opens it*): Aaugh, aaugh.

KAJETÁN: Don't do that . . . Open wider . . .

EDITH: It's gone. Forever. Do you think it'll stay inside me forever?

KAJETÁN (*grabbing the magazine and smacking it down on the table again*): This is your doing!

EDITH: I just . . . are you angry?

KAJETÁN (*to the audience*): She's not as dumb as she looks. I'm so pissed off at her, that I am perhaps merely manipulating this picture of her a little bit.

EDITH: Are you angry?

KAJETÁN: Terribly! (*Holding the magazine up to her face.*) What do you see?

EDITH: Both of us sitting by our swimming pool?

KAJETÁN: You see you and a fat tub of lard sitting by our swimming pool!

EDITH: Big deal . . . (*cutely*) just a little relaxed belly . . .

KAJETÁN: A little? You mean this beached whale? Fuck! (*beat*) Jesus, you're smiling right into the camera . . . ! You . . . you knew they were taking pictures of us?

EDITH: Well, sort of . . . Yes.

KAJETÁN: I can't believe it . . . you sold me out! For money!

EDITH: Look . . . Sit down for a minute. (*She puts on a serious face.*) We need to talk. Sit down. I have to sit down too. Oooh, that SIM card is jabbing me in the stomach . . .

KAJETÁN *grabs a handful of fish-shaped sesame crackers from a bowl.*

EDITH: See . . . I just wanted my family to be proud. To let them know that they lived for a reason. Now that I've been in the magazine, our neighbors will show some respect to my parents, because everyone reads this.

KAJETÁN: Don't try to scare me! Not everyone reads this . . . this sleaze!

EDITH: Everyone does. And don't look down your nose on people. You artists. Thanks to magazines like this, people today still know how to read. They are our primers, you see?

KAJETÁN (*to the audience*): Comenius is somewhere bleeding on a dentist's chair right at this moment!

EDITH: I never leave anything to chance. While they were taking our pictures from the roof, I came in to change into my outfits a few times.

KAJETÁN (*to the audience*): I take it back. She is dumber than a bag of hammers.

EDITH: Who are you talking to? Are you taking your vitamins? Why did you try on my thong this morning? And why do you think that I am some kind of stupid little chickie who bleaches even her nostril hairs? I wasn't born yesterday, honey. Thanks to you, my career is taking off. Up until now, I was just a piece of your decoration, but I am a babe! And I was on the cover of a magazine! In a couple of weeks, I'll be giving interviews and no one will ever ask where I came from.

KAJETÁN: I need to get some fresh air. (*He exits.*)

EDITH (*to the audience*): And whichever one of you is laughing at me and my strategy, well, you are just a . . . a backward cunt!

Quiet.

EDITH (*a sound suddenly erupts from her throat*): X – X – X – X – X – X – X – X – X – X – X!!

Quiet.

EDITH: In Elle magazine, they recommended that you scream "X" twenty times one right after the other. It's good for firming the muscles of your neckline.

Quiet.

EDITH: X – X – X – X – X – X – X – X – X – X – X – X – X – X – X – X – X – X – X!!!

Quiet. Fade out.

THE FRENCH LESSON

A little room in IVAN*'s apartment. Filled with CDs and dictionaries. Very tidy.* KAJETÁN *in his jacket storms in towards* IVAN *and embraces him.*

KAJETÁN: I'm so pissed! They're worse than fleas!

IVAN: What happened? Shoes. Shoes off, please.

KAJETÁN (*taking off his shoes*): She hired some paparazzi to take pictures of us near the swimming pool. Look.

IVAN (*flips through the magazine*): You eat helium for breakfast?

KAJETÁN: Just rub it in! God! They say that everyone reads this shit—cover to cover.

IVAN: It's true. Sorry. People are interested in this more than in the afterlife.

KAJETÁN: No wonder—it provides the answers to burning questions like . . . "What am I worth if I'm not wearing my antiperspirant?"

IVAN: And wait until they print our story—"One Fateful French Lesson."

KAJETÁN: I still have you, though. You're always able to comfort me. As if I were able to hug myself. Give me a kiss . . . What's wrong?

IVAN: We need to talk.

KAJETÁN: Okay, what?

IVAN: Sit down.

KAJETÁN: I'd rather stand. I'm losing weight. Ok. What is it?

IVAN: I met someone.

KAJETÁN: Aha.

IVAN: His name is Radek. He is . . . Well, to me, he's just . . . well, he's . . . he's in the kitchen.

KAJETÁN: Here? In the next room?

IVAN: Yeah.

KAJETÁN: Hiding from me?

IVAN: No. He's trying to fix the stove.

KAJETÁN: I told you that I'd send someone to . . .

IVAN: But I can't survive two months without eating.

KAJETÁN: Well, just call him in here.

IVAN: He won't come.

KAJETÁN: Is he shy?

IVAN: He's just afraid that they will gawk at him, too. You know how it is.

KAJETÁN: We're here alone.

IVAN: I doubt it.

KAJETÁN: We are.

IVAN: No one ever knows with you. People are always following you. Radek doesn't want to belong to a world like that. He says that when you're famous, someone somewhere can drink from your bowl of energy.

KAJETÁN: Some kind of smart-ass, is he?

IVAN: He's studying psychology and personal relations. I have a weak spot for smart guys.

KAJETÁN (*cracks the door open to the kitchen*): Hi. You're Radek, aren't you?

RADEK (*offstage*): Uh huh. Ivan's told me about you.

KAJETÁN: What's with the stove?

RADEK (*offstage*): It made up its own mind. I'm just trying to help it reveal its true nature. In reality, inorganic matter lives exactly the same way we do.

KAJETÁN: Maybe it thinks it's a food processor. (*He turns to* IVAN.) I think you're gonna starve to death. (*whispers*) What about his dick?

IVAN (*whispers back*): Yours is nicer.

KAJETÁN: That's what I thought.

IVAN: I love him. He's so pure—he has principles. He slaved at night in a bakery just so that he can save enough money to take me to Croatia. Well, we're going in December, but isn't that the sweetest thing?

KAJETÁN (*to the kitchen*): Do your folks know?

RADEK (*offstage*): What?

KAJETÁN: That you're a homo?

RADEK (*offstage*): Yours?

KAJETÁN (*closes the door*): You're trading me in for that child?

IVAN: What kind of question is that, Kajetán? What do you mean, "trade?" I never really had you to begin with. You show your face here once a month, unpack pictures of your new girl friend, we have sex, watch a movie, and then bam . . . just every so often, I get a text message. A funny one.

KAJETÁN: You know I'm not a fag. I can't help it. It would be so much easier for me, but I'm just not. Women fascinate me.

IVAN: No, you just don't know what you want? You just take it all—whatever comes your way. And once you do have everything, you just throw it in the garage where it rots in a pile. And then you promise that you'll take the stuff out in the morning, recycle it, and start clean all over again.

KAJETÁN: Cette la vie.

IVAN (*corrects his French*): C'est la vie.

KAJETÁN: Who's gonna to teach me French now?

IVAN: Come on, we only studied French on our first date.

KAJETÁN: I'll buy you a new stove, so you don't have to go to the student cafeteria. See you. (*He leaves.*)

Black.

WEBBED HANDS

The Aquabelles stand in the water about to begin training.

PAVEL (*offers his friends a glass containing a type of gelatinous substance*): Gentlemen, this is gelatin. Here—we can put it in our hair and it'll stop flying around like we're some rednecks. I stole it from my mother-in-law when she was baking.

KAJETÁN: I'm not gonna. It burned the hair right off a poor girl's head. They showed her bald little head on TV.

PAVEL: You shouldn't believe in children's fairy tales. It smells pretty good.

KAJETÁN: We'd be better off eating it, my friends. (*To* PHILIP.) You're kind of blue.

PHILIP: I think I should tell you guys something. I've been here since our last practice.

PAVEL: What do you mean—you've been here since our last practice?

PHILIP: I never went home. I just stayed in the water. When you left, I went to the bathroom, came back, turned the lights off and got back into the water.

KAJETÁN: You stayed here? How long . . . six days?

PHILIP: Yeah.

PAVEL: Why? Crisis at home?

PHILIP: Look at my hands. Against the light. Do you see it?

A cell phone rings.

KAJETÁN: Shit. Sorry guys. (*Answers the telephone.*) . . . Of course, I know about the broadcast. It's postponed, okay. Good-bye. (*Hangs up.*) Shit. Guys, I'm just gonna drink the grog right out of the thermos, okay? God, it's been such a bad day. (*Wet, he patters over to his bag.*)

PAVEL (*peers at* PHILIP*'s fingers*): Yeah, there is something there. Something is sprouting down there in between your fingers.

KAJETÁN: Probably eczema or something.

PHILIP: I'm growing webs between my fingers.

PAVEL: You're just imagining it . . .

KAJETÁN: Well, just drink up, my little frog prince. Come on, guys let's get a move on. Let's try the "albatross" again.

PAVEL *turns on the music. The men put on their nose clips and swim. They dance.*

THE WORLD AFTER FREDDIE MERCURY
───

A picnic after practice. The men are wearing bathrobes and towels. They drink, eat, read the newspaper, and sometimes enthusiastically gesticulate. Only PHILIP *eventually leaves the group and climbs back into the water.*

PAVEL: I really love feeling the pins and needles in my toes and when my head spins after we do our turns. When we're swimming under the surface of the water hip to hip . . .

KAJETÁN: . . . when we come up for air, we stroke the water off the palms of our hands, and together as one man, we shoot our hands into the air and make them into fists . . .

PAVEL: . . . and we exhale the last little bit of breath that we've saved . . .

PHILIP: I am in my own element.

PAVEL: My head is swimming already. You're a real dragon the way you keep filling me up . . .

KAJETÁN: I don't want to drag us out from this lethargy that has recently lain us down, like a . . . like a lover having a hypoglycemic attack. Gentlemen!

PHILIP: Is it possible to swim backwards—I mean, back in time? Can animals?

KAJETÁN: Not long ago, my mom thought long and hard over a cup of coffee, and she, even if she is sort of temperate and serious . . . she just said: "It's not as fun as it used to be since Freddie Mercury died."

PAVEL: It's true, we're completely cramped, and what's more you're such a scrooge.

KAJETÁN: You really wanna piss me off, don't you, Pavel. I could give a damn about money! I could just as easily throw it away, asshole!

PAVEL: And half the world's population is dying of hunger . . .

KAJETÁN: If everyone in the world could fit into my kitchen, they'd be more than welcome . . . what's eating you? What's gotten into you about me? Does the TV gig bother you?

PHILIP: Stop fighting. (*Dives under the water.*)

PAVEL: We made a pact. We'll never collaborate with them.

KAJETÁN: With whom?

PAVEL: With the void.

KAJETÁN: You are still living in *The Neverending Story*, my boy. Wake up! The Commies are gone!

PAVEL: They're not. They are inside of each and every one of us. Like some kind of cancer.

KAJETÁN: It's holding you back. The stuff blew over. Should I be bitter and fret about it? Sorry. Life is a cabaret. A game. No one is oppressing anyone anymore. You're not going to ruin your life just because Czechs have bad taste.

PAVEL: I didn't want it this way. It's all about consumerism. It has no class.

KAJETÁN: So put on your T-shirt with Che Guevara, strap yourself up with bombs and dive between the shelves of detergents in Walmart and clean the world! Idiot!

PAVEL: I'm so pissed off, I could just kill someone. It's horrible.

A moment of silence.

KAJETÁN (*looks in his bag*): Because of you, I brought your favorite gin. You like it don't you? . . . The juniper just pulses . . .

PAVEL: I am so wasted . . .

PHILIP *surfaces. He makes his way over the banks of the dam on his hands and knees, then crawls on all fours toward the toilet.*

KAJETÁN: Have you gone insane?

PHILIP: I'm going to take a leak.

KAJETÁN: No, you're crawling to take a leak.

PAVEL: What's wrong with you?

PHILIP: I want to be an otter. (*He disappears behind the door.*)

KAJETÁN: He's pretty wasted, isn't he?

PAVEL: He barely drank anything.

KAJETÁN (*lights up*): It also pisses me off that the world is so shallow and washable . . . and what's more, there are cameras everywhere, right? . . . But what can we do? Times are long gone when even the Farmers' Almanacs were written in verse.

PAVEL: I don't like the looks of Philip.

PAVEL *and* KAJETÁN *watch as* PHILIP *crawls carefully on all fours back into the pool.*

PAVEL: Why did you keep yourself locked up here for so long?

PHILIP: I just don't want to waste time anymore. (*After a while.*) I think we have the right to make our own choices. (*He munches on nuts.*) And I've decided to retreat back to the water.

A short silence. The men watch each other silently.

KAJETÁN: Do you expect me to say something now? Should I shake my little bell? What's led you to this?

PHILIP: I feel like I don't have much time left. I don't want to roam about anymore. I wanna stay home. In my own element.

PAVEL: Like an otter.

PHILIP: Yeah.

KAJETÁN: You are so much like Pavel here. He'll start off with humanitarian terrorism, and off you go now and establish the Green Party in a lake? Hey, guys?! The revolution is over, and what's more, it wasn't even a revolution at all. (*He sobs.*) I love you, guys. What's happening to you?

PHILIP: Kajetán, I've been trying to keep it from you. For a long time now, I've had no idea what's going on between people. It all started when nothing I heard made sense to me anymore—on the radio, on the street, on TV. Nothing. Then I couldn't put words in the newspapers into any kind of context. Like in the store or at the train station, I just stood there and I didn't know anything at all. I just watched people. Then I breathed through my mouth for a second, hoping that I could catch myself. But nothing. And these failures became longer.

PAVEL: What about your girlfriend?

KAJETÁN: Which one?

PAVEL: Kamila's sister.

PHILIP: She left me tons of guilt trips on my answering machine. It stopped a couple of days ago.

PAVEL: Oh. Markéta and Simon say hi.

A moment of silence.

PHILIP: My only joy in life is our secret synchronized swimming meet.

Silence.

KAJETÁN: Boys, let's put on some Tom Waits and I'll open another glorious bottle . . .

KAJETÁN *puts on a CD. Someone once said that Tom Waits sings as though he is gargling a handful of pebbles . . . The tension is released.*

KAJETÁN: All the misery in the world—plagues, wars, AIDS—run around inside my head. But in the end, I'll still park myself on that bloated picture of me beside the swimming pool . . . I am such a loser. And on top of it all, they drew the arrows and put the headline "Whoa! Are you fat!!"

PAVEL: That's pretty brutal. They really got you!

PHILIP: I haven't seen it.

KAJETÁN *shows him the magazine.*

KAJETÁN: And I told my poor girlfriend that I thought my career would be much different. I told her, "It's such a waste for me. Jesus, I graduated with a Major in Philosophy!" But she just asked me if I went to school with any Generals.

For the first time, they laugh together.

PHILIP: Why did they take pictures of you, when you had no idea that they were there? That was a stupid question, wasn't it?

PAVEL: Lucy would never have done that. She had class.

KAJETÁN: Stop bringing Lucy into this. It's over. She has two little kids, a husband, and it's over. That was a long time ago.

PAVEL: You shouldn't have let her go. I have to tell you this openly.

PHILIP: She had pointed ears . . .

KAJETÁN: Yeah, she did. But guys, I haven't told you how my new girlfriend went nuts and swallowed her SIM card.

PAVEL: Nooo . . .

KAJETÁN: Just to fucking punish me. (*He freezes for a moment.*) . . . Hey, I have an idea. I have an idea. Let's call her. Let's call her stomach!

PAVEL: We are so wasted . . .

KAJETÁN (*dials the number*): Let's see who fucking picks up the phone . . .

PAVEL: Suddenly I feel so great . . .

KAJETÁN: Hey, it's ringing . . . Oh God! Someone answered! Hello?

VOICE OF THE STOMACH SPIRIT: Hello? Is that you, Kajetán?

KAJETÁN: And . . . You are . . . ?

SPIRIT: You wouldn't believe it.

KAJETÁN: Who?

SPIRIT: The Spirit of the Stomach.

PAVEL: Fuck.

SPIRIT: What would you like to know?

KAJETÁN: Come off it, okay . . . Did you steal Edith's cell phone?

SPIRIT: No. The SIM card is lodged firmly in her stomach. The foamy stomach juices and intestinal villi are delicately tapping on it.

KAJETÁN: Ah . . . ehm . . .

SPIRIT: Gentlemen, have fun with your little encounters. But, from now on, they will be a little . . . different. Your fun is only apparent. The electric eels of your conscience are slithering under the hoods of your heads, and request that you listen to them. Instead, you are trying to keep them away with your gilded hands of oblivion . . .

PHILIP (*surfaces*): I am an otter.

SPIRIT: I have to go now. Thank you for calling. Good-bye.

Busy signal.

The men stare thoughtfully at the ground and drink.

USED WEAPONS

The kitchen in PAVEL's *apartment.* PAVEL, *his wife* MARKÉTA, *and seven year old* SIMON *sit at the table. The dense atmosphere precipitates into small crystals on the lampshades. Dinner.*

PAVEL: I'm afraid for both of them. They don't know what to believe in. And Kajetán's sluts . . . Aren't you talking to me?

MARKÉTA: What happened this morning really got to me.

PAVEL: What?

MARKÉTA: When you yelled at me about the magazine.

PAVEL: We can't support them. Don't ever buy it again.

SIMON: Whoa, uncle sure is fat.

PAVEL: Don't speak like that. (*To Markéta.*) You see. He's already beginning to talk like the magazine. They have no respect for people.

MARKÉTA: Everyone who goes past the magazine stand reads them.

PAVEL: We don't.

MARKÉTA: So, we can't go to the cinema either?

PAVEL: Why are you doing this to me? Why are you making such a big campaign about this? Why are you making me look like the bad guy in front of Simon?

SIMON: I want to go to the cinema. Vojta and Matthew are going.

PAVEL: It's highway robbery. Overpriced tickets. Then they shovel popcorn into your kids' faces, and expect you to wash it down with Coke, and I have no idea what else!

MARKÉTA: You haven't laughed in such a long time. Have you been putting gel in your hair? It looks like a helmet.

PAVEL: I see how everything is falling apart around us. We're behaving like we're some kind of computer chip in completely strange machines.

MARKÉTA (*endearingly*): I can't take this anymore, Pavel.

PAVEL: I'm just protecting my family from this mess, do you get it? I made a vow to my dad when he died, and I'm not gonna give up.

MARKÉTA: And what we feel is of no interest to you?

PAVEL: Of course it is. But the important thing is to be ourselves. Everything else is insane.

SIMON: Why can't I go to the cinema with the other kids?

MARKÉTA: I can't take this anymore. This isn't a life. It's an army barracks.

PAVEL: Markéta, I—

MARKÉTA: I'm leaving. I'm packing our things and tomorrow we're out of here. I have to get some air. (*She runs out of the room.*)

A moment of silence.

SIMON: Why can't I have computer games like everyone else? Robert has one, and he's a Gypsy. I don't have a single one.

PAVEL: Markéta, just—

SIMON: I wouldn't play with it all the time. I like playing the piano and my art classes, but I wanna play computer games too. They're not all murder games— there's Formula Racing, too. Or the one where the prince looks for the lost treasure. But that one's also got a lot of bloody monsters, too. That's true. Like when one of 'em cut off the prince's arm. I had to cover my eyes that time. But, it's not that scary.

PAVEL *runs out of the kitchen. The little boy slowly drinks his cocoa and squints his eyes in several different ways as he looks into the light. After a while,* PAVEL *and* MARKÉTA *return.*

PAVEL (*whispers*): We can't let ourselves go at each other like this.

MARKÉTA: I don't want to fight with anyone all the time. Politics don't interest me. I want someone to hold me. I want to laugh—to enjoy the little things in life.

PAVEL: But you can see into these swindles just like I can. We can't let anyone manipulate us. You're educated too and you can see that crap in the newspapers . . .

MARKÉTA: This is making you sick. You're completely paranoid.

PAVEL: Philip asked about you. Now he is the sick one.

MARKÉTA: I have to see him.

PAVEL: He's my friend. This is difficult for me.

MARKÉTA: Simon's father called.

PAVEL: Aha. Aha. So that's it. Aha.

MARKÉTA: That's not it. Really. It's not.

PAVEL: This is betrayal . . . So the little weasel returned from Australia?

MARKÉTA: Not now. Not in front of Simon . . .

PAVEL: People keep betraying each other—like they're on some kind of treadmill . . . You really shut me out!

MARKÉTA: Pavel—

PAVEL: What do I have to do to make myself attractive to you? Roll in the dough, or smile at whatever kind of criminal or swindler comes my way, go to fancy dinner parties—smoked meat with blockheads who've never read a book in their life, and who buy their own children?

MARKÉTA: Wait just a minute . . .

PAVEL: Everything is just burning up around me . . . Two of the closest beings have betrayed me . . .

MARKÉTA: Simon, go put on your red pants and run over to Matthew's, okay?

The little boy leaves.

PAVEL: For years, the kid never enters into his head and—

MARKÉTA: Listen to me for a minute . . .

PAVEL: Shit, who can I count on? Who can I—?

MARKÉTA: Shut up for a minute. This has nothing to do with Simon's father. Put down the towel and listen. It doesn't. You never listen to either one of us. You are continuously afraid of something and you just keep waving your guns . . .

PAVEL: You are traitors.

MARKÉTA: You can't be so hard, so unfeeling—I have a soft spot, too. I—

PAVEL: I don't want to end up like my old man. When that woman left him alone. I don't want to stand at the gate every Sunday, waiting for the mailman, just in case I get a letter from her. I respect you—I treat you okay, don't I?

MARKÉTA: But that's not enough. It's not enough—to be "in love" . . .

PAVEL: You women are repulsive masochists. If a guy doesn't wipe the floor with you, so that you can cry about his affairs with your girlfriends, you'll go mad. It doesn't matter that the man is just a selfish asshole. To you, it's just some kind of "peculiarity." He's just a "little rascal." That makes me sick!

Without a word, MARKÉTA *gets up from the chair and leaves.*

PAVEL: You're already gone. They brainwashed you. In the beginning, you used to laugh at that shit, but they got to you. They've got you eating out of the palms of their hands. You're already thinking according to their schemes. You start drooling when they ring their little bell. You used to be my friends, my loves, my inspiration . . . and today, you're just an ordinary, programmed . . . (*A brief moment.*) . . . nothing. (*A brief moment.*) It's because I'm angry when we have sex, isn't it? You despise me because I get fuck-all for my work at the school, isn't it? Or because every illiterate scoundrel gets more money in this country than I do? Or have your folks spoken badly about me again? Those Commies that just keep laughing into our faces!

He cries. He destroys the dining room table. He cuts his palm, and starts to bleed. He puts his hand to his mouth. He kicks and breaks the kettle.

DREDGING

As a change, complete silence. The pool has glass walls, and the water reflects the rays of light. PHILIP *floats in the center of the pool like a piece of cotton batting.*

PHILIP's VOICE: Hundreds of bubbles pass my face making my nostril hairs and eyelashes stand on end. Can the bubbles stand on end? Plink, plink . . . A few of them pull away and float to the surface . . . It's getting late. I'm pressed for time . . . the other worlds are knocking at my door and yelling: "Where did you forget yourself? How long do we have to wait for you? . . . Swim." Perhaps none of you on dry land will be angry. Perhaps you will not miss me painfully. Please don't blame me for anything—I simply cannot stay here any more . . . I mastered the moves. I can put my arms at my sides, and turn with just a small kick of my feet . . . I will carry all the pictures of us together through the whirlpools—have no fear. They will continue to reflect a faint light in my memory like a garland of roe, like scales. Sometimes an intruder will get through in here . . . (MARKÉTA *swims toward* PHILIP.) . . . I do not need to explain anything to her . . . I swim behind her through the dark waters . . . an icy stream washes my eyes . . . (MARKÉTA *gets out of the pool and leaves.*) . . . I have already stopped speaking coherently . . . so I had better say goodbye . . . (*His motions slow down. He smiles and swims directly into the glass wall, hitting his head on the side of the pool . . . then swims out of view.*)

ACT TWO

THROUGH THE GLASS

Once again we can see into the pool. And once again we can see PHILIP. *But no matter what we do, we are unable to make substantial contact with him. He appears on the other side of the glass, engrossed in his own rhythm, with no expression on his face and with no human gestures. It seems to us as though we are visitors at an enormous aquarium in a zoo. Lumps of macerated food float around* PHILIP*'s head, and they add a cloudy, pond-like appearance to the water.*

CAGED IN

PAVEL *is completely drunk sitting amidst the remnants of the room that was once his kitchen. It is a time of great fatigue, when desperation has already been replaced by exhaustion.* MARKÉTA *enters.*

MARKÉTA: I came for some things. Simon's roller blades and stuff. Are you okay?

PAVEL *tries to tear open his eyes. No matter what he does, he does not succeed.*

MARKÉTA: Are you drunk?

PAVEL *mutters a bunch of mumbling sounds that make no sense. He only drools from his mouth.*

MARKÉTA: If there is something, give me a call. And close the fridge. (*She goes to leave.*) I dreamt about Philip last night. Has something . . . happened to him?

PAVEL *looks at her, but once again his eyelids roll shut.* MARKÉTA *leaves.*

A SINGALONG

KAJETÁN *sits in the studio at the moderator's desk. Technicians move around him as they are preparing the taping of the program.* KAJETÁN*'s cell rings.*

KAJETÁN (*into the cell*): Yeah? Pavel, hey . . . What's up? What's wrong with your voice? Have you been on a wild binge since the morning? (*He listens for a bit.*) What? . . . I didn't get that . . . he shit in the water? Who found him? That's horrible, I—

ASSISTANT DIRECTOR: We're rolling.

KAJETÁN: Hey, look. They want me now. We're gonna start rolling. I . . . I'll be right over after . . . You go on ahead of me. You're just two blocks away, okay . . . Just—

ASSISTANT DIRECTOR: Excuse me, would you kindly . . .

KAJETÁN *puts his cell into his pocket, and the lights come up immediately.*

KAJETÁN: Another week has gone by, and now its time once again to play your favorite song contest *Let 'Em Have It!!!* Even in the brightest days, we can see stars—on the streets, sidewalks, floors and carpets. But they haven't been discovered . . . yet! But now you, too, have the chance to show us, that even you are a star and deserve fame and shine in the heavens! Sing for us!

A commercial break. The lights dim for a moment. KAJETÁN *asks his* ASSISTANT *something. We only hear* "taxi in front of the building." *The lights come back up.*

KAJETÁN: Yes, any differences between those who are famous and those who are under Mount Olympus will truly be wiped away clean. The day will come when everyone will be famous. When a million stars will shine in the Czech Republic, attracting the cosmic nomads, those extraterrestrials who land on the Letna Plain and . . . and HEAD RIGHT TOWARDS OUR SHOW! The Umbilical Cord to Fame! Who will Fortune select today? Hold your breath; let's select our lucky contestant!

Another commercial break. KAJETÁN *apathetically sits behind the table. His assistant explains something to him.*

KAJETÁN'S VOICE: I'm losing my friend. I'm falling into some kind of strange solitude. Who out of all these puppets can replace him?

KAJETÁN: What?

KAJETÁN'S ASSISTANT: I found a new French teacher for you.

KAJETÁN: Not today.

Lights.

KAJETÁN: So. Today's lucky number is—number 52!!!

The camera pans the audience, where it singles out a woman around fifty years old. She trembles with stage fright. She makes her way to KAJETÁN's *table.*

KAJETÁN: Welcome to LET 'EM HAVE IT! Mrs. Prosper. What do your friends call you?

MAGDA: Magda.

KAJETÁN: Did you come by yourself, Magda, or is there a certain someone special in the audience who's rooting for you?

MAGDA: My husband is sitting over there, and so are my two daughters and my son.

Like all contestants' families, MAGDA's *family thunderously applauds.*

KAJETÁN: Shut up.

MAGDA: Sorry?

KAJETÁN: Nothing, sorry . . . Just . . . (*He unravels a bit.*) . . . Isn't she an elegant woman . . . what do you do? I mean, for a living? (*Drinks water.*)

MAGDA: I'm a teacher at a little elementary school.

KAJETÁN: And what brings you here?

MAGDA: I don't understand.

KAJETÁN: Why did you come here?

MAGDA: Why, to sing, of course.

KAJETÁN: Just like that?

MAGDA: Well . . . yes.

KAJETÁN: Millions of people will be watching. Is that what you want?

MAGDA (*at a loss for words for a minute*): My family said that it would be fun to give it a go.

KAJETÁN: Aha. So they really don't respect you too much, do they?

MAGDA (*looks around*): They do.

KAJETÁN: Well, let's just see about that. Let's give it a listen. What are you going to serve up for us today? What top forty trash hit are you going to bash us with today?

MAGDA: You mean which song?

KAJETÁN: What else?

MAGDA: "My Heart Will Go On."

KAJETÁN: So, ladies and gentlemen, let's hear it for our teacher Magda and her rendition of "My Heart Will Go On!"

Commercial break. The ASSISTANT DIRECTOR *rushes up to* KAJETÁN.

ASSISTANT DIRECTOR: What's wrong?

KAJETÁN: And what's wrong with you, my little idiot! What are you here for? You're just a little gopher who fetches me coffee at my every beck and call?

DIRECTOR´S VOICE: Kajetán. Please, what's gotten into you? Why are you so aggressive? Mrs. Magda, please, try to stay calm. Take a deep breath and let's give it a go, shall we? Audience, I'd like to hear a stronger applause. Let's go!

Lights.

There is no doubt that MAGDA *can sing. However, she is quite nervous, and the shock from* KAJETÁN *has affected her performance. She starts to sing one octave higher than her range, and she has trouble controlling her breathing. Nonetheless, the audience thunderously applauds. Even* KAJETÁN *applauds.*

KAJETÁN: Marta, have you been on board the Titanic?

MAGDA (*shaking with relief*): No, no I haven't. (*To the audience.*) Thank you.

KAJETÁN: My pleasure. So what will your little pupils say about that?

MAGDA (*trying to laugh*): Oh, hopefully they weren't watching me . . .

KAJETÁN: But everyone is watching. Do you still think that you'll have their respect when you dance here in your caftan karaoke dress crowing like a turkey?

MAGDA: Well I . . .

KAJETÁN: Why do you expose yourself and make such an idiot of yourself? For what reason? I'm sure that you can sing—when you're at home alone in your little house or with your friends sitting around the campfire. That must be very pleasant, because you have a beautiful voice. But here? This is just entertainment for the greasy riffraff who don't know how to entertain themselves and just want to kill time . . . but you are . . . (*His voice cracks.*) I mean you are a . . . teacher. You are a lady, aren't you?

KAJETÁN'S ASSISTANT *comes to* KAJETÁN *and gives him a piece of paper.* KAJETÁN *throws it back at her without reading it.* MAGDA'S SON *stands up in the audience.*

SON: You're insulting my mom, you asshole!

KAJETÁN: And who are you? Is this your son, Magda? Don't you dare come here, you little bastard. Don't you see? It's a complete enlightenment here. It's just some type of illumination—the magic lanterns cast their rays of light on you, and you become a Star. Do you want to be a shining star like your mother? A show business mutant from Chernobyl?

SON: Stop insulting her! (*To his father.*) I'll punch his fucking lights out!

A quick commercial break after the lights dim. We can hear the DIRECTOR'S VOICE *saying "Kajetán, you're crazy! This is a live broadcast! You're in for it!" and so on . . .*

KAJETÁN (*holding his hands up so he can see the audience*): Young man, do you know how I came to be a TV host?

SON (*to his father*): He made a fool out of mom in front of the entire country...

KAJETÁN: Do you want to know how? I got drunk with my friends Pavel and (*His voice cracks.*) . . . and Philip after one of our water trainings. We dared each other to come onto this stupid program and croon that song "People" by Barbra Streisand in front of the entire country. You know Barbra? Do you also think she should have the title role in the musical *Mother Theresa*? (*He removes the microphone from his jacket.*) A while ago, it would seem to you like some brutal sense of black humor, but today—it doesn't surprise you at all? Well, I "won" and then I went on the show. And so I got up there, completely plastered in front of everyone and wailed "*People. People who need peeople!*" and the guys sat by the TV splitting their guts laughing and Ivan—you don't know him—left me about twenty ghastly messages on my answering machine. But wait! They not only cheered me on at the TV station, they offered me a job—they asked me if I wanted to moderate the fucking thing! They said I have flair and I'm the right type! Jesus! I thought my friends and I would just kill ourselves laughing! Only, and here's the thing, my boy, they fired me from the newspaper, and that was that! I took the job moderating. (*beat*) I'm a star!

MAGDA'S SON *runs onto the podium and attacks* KAJETÁN. *He wails on him. Assistants, technicians and a security guard try to tear them apart.*

Black out.

QUEEN OF THE ABYSS

A STRANGE VOICE: We are back in Kajetán's apartment—or rather, what's left of it. The furniture is covered in black skirts and scattered amongst the pieces, they prowl on the unattended pilgrims of the spiteful, sleazy abyss. The air sparkles and crackles with electricity. From the cornucopia of the acrid, greasy smoke emerges the Queen of the Abyss. Previously known as Edith. The glands on her face swell up like the bladders of a toad, and her prickly fingers stretch and stretch until they reach the faces of the audience.

EDITH: My power is increasing! My beauty tattoos a picture onto your gray brain cortex. A picture of me. Remember me!

The cell phone hanging around EDITH's *neck rings.*

EDITH (*her voice is back to normal*): How can my phone be ringing when the SIM card is in my stomach? It's simply not possible, is it? (*Into the cell.*) Hello?

VOICE OF THE STOMACH SPIRIT: It is I, your Ladyship.

EDITH: Who are you?

SPIRIT: Your humble servant. Now is the perfect time to prepare for war.

EDITH: Really?

SPIRIT: Go boldly towards it. Entire hordes of pathetic losers are simply waiting for your command, your Darkness. An unparalleled chic of paralleled servants.

EDITH: They worship me?

SPIRIT: Like majorettes worship their go-go boots.

EDITH: My followers! Run out into the streets. Invade the apartments, houses and hiding places. And become detectives! Spy on the celebrated! Spy on their every move! Find out who they're sleeping with, who they're kissing, how much weight they've put on, where they're hiding their plastic surgery scars, what they ate, where they got drunk last night, whether their make-up isn't concealing up some bruise! Let 'em have it! Rise up to the summit after we've kicked their asses! Redeem yourself with their blood! In broad daylight and in the deep, dark of the night! (*Still affected.*) Chachachachachacha! (*Applying lipstick.*) X – X – X – X – X – X – X – X – X – X !

SPIRIT: Don't forget the fashion police.

EDITH: Oh yeah! Peer into their closets! Live by it! Tell the world what these kitsch demigods have dragged out of their closets! Tell us about it! Call us, write us, send us pictures! Brand their shoulders with the names of their elitist rags! A hideous, festering sign! (*After a moment.*) Okay, can I go pee now?

SPIRIT: Run! Everything is now in motion. Don't be afraid, when the blinking rusty card comes out of you. Don't get in its way. It is now above the power of your calling. It would tear your apparatus to shreds. Flee, go quickly! Get out!

MY PAIN, YOUR PLEASURE

KAJETÁN *sits in the back seat of a taxi. Blood is flowing from his broken lip into his white handkerchief. During the ride, he sometimes gives the taxi driver directions and tries to stop the bleeding with the handkerchief. He calls someone. On the screen above the taxi, we can see the facial details of a different* KAJETÁN. *Without blood on his lip and with steely gray, icy eyes.*

KAJETÁN ON SCREEN: Even I have moments when I get extremely angry. Moments when I try to suffocate the infantile, gullible, mischievous feeling inside myself and I want . . . I want to hurt someone. Then I despise people for giving me their strings so I can pull them. Then I take revenge on them for my banal life. (*beat*) That's when these warped ideas come into my head. Warped ideas, twisted like horns of a mountain goat, or like a corkscrew that's just impaled a flabby genie.

The camera pulls away from KAJETÁN*'s face. Two pudgy, bald men stand next to him, nervously shuffling their feet.* FANS *of Sparta and Baník soccer teams.*

KAJETÁN ON SCREEN: Let's finish one thing. There's so much talk about violence and hostility, but most of it is only media smoke, a fleeting, ephemeral fart of steam. (*beat*) At the television station, they said "more adrenaline." I knew from the paper that before the Sparta and Baník match, two exceptionally brutal commandos from both camps were going to meet in a secluded forest on the outskirts of Prague and have it out with each other—man against man. (*beat*) No place on Earth is completely hidden. So we tracked them down and offered them the chance to thrash it out at the studios. For this, they wouldn't get a dime—they'd have to sign a waiver that they were doing this on their own free will—and it would be a live—unedited—broadcast. (*beat*) So now we'll see an authentic massacre of two mobs who carry on completely without a script, without a director, and whose ending is determined only by the actors themselves. (*beat*) So, don't call us here. Don't write us, just watch. (*beat*) What's more, most of us despise these hooligans. We're so terrified of them that our personal feelings should not dramatically suffer. (*beat*) What do their leaders have to tell us?

BANÍK FAN: Only belts, chains, and knives!

SPARTA FAN: Sparta!

BANÍK FAN: Baník!

SPARTA FAN: You're dead meat!

Behind KAJETÁN, *they form two groups. In spite of their aggressive appearance, the men seem rather uncertain in front of the cameras.*

KAJETÁN ON SCREEN: They are fathers with families, somebody's brother or son. So, just looking at them, someone will of course suffer. But as for the rest of you—enjoy yourselves. When do you get to witness a real war?

The hoards behind KAJETÁN *begin to fight and shout. Fade out.*

Below in the taxi, KAJETÁN *puts the telephone into his jacket pocket and leans forward to the driver.*

KAJETÁN: Over there, behind the green Ford on the right. Here, yeah. Here is fine. I'll just jump out near the corner.

Fade out.

THE VILLAGER

MARKÉTA *and* SIMON *take a walk in the field. An autumn chill makes their noses pink. They point to some movement that they have seen. Perhaps a rabbit. In the storm clouds above, we can hear thunder. An elderly man, a* VILLAGER, *wearing rubber boots comes up from behind them. He has gray stubble on his chin, and he frequently adjusts his gray cap.*

MARKÉTA (*catching sight of the man*): Hello. This is your property, is it? I just wanted to show my son your animals.

VILLAGER: I already brought the cows in from the pasture.

MARKÉTA: We've seen the sheep, the ducks, the chickens, and the lamb. So we're quite content.

SIMON: And the rabbits.

MARKÉTA: And the rabbits.

VILLAGER (*pointing upward*): Those angels flew above the barn in one solid band. Just one right after another. Then they turned around over there, circled above the bell tower—one sort of dropped behind—and then they carried off around the two poplar trees. Then they all disappeared behind that hill over there . . . (*The man continues to paint the birds' path in the sky. It begins to rain, and a couple of drops of water dribble down his erect, calloused index finger with cracked fingernail. He wipes the rain from his face with his other hand.*)

Fade to black.

ON THE SHORES

On the banks of the lake. In spite of the fact that it's late October, the sun is still quite strong. The rushes blow in the wind. PAVEL *and* KAJETÁN *slowly come toward the water. They carry a massive wooden trunk on their shoulders. Both of them are wearing dark suits, shirts opened wide, no ties. The pebbles shoot out from under the heels of their black dress shoes. Their load is heavy, and they walk unsteadily.*

KAJETÁN: Steady, steady . . .

PAVEL: It's slipping.

KAJETÁN: Where to?

PAVEL: I thought over there toward the floodgate, you know? It seems nice to me. (*He loses his balance.*) Jesus, I almost dropped him.

KAJETÁN: He's heavy. A man could say such a tiny man! Let's switch shoulders, okay?

PAVEL: To hell with physical training!

KAJETÁN: He's moving inside. He's not making it easier at all for us. It's beautiful here. That's a heron, isn't it?

PAVEL: Where?

KAJETÁN: Over there.

PAVEL: That's a branch.

KAJETÁN: I mean behind it.

PAVEL: Another branch.

KAJETÁN: Aha. Two branches.

PAVEL: I think that this a fine place. It's hidden from the road. And there's a big dam. A beaver dam.

KAJETÁN: It's a beauty!

PAVEL: You're standing in the water.

KAJETÁN: Another beauty. Shit!

PAVEL: Please . . .

KAJETÁN: I'm sorry. (*He knocks on the trunk.*) We're here! But it's quite cold. Prepare yourself. My foot is freezing up.

PAVEL: Slowly . . . slowly . . . let it down.

The men place the trunk on the top of the floodgate. PAVEL *then opens the side of the trunk facing toward the water. Something slips out of the trunk and flops into the water.*

PAVEL: That's it . . .

They both look at the surface of the water. Rings appear on the surface of the water and will disappear in a moment, until the surface becomes completely clear—if we don't count the little rings made by insects.

KAJETÁN: It'll be great for him here. He can just frolic. They say it's quite deep here.

PAVEL: And there's lots of fish.

KAJETÁN: Yeah . . . but I was just thinking about . . .

He realizes that PAVEL *is wiping his eyes, and he stops.*

PAVEL (*after a moment*): What are you thinking about?

KAJETÁN: Christmas is just around the corner.

PAVEL: Do you want to throw him presents?

KAJETÁN: Like potato salad and other holiday stuff . . .

PAVEL: You idiot . . . (*He smiles and then starts crying.*)

KAJETÁN: There's just the danger that he might be caught like all the other carps for Christmas. Do you think that you could eat him? (*beat*) I don't know. If you put him in some kind of batter, maybe. But maybe he'll destroy the net and become a carp super hero.

PAVEL: This isn't a breeding pond.

KAJETÁN: Really?

PAVEL: It is not. (*After a while.*) We can just keep this quiet. There's too much talk. Everywhere.

KAJETÁN: You're right. Today, no one sticking a finger up your ass without telling the world about it.

PAVEL (*laughs*): Sometimes I'm afraid of the silence.

KAJETÁN: Let's try it for a moment, okay?

The men walk along the wet shores of the lake. Each independently, aimlessly, pondering. They smoke, squinting into the unusually strong autumn sun. The wind blows through their hair.

PAVEL: We don't have Philip anymore. (*He sits on one of the stones.*)

KAJETÁN's *cell phone rings.*

KAJETÁN: Fuck, I forgot to turn it off. (*Into the cell.*) What? (*He listens for a while, and then turns it off.*) I can't believe it . . .

PAVEL (*sarcastically*): That your babe?

KAJETÁN: No, she's been gone for a while. They just called from the TV station. They said they're not going to fire me because of the fight.

PAVEL: You had a fight?

KAJETÁN: With a little punk who had a pretty big chip on his shoulder.

PAVEL: You do have a pretty good shiner there.

KAJETÁN: He chipped my tooth. They phoned from the TV station to tell me that they're not going to fire me because of that fiasco. But that they actually liked how brutal I was, that it's "in" now. They offered me a special game show where all I do is harass people. (*He looks at the telephone display.*) I always start shaking when I see Philip's number in the list. It's suddenly so empty and creepy. I get goose bumps. It terrifies me how it just keeps offering a dead figure to me. Look. What's even stranger though is that I don't dare delete it because then I'd cut myself off from Philip forever . . . (*He takes a deep breath and throws the cell phone into the center of the lake.*)

PAVEL: You just threw away a perfectly good cell phone!

KAJETÁN: Fuck it...

PAVEL: Wow. I'm impressed!

KAJETÁN: I have two more at home.

PAVEL (*smiles and his stubbled sleep-deprived face once again becomes beautiful*): Let's just hope that the Mermaid from the Lake doesn't call you.

KAJETÁN: Or the Spirit of the Clam.

PAVEL (*frankly*): You're so funny.

KAJETÁN: A grimacing, fat prankster. I live in debt. All day, I never take time for myself. I never pray, I never meditate, I never read old letters, I just keep talking, keep eating. I'm cynical, I'm witty, I'm superficial, I'm indifferent, I'm never on time, and I could keep talking about myself like this for ages. It's as if someone cut off an artery that kept me in touch with the world around me. And only the Brother Pig remained.

PAVEL: We're exhausted.

KAJETÁN: What about Markéta?

PAVEL: We met each other yesterday. She said I smell of alcohol . . . She looked so beautiful. She cut her hair into a bob. But . . . you know, I'm probably a bit allergic to her. I lose my temper and I'm always pissed off. I never let her finish. I always blame her for something. (*After a while.*) That she always deserved something more than that—something more than me.

KAJETÁN (*after a while*): Do you want me to talk you out of it?

PAVEL: Of course, I do!

KAJETÁN: She couldn't have had a better man. Actually she could have, but he just swam away. And for her, I am too . . . amphibious. Would she want me?

PAVEL: Yesterday, she said that she only wants me. I couldn't sleep at all last night. I kept pacing. I love her. I hate her for being so fabulous! That's the unbearable thing about her. Luckily, she does have her faults too—she drools when she sleeps, and that keeps my head above water.

KAJETÁN: I also just recently fell in love. But this time, I think it's the one.

PAVEL: Another jubilee notch in your belt?

KAJETÁN: No, no, no. This one is like she ran away from *The Matrix* or something. I don't need another coloring book.

PAVEL: What's her name?

KAJETÁN: Stella. She's so . . . boyish.

PAVEL: Let's just hope.

KAJETÁN: Someone's watching us.

PAVEL: Where?

KAJETÁN: Don't be conspicuous, but look over there. To the right of the willows. Those two.

PAVEL: Are they after you?

KAJETÁN: No doubt about it.

PAVEL: They're coming this way.

One of the women is very skinny and the other is plump—as it should be for a pair of comedians. In reality, there is no joke. These two are voluntarily folk spies, of the Queen of the Dark Descent . . . Footmen of Lucifer's SIM card! Both are biting into a peach.

FIRST: I admire Cher. She's a nice woman, even though she's had a few "repairs" done. But I despise Celine. When I see her on TV, I just turn her off immediately.

SECOND: But Celine sings beautifully, doesn't she?

FIRST: She may sing all right, but she's horrible otherwise. She's just with her man for his money. She's only sucking the money out of him.

SECOND: It's not her fault. And her poor little Rene-Charles suffers.

KAJETÁN: Little Rene-Charles does not suffer.

PAVEL *quickly retreats from the oncoming pair. He takes off his shoes and socks, rolls up his pants legs, and walks into the shallow water.*

FIRST: I wouldn't even shake hands with her. She makes herself look like an innocent baby, but everything she does is so calculated. Like all those French-Canadian people.

SECOND: While Cher is just stitched together from a dozen other people—no one seems to care! She's had more facelifts than she's had sets of teeth! She's so embarrassing—she still struts around like a drag queen, but she should already be collecting her pension, shouldn't she? And she pretends to be a young chick.

FIRST: She can still put the young sticks in her pocket.

KAJETÁN: Isn't she a robot?

SECOND: No, Joan Rivers is a robot.

KAJETÁN: Everyone knows that. But Cher's not?

FIRST: Oh God, I thought so . . .

SECOND: Good morning! You know her personally, don't you?

KAJETÁN: I was there when they changed her head.

SECOND: Really?

FIRST: That's pretty disappointing . . .

KAJETÁN: Cher roots for Sparta and Celine for Baník.

SECOND: Sorry?

KAJETÁN: Nothing. And do you know them personally?

SECOND: Everyone knows them personally. I even keep everything about you filed away. I have something on everybody.

FIRST: What are you doing here? Are you on a date?

KAJETÁN: I have a store here. A convenience store.

SECOND: Where?

KAJETÁN: Right here. You're standing in it. (KAJETÁN *brings a couple of branches, stones, and leaves, and puts them in a pile. He sprinkles some of the leaves with dirt, others he cuts with his car key.*) Do you want to buy anything? (*Offers the leaf with dirt.*) This is a pizza with some special sauce. (*Offers a branch.*) This is a hot dog. (*Offers the stones.*) These are cookies. They're not baked yet—you still have to wait. Make a hole in the ground here, and I'll pour some milk into it. But we don't have any Dr. Pepper.

SECOND (*whispers into* FIRST*'s ear*): They say he takes drugs . . .

KAJETÁN (*offers a palmful of soil*): These are drugs, but they are only for my whores.

FIRST *whispers to* SECOND.

KAJETÁN: Who will have what? Hello? We are open. So what'll it be?

They stare.

KAJETÁN: Come on now, what'll you have?

SECOND: Me? I don't know . . . a branch.

KAJETÁN: Hot dog!

SECOND: Okay, a hot dog.

KAJETÁN: One fifty.

They look at each other. SECOND *digs into her purse, and pays.*

KAJETÁN: And what will you have?

FIRST: I'll just have something small.

KAJETÁN: Do you want a bit of these drugs? They're still warm.

FIRST: OK.

KAJETÁN: And are you my whore?

FIRST (*turns pale*): I don't know.

KAJETÁN: OK. Five bucks.

FIRST: But . . .

SECOND: It's better to give it to . . .

FIRST *pays with a trembling hand.*

KAJETÁN: And because you were such fine customers, allow me to introduce someone to you. Pavel!! Come over here. My customers here have something on everyone. But I think that they don't have anything on you. Do you have anything on him?

PAVEL *wades back to the shore.*

FIRST: I don't know him.

SECOND: Neither do I.

KAJETÁN: That's Pavel. My best friend. They've never written about him anywhere?

FIRST: I don't know.

KAJETÁN: Pavel, what are you doing?

PAVEL: I'm catching flies that have fallen into the water and I'm bringing them to the banks. I'd like to do this until I die.

KAJETÁN: Pavel is a paramedic. Today, he's already rescued 54 flies and june bugs. But they didn't have any medical insurance—you know how it is.

FIRST: I see.

KAJETÁN: And do you know what Pavel is famous for? Most famous for?

SECOND: We don't know. I don't have him anywhere . . .

KAJETÁN: He has a beautiful and fantastic dick! Pavel, please be so kind and show my lovely customers your colossal member!

PAVEL *looks at him for a moment, then the worry from his face disappears. He unzips his fly very quickly, and he exhibits his penis to the women. They become terrified and run away.*

PAVEL: That was such a great feeling! Beautiful! Such a relief . . . Thanks!

KAJETÁN: I know why I don't come into nature very often. Here, I always realize how silly my life is. Every day, I promise myself, that tomorrow, I'm gonna make a clean start. Like a clean slate, and then shit. But I really want to be there when the life on this earth is born and comes up! I really want to be invited to this miracle . . .

PAVEL: At least you don't shrink back in fear, like me. There will be a sign on my grave: He died after a difficult fight, as a result of self-censorship. How the wind blows through the chest, you see?

KAJETÁN: Look over there at the cattails, at the reeds. I had a feeling that I saw Philip. He came to the surface for a minute . . .

PAVEL: I guess I love my son, man. Although, he's sometimes so unpleasant and strange. For five minutes, I've been thinking about the grimaces he makes when Markéta cleans his ears . . .

KAJETÁN: I can't get your penis out of my head. Such a Masterpiece!

PAVEL: Really? Should I rely more on it?

KAJETÁN: The rest of your body is average, almost lousy. Are you smiling?

PAVEL: Yes.

KAJETÁN: Do you think that we're as strong as each other? That if we started to eat each other, there wouldn't be anything left of us?

PAVEL: Like two piranhas?

KAJETÁN: Like two middle-aged piranhas. Where are you running?

PAVEL: A bee flew over there. I'm going to save her life. (*He picks up the bee between his fingers.*) She's still falling back into the water.

KAJETÁN: Take this twig.

PAVEL (*watches the bee closely*): She's soaking wet. Look. You can make fun of me all you want, but it really got to me. I'll have to focus on it. It'll be my vocation. Maybe it's my calling. I will be closer to Philip . . . Our secret aqua belle club has fallen apart anyway . . . Will you help me? There's a ladybug over there.

KAJETÁN: I have my own little store on the banks. If you don't catch them in time, you can bring them here to me. I also sell meat products.

PAVEL: Idiot! Hurry. Grab the ladybug.

KAJETÁN: I have my shoes on. Fuck the shoes. Cold . . . (*He rescues the ladybug.*) Ladybug's sluggish . . . but no, she moved! Oh wow, look, she's alive!!

PAVEL: You threw down the bee . . .

KAJETÁN: I'm taking the ladybug and taking her to the store. She'll get a little hot milk with some honey. Oh no, she has to wait. There's a horsefly . . .

PAVEL: Watch out for the algae, it'll grab you around the ankles.

KAJETÁN *takes a couple of steps, and he kicks the water for a moment. Then, for a moment, he completely disappears into the water.*

KAJETÁN (*surfaces*): We're Laurel and Hardy, have you noticed?

PAVEL: When you're already soaking wet, why don't we dance for the last time for Philip?

KAJETÁN (*fishes out the horsefly, and throws it on the banks*): That's a good idea.

PAVEL: What about number . . . three.

KAJETÁN: The R.E.M. theme?

PAVEL: Yeah, that one.

KAJETÁN: Ideal.

PAVEL: I'll sing. But pay attention to the beginning of the second verse. It's only a quarter turn; a swing of the calf, and then surface—like this. Let's go.

KAJETÁN: Are you going to wear your jacket, too?

PAVEL: In my jacket.

The pair of Aquabelles begins to dance. When they surface, the water pours out of their sleeves and pockets. They are secretly watched by the old fisherman from the reeds. But he only watches them for his own pleasure. The stones at the bottom of the lake will turn over to their other side at once. On the screen, we see the empty room of PHILIP's grandmother.

Fade out.

THE END

OPENING THE DRAWER
AND
PULLING OUT THE KNIFE

Ivana Růžičková

Ivana Růžičková
Photo courtesy of Aura-Pont

Ivana Růžičková, born April 24, 1981, was inspired to work in the theatre through her contact with the Drama Studio in Ústí nad Labem. She recalls that early on she became "fascinated by theatre as a form, the expressive possibilities and limits of the play." Her first attempts at writing, at the age of 19, were intense reflections of her personal life. In 2003 she attended World Interplay, the largest international festival for young playwrights held in Australia each year. Her fourth play, *The Moment before I Opened the Drawer and Took out a Knife*—rewritten for World Interplay as *Opening the Drawer and Pulling out the Knife*—won third prize in the 2002 Alfréd Radok Awards. Although the play has yet to receive a full production, Růžičková continues to "play with it." The latest version is called *The Knife is in the Drawer*, and she writes "it uses the same words to tell a completely different story."

Currently she is studying social anthropology and works as an editor for the Czech edition of *Cosmopolitan* magazine.

Drawer *was originally a poem, then a letter, and finally a play. It came out of a need to express my feelings, and writing it became a sort of exploration of the situation I was stuck in at the time. An experiment, an opportunity, a wish, a question, an exclamation point. Which is why I leave it open to constant revision and new scenes. Anyone it speaks to can recreate it at any time. Cross out all the dirty words, for instance; or find a better solution than the one my characters found.*

—Ivana Růžičková

Opening the Drawer
and
Pulling out the Knife

by

Ivana Růžičková

Translated by
Ivana Růžičková

Language editing by
Irena Kovarova for Immigrants' Theatre Project 2004

CHARACTERS

WOMAN 1 (Puppet)
WOMAN 2 (Puppet)
WOMAN
MAN

Author's Note: The MAN and WOMAN parts can be replaced with two women or two men. The PUPPETS can be any gender as well.

The purpose of this play is not to depict long slow depression. The play is actually full of anger and rage. The individuals are furious, mad and outrageous and they desperately need to get to some final conclusion. With a knife in their hands they're waiting for their paradise.

The play consists of two parts based on the same text. The characters are saying similar things, but getting to different conclusions. The puppet play is about the desire to stay, but not having enough reasons to do so; the drama part is about the need to separate, and waiting for the courage to do that.

Part One, seeking the reason to stay

I'M OPENING THE DRAWER

Puppet foreplay

" . . . at first she made herself some coffee but then she had absolutely nothing to do."

"Do IT . . . bitch."

A small bedroom. The bed is in the middle of the room; on it lies a sleeping puppet, WOMAN 2. *Another puppet,* WOMAN 1, *is sitting by a table in front of the mirror. She's nervous; every once in a while she peeks at sleeping* WOMAN 2. *As the play progresses she walks about, talks on the phone, opens the window and shouts out her lines to the people on the street.*

WOMAN 1: I'll count to three and everything will burst like a bubble! One, two, three . . .

(*Imitating* WOMAN 2.) "Sorry honey, you are an angel, but only for like twenty percent."

Sure.

Am I?

Unnecessary lamb
On your plate
Portioned out, served, spiced . . . hey, do you love me at all?

Twenty percent angel.

(*She picks up the phone, dials a number, waits, whispers.*) Not yet. Your orders are missing the exclamation points. (*She hangs up.*)

Another night in this city.

Used . . .
To be used.
To be THIS used.
Like this. Used. Will.

(*She turns to* WOMAN 2 *on the bed.*) Will you use me again?

WOMAN 2 *snores and turns to the other side.*

Connection interrupted! I don't care anyway.

The phone rang yesterday morning at seven.

(*She imitates* WOMAN 2.) "That girl must be pretty pissed."

This morning I'll write the instructions for HOW TO ABUSE . . . No.
HOW TO RE-USE . . . err, THE USING OF PEOPLE!

Oh yes, my dear, each of us has gone through our own Hell.
Heaven as well. I still remember that.
But I don't want to, now.

I DON'T WANT TO always be like this. Drunk and bored.
With you.
In this big BIG HUGE house.

I'm using wrong words.
I'm asking inappropriate questions.
I'm getting incomplete answers.

Rule number one: Absolutely no emotional investment, darling.

I'm an animal myself.

(*She pulls up her skirt and wags her tail.*) Arf! Arf arf! Grrr arf! (*She runs around the room on all fours.*)

With you I'm a cube of ice.
Melting.
Under your flaming look.

Doesn't that sound nice?

I wanna buy trees and discounted monthly Metrocards.

Personal emergency.

I'll stab myself before you finish your cigarette.
I'll tear off my clothes and show you my body. Crucified.
Your hair, my blood.
Neighbor's eyes.
Landlord's super is quitting.

I'm either a few moves ahead or behind. Never where I should be.

So be it.
Sharp and sour taste of your lips and afternoon cigarettes.

Sugar (spilled out)
Tension (high)
Food (unfinished), who the Hell would eat this cow tongue anyway?
Insufficient number of sleeping pills.
Sweet dreams.

(*She bends over sleeping* WOMAN 2.) LAUGH!
NOW. Attention, please.
Take a deep breath and don't care about what doesn't matter.
All zebras and wild boars. Ignore.

Midnight litanies.
Midnight lovers.

My expression will always be the same. EVEN WHEN I HATE YOU.

Monday.
Hmmm . . .

(*She opens the window and shouts.*) It is Monday. (*She shuts the window.*)

Monday depressions.
A blow.
By all means.
TAKE IT ALL.

Solitude is female.
To lie on the ground. To hang from the ceiling.

(*She lies on the ground looking for something, spots it under the bed, stretches out her arm and pulls out a bottle.*) Vodka and other extenuating circumstances.

Long arms, bony fingers, trimmed nails.
And that terrible feeling that comes every night when I'm looking for you in the sideboard.

(*Now, she's really hunting around for something. She finds the December edition of* Harper's Bazaar.) They are asking me: "Are you ok? Do you have a problem? What's wrong?"

Talk to me! (*She kicks the wall, kicks the bed, kicks* WOMAN 2.)

WOMAN 2 (*wakes up*): What's your problem? Anything wrong?

WOMAN 1: I have just memorized all the right answers.

WOMAN 2: Good for you, honey, anything else?

WOMAN 1: No.
Except for the fact that I AM
Under your skin.

WOMAN 2: Okay.

WOMAN 1: In your blood.

WOMAN 2: Can we discuss this in the morning, love?

WOMAN 1: I'm not gonna be here in the morning. I mean . . . I will.

WOMAN 2 *pulls a blanket over her head and continues sleeping.*

WOMAN 1 (*takes the phone and dials a number, whispers*): We have just GOT there. (*She hangs up.*)

Who are you?
And why do you always look somewhere else, damn it?

Our senses are only filters for reality.

Rushed misunderstandings.

MY HELL
is your friend, isn't it?

(*She shouts out the window again to the drunks, pedestrians, and prostitutes.*)
I want to turn off the street lamps
And refuse to sleep
And seek help in the yellow pages. (*She shuts the window.*)

I'm pampering my little suffering.
I'M NOT LOOKING FOR AN END TO MY DISTRESS.
I'm not looking for anything.
I'm not looking back.
I sleep with my eyes open. I SLEEP WITH YOU
In the cold nights

Discomfort
Breath.
Cut.

To go to Hell!
To sit on a toilet.
To finish up a cigarette.

When I wait for a tram.
I am always IMPATIENT.

(*To* WOMAN 2.) Do you know what I want from you? Any idea?

I WANT TO decipher all of your coded messages.
And
I want your money.
Spend it, count it, watch it, waste it.

And then I can calmly shut myself in the freezer and freeze.
Just like a beef cutlet.

A little different taste of paradise.
Sour and you like it, huh?

STAND IN THE CORNER AND SHUT UP.

Listen to me.

(*She lights a cigarette.*) I'm burning in your flame.

(*Dials a number again, waits, quietly.*) The solutions that you're proposing are absolutely unacceptable to me. (*She puts the phone down.*)

FRIENDS FOR ONE TIME USE ONLY.

Emotional wreck.

Honey, I wanted to tell you that I've got no money.
I have YOU, at least. (*She opens the drawer and pulls out a vibrator.*)

(*She reads the instructions.*) FAST FORWARD. Actually it doesn't have to be FAST as long as it is FORWARD.

(*She tries to use it.*) Oh, yes, I'M SEEKING THE WAY TO MY OWN GATE.

Thank God for the progress.

Ooh ahh oohh

WOMAN 2 *starts to wake.*

(WOMAN 1 *stops abruptly before climaxing.*) Uncertain result—when it's not possible to win.

Three forty-seven.

And what if all of this misses the point?

(*To* WOMAN 2.) TALK TO ME!
Or we'll never get anywhere.

Stand by your spike mark.

BITTER TRUTH.
Truth like the taste of bitter almonds and over-ripe oranges.

(*Very loud.*) JUMP! ON ME! AND DO IT WELL!

Ooh ahh oohh

WOMAN 2: Veronica!

WOMAN 1: I can't sleep.

WOMAN 2: So watch the fucking TV or something.

WOMAN 2 *tries to sleep again, pulls the cover over her head. There's quiet for a while.*

WOMAN 1: 50% MISERY. 50% YOU.

(*Imitating* WOMAN 2.) "Look baby, I'm not living your life. Nobody's going to do that dirty job for you."

Maybe I really am
drunk after one glass of champagne.

EMOTIONALY UNAVAILABLE AT THE MOMENT.
PLEASE STAND BY.

Your friend.
Your truth.

When I am looking at your clit

(*She smiles.*) Your BIG truth, my LITTLE friend.

(*Imitating* WOMAN 2.) "Why do you always get me hard and hot and then let me cool down?"

She laughs.

WE SHOULD JUST SAY, "FUCK IT!"

Well look at it this way
Up until a certain point the discomfort is an advantage.
And then?
Then you come and I roll over.

(WOMAN 1 *puts on dark sunglasses, starts putting on sunscreen.*) No, wait a sec!
I'm not ready quite yet . . .

(*She combs her hair and puts on perfume.*) Not yet. I'm still not ready for your lies, honey.

SO THIS IS ME.

(*She lies on the bed and opens her legs.*) And this is the way I bare my soul.

Here we go. All the sins of Veronica.

Just so you know, tomorrow I'll give you a list of your new enemies.

WOMAN 2 *wakes up, rubs her eyes, blinks and looks straight into* WOMAN 1's *crotch. She's a bit confused.*

(WOMAN 1 *starts stimulating her own clitoris.*) What are you staring at, don't you wanna help me?

WOMAN 2 (*helps, she enjoys it; when it's all done*): That was good. What else have you got?

WOMAN 1: A knife. In the drawer.

Curtain.

Part two, waiting for the reason to leave

ARE WE GONNA PULL THE KNIFE OUT, HONEY?

A drama

"About the impassable distance from one side of the table to the other."

A not very attractive WOMAN *and a not really attractive* MAN *are sitting at a table on opposite ends facing each other. On their bodies there's a sign of constant tension, light nervousness. Dialogue is fast, exchanges are quick and uncompromising.*

It's dinnertime and on the table are pots with lamb and mashed potatoes. In the middle of the table is a little vase with a dried flower. Plates in front of them are still empty.

MAN: So?

WOMAN (*gets up and scoops food out onto plates, rhythmically; each time the scoop hits the plate, comes one line*): So . . .

I'll count to three and then the bubble will burst.

MAN: So . . . as usual.

WOMAN: Twenty percent angel.

MAN: . . . as usual.

WOMAN: Unnecessary lamb.

MAN: Whatever you want.

WOMAN: Do you want . . . ME?

MAN: Now?

WOMAN: I always admired your talent for asking the right questions.

MAN: Bitch!

WOMAN: I hate nights in this city

MAN: Connection interrupted.

WOMAN: THE PHONE RANG AT SEVEN O'CLOCK IN THE MORNING.

MAN: That's all you have to say about it?

WOMAN: That girl must be really pissed off.

MAN: Do you want me to give you the instructions to . . . ?

WOMAN: ABUSED!

MAN: Do you want me to . . . ?

WOMAN: RE-USED!

MAN: Do you -

WOMAN: USED! (*pause*)

Eat or it gets cold.

MAN: Each of us has gone through our own Hell.

WOMAN: Heaven.

MAN: Our own variation of Hell.

WOMAN: I don't want to always be like this. Drunk and bored
With you
In this huge house.

MAN: Rule number one: Absolutely no emotional investment.

MAN *starts eating with gusto.* WOMAN *watches him.*

WOMAN: I'm half animal, half wind.

MAN: Arf! Arf arf!

WOMAN: Melting
Under your flaming look.

MAN: Too bad. I don't want you like this.

WOMAN: Give me discounted monthly Metrocards.

MAN: Whatever you want.

WOMAN: Personal emergency. (*She grabs her fork and knife.*)

MAN: Anytime you want.

WOMAN: I'll stab myself before you finish your cigarette. (*Stabs at the lamb on her plate.*)

MAN: You have always been a few moves ahead or behind. Never where you should be. Never.

WOMAN: I still like your style.

WOMAN *chews lamb.* MAN *angrily approaches the* WOMAN *and takes her hair, yanking her head to his chest.*

MAN: My style?

WOMAN: Sharp and sour taste of your lips and afternoon cigarettes.

MAN *pulls harder.*

WOMAN: The roughness of your skin and size of your penis.

MAN *pulls even harder until* WOMAN *starts to cry with pain, trying to loosen the grip.*

MAN: Shut up!

WOMAN: Let go!

MAN: I DON'T WANT TO.

He lets go of her hair, steps aside and turns his back to her.

Pause.

WOMAN: Unfortunately I don't have enough sleeping pills.

MAN: So what?

WOMAN: Don't make fun of me!

MAN: From now on all my moves will be off the chessboard.

WOMAN: Again?

MAN: I didn't know you were such a blockhead.

WOMAN: Unnecessary lamb.

MAN: Or even better GRILLED LAMB.

WOMAN: You are a beast.

MAN (*amused*): What, Zebra? Wild boar?
(*sharply*) I already told you once:
BITCH!

WOMAN: night talks with demons
Midnight litanies
midnight
l.o.v.e.r.s.
LOVERS

MAN (*angry*): YOU WILL ALWAYS BE BITTER, I WILL ALWAYS HATE YOU.

WOMAN: Every Monday?

MAN *hits the* WOMAN.

MAN: By all means.

WOMAN: You take it all.

MAN (*sarcastically*): I'm so moved by your desperate screams.

WOMAN: For the first time.

MAN: So!

WOMAN: I'm going to leave in the morning anyway.

MAN: No breakfast.

WOMAN: I'll have one. But -

WOMAN *starts eating.*

MAN: Your self-centered yapping.

WOMAN (*her mouth full of food*): No more sweaty hands, expensive bills and senseless phone calls.

MAN: I used to love you.

Pause.

WOMAN *finishes chewing; and swallows.*

WOMAN (*slowly*): I hate sentences in the past tense.

MAN: And I hate you.

WOMAN: In the morning?

MAN: Anytime.

Their exchanges become faster and faster.

WOMAN: Solitude is female.

MAN: Words are traps.

WOMAN: Vodka and other extenuating circumstances.

MAN: Don't count on me.

WOMAN: I hate that terrible feeling when I'm looking for you in the sideboard. (*She opens the drawer in the sideboard.*)

MAN: I am not hiding myself from you.

WOMAN *slams the drawer shut rattling the forks and knives. A second of silence.*

WOMAN: They ask me: Are you ok? Do you have a problem? Is there anything wrong? Talk to me!

MAN: What's your problem?

WOMAN: I'm burning.

MAN (*takes her face softly into his hands*): Me too . . . you know. In your flame.

WOMAN: I have to memorize all the right answers.

MAN: We've already been there.

WOMAN: And here? (*She takes off her panties, and opens her legs.*)

MAN (*looks*): Here as well.

WOMAN: I don't enjoy this hide and seek game.

MAN (*sarcastically, eyeing her crotch*): You have nothing to hide anymore, I am afraid.

WOMAN (*crosses her legs*): Are we going to go back now?

MAN: Back to the beginning?

WOMAN: How many times have we done this already?

MAN: It's better to ask how many more times we will be doing it.

WOMAN: Once in the morning and once in the evening.

MAN: No!

WOMAN: You do whatever the Hell you like.

MAN: Our senses are just filters for reality.

WOMAN: I wanna be anywhere where I can satisfy my urge. The urge to be with you.

MAN: A big urge.

WOMAN: To be with you!

MAN: So come. (*Rises from the table.*)

WOMAN: I don't want.
Not now.
Not like this.

MAN: I don't understand what you want. (*Sits down again, loosens his belt, and unzips his trousers.*)

WOMAN: I'm under your skin.

MAN: Your choice.

WOMAN: Rushed misunderstanding.

MAN: Your fuckin' decision!

WOMAN: HELL.

MAN: Your girlfriend?

WOMAN: Turn off the light.

MAN: I won't, I'm having dinner. (*Takes fork and starts to play with his food.*)

WOMAN: Give me one more chance.

MAN: I'll look for help in the Yellow Pages if you want me to.

WOMAN: I don't want to sleep with my eyes open.

MAN: When I sleep with you I always get cold.

WOMAN: I feel cold. (*She starts eating slowly, without interest.*)

MAN: I'm off but maybe I'll be back later tonight.

WOMAN: DON'T GO!

MAN: I'll be back.

WOMAN (*points to his plate*): My heart is sliced on your plate.

MAN: That's fine. Either way. I don't have enough suffering in my circulatory system.

WOMAN: You have to be satisfied with small pains.

MAN: Well, you're not going to satisfy me. (*He starts to stimulate his penis.*)

WOMAN: Done, or not yet?

MAN: Discomfort.

WOMAN: Breath.

MAN: Slice.

WOMAN: It hurts.

MAN: Spread yourself out like a table cloth.

WOMAN: Sometimes I don't understand you at all.

MAN: Don't lie.

WOMAN: Your words.

MAN: Words don't lie. People lie.

WOMAN: Loss of happiness.

MAN: How can somebody lose happiness?

WOMAN: Like this! (*She pulls out a sharp knife from the drawer, sweeps the vase off the table, and stabs the knife there exactly half way between him and her.*)

MAN *stops masturbating. Both stare at the knife, then their eyes meet.*

MAN: To lose patience.

WOMAN: To lose hope. To lose keys and be unable to get into your own house.

MAN: Just when I was feeling good.

WOMAN: You bastard.

MAN: What?

WOMAN: There is nothing left for you to do here.

MAN: Is that what you think?

WOMAN: That's what I hope.

MAN: When I am waiting for a tram, I am impatient.

WOMAN: What, you're not hungry anymore?

MAN: I don't want . . .
To beg forgiveness.
And to pay fines if I drive faster than the speed limit.

WOMAN: A little different taste of paradise.

MAN: Why do you want to spit into my wounds?

WOMAN: Better to lick them.

MAN: Die!

WOMAN: To multiply the pain.

MAN: On purpose.

WOMAN: I only thought that . . .

MAN: You're lying to yourself.

WOMAN: Everybody is moving away from me. Mostly those I wanted to get closer to.

MAN: Who for example?

WOMAN: And they say there is friendship!

MAN: I've never heard that before.

WOMAN: That's what they say.

MAN: FRIENDS ARE ONE TIME USE ONLY.

WOMAN: You're a piece of shit.

MAN: I HAVE NO MONEY.

WOMAN: You've got me.

MAN: I don't want YOU.

WOMAN: Fuck you.

MAN: Don't you even dare touch me.

WOMAN: Who's talking about touching?

MAN: Stop tossing and turning, ok?
Give me your hand.

WOMAN: No.

Pause.

MAN: Could you check my crotch for a sec?

WOMAN: What?

MAN: Just to see if everything is in its place.

WOMAN: Go ahead. (*beams*)

MAN (*taking off his pants, he stops suddenly and pulls them back on*): No way.

WOMAN: Don't start what you can't finish.

MAN: Go to Hell.

WOMAN: Fast forward!

MAN: It doesn't have to be FAST as long as it is FORWARD.

WOMAN: Bullshit.

WOMAN *checks the time.*

MAN: NINE FORTY SEVEN IN THE AFTERNOON.

WOMAN: Evening. Nine in the evening.

MAN: Whatever. How old are you anyway? Aren't you too young for me? Go home! What are you still doing here?

WOMAN: I'm hungry but I don't wanna eat anything.

MAN: In the morning it was the other way around.

WOMAN: Black and white, as a matter of fact.

MAN: Who sent you here anyway?

WOMAN: Provocation. Not confrontation.

MAN: Broken mechanism of a typewriter.

WOMAN: Automatic transmission.

MAN: Don't you think I should be a bit more attractive for you?

WOMAN: UNFINISHED CONFESSION.

MAN: More sexy.

WOMAN: UNFINISHED DECLARATION.

MAN: As for me, it was never a big thing.

WOMAN: This is how I spend my days.

MAN: Mainly the nights.

WOMAN: Lost in this city.

MAN: Where you evidently do not belong.

WOMAN: And you?

MAN: What about me? I don't give a fuck.

WOMAN: Hanged.

MAN: Harsh truth.

WOMAN: I had a dream about licking my clitoris.

MAN: Again?

WOMAN: Hold me!

MAN: Sorry.

WOMAN: The watch says there's a lot of time . . .

MAN: The watch lies.

MAN *approaches* WOMAN. *He forcefully turns her chair to face him, kneels down, and puts his head into her naked crotch. He holds her tight.*

WOMAN: Let go!

MAN: DON'T WANT TO.

WOMAN: Close the curtains.

MAN: Open your legs!

WOMAN *cooly, opens them.* MAN *starts licking her.*

WOMAN: Lower.

WOMAN (*breathes faster, she embraces him with his legs*): I love you.

MAN (*stops, steps aside, wipes his mouth with his sleeve, and spits out*): You're evil.

MAN *sits back at his place and starts to slowly eat the rest of the dinner.*

MAN: By the way, I don't like when you pluck your eyebrows.

WOMAN: I also shave my pussy.

MAN: And under-arms.

WOMAN: I HATE YOU.

MAN: Call me, sometime . . .

WOMAN: WHY DON'T YOU JUST SAY "FUCK IT!"

MAN: Just a few minutes after a whipping?

WOMAN: I'm pouring down.

MAN: From now on you don't have to explain anything to me, honey.

WOMAN: Honey?

MAN: DON'T BE ASHAMED OF ME.

WOMAN: Please!

MAN: I DON'T HAVE TIME, NOW!

WOMAN: Could you open the window for a sec, please?

MAN: But of course I DO love you.

WOMAN: Yeah, sometimes I'm in that mood too.

MAN: Desperation.

WOMAN: Too much time on your hands. (*She spears a big piece of meat from the pot.*)

MAN: IS THIS YOU?

WOMAN: No, this is the way I bare my soul. (*She throws the meat onto his plate.*)

MAN: Snake.

WOMAN: SSSsssssss.

MAN: So tomorrow you finally leave, right?

WOMAN: Tomorrow I will finally finish the list of your new enemies.

MAN: A list?

WOMAN: If you want me to.

MAN: Don't you understand that I'm simply tired of you?

WOMAN: Maybe . . .

MAN: Will you leave?

WOMAN: Tomorrow.

MAN: Good.

WOMAN: Now, help me finish this dinner.

MAN *pulls the knife out of the table, stabs some meat from her plate and puts it in his mouth.*

MAN: With pleasure.

Peacefully, without a word, they finish off the lamb. The WOMAN *puts her panties back on and leaves.*

THE END

THEREMIN

Petr Zelenka

Petr Zelenka
Photo courtesy of Hynek Glos

Petr Zelenka, born August 21, 1967, graduated in scriptwriting and dramaturgy from the Film Faculty of the Academy of Performing Arts in Prague. In 1993, he made his directorial debut with a film about punks, *Visací zámek*. Four years later, he premiered his most highly awarded film, the episodic *Buttoners*, which won the prestigious Czech Lion for best script, direction and film. The popular film *Loners* (2000) was based on a Zelenka story. His films *Year of the Devil* (2003) and *Tales of Common Insanity* (2005) were both awarded main prizes at the International Film Festivals in Karlovy Vary and Moscow. In 2008 his latest film *The Karamazov Brothers*, and brought more Czech Lion awards for best direction and film.

Zelenka began his career in the theatre translating the plays of Michael Frayn. His debut as a playwright—and his first time as a theatre director—was with *Tales of Common Insanity*, which in 2001 won the prestigious Alfréd Radok Award for Play of the Year. His recent play, *Coming Clean* (2007), was commissioned by the famous Narodowy Stary Theatre in Cracow, Poland. Zelenka's plays have been translated into over ten languages.

For a filmmaker there is definite beauty in theatre. At the premiere of a film, only a couple of people remember how it all began—and some of them have made three or more films in between. While opening night at the theatre is a climax of the compact in which everybody takes part. The process of creating a play from the first outline of the text to the thrilling first encounter with the audience is magical and highly creative. Whatever the result might be, it has a wonderful human touch.

—Petr Zelenka

From left to right: Martin Myšička, Ivan Trojan, Jiří Bábek, and David Novotný, in *Theremin* (2005), Dejvické divadlo, Prague, directed by Petr Zelenka

Photo courtesy of Hynek Glos

Theremin

by

Petr Zelenka

Translated by

Štěpán S. Šimek

CHARACTERS

LEON SERGEIEVICH THEREMIN—Russian inventor, musician, and industrial spy. He is a kind but stern good-looking and slender man with penetrating eyes. There is something priest-like about him. In his 30s.

HANS GOLDBERG—His manager, business partner, and friend. Despite his Russian Jewish heritage, he still remains an optimist. In his 40s.

SAMUEL HOFFMAN—Private investigator and a baseball fan. A simple but warm human being. He is in good physical shape, maybe even a jock. In his 30s.

LAVINIA WILLIAMS—Dancer, Theremin's assistant, speaker of six languages, and later his wife. A Communist and a political activist. She is a beautiful woman of Haitian and Irish heritage. In her early 20s.

KATHERINE THEREMIN—Theremin's first wife. A Russian. An insistent but fully dignified woman with a bit of a martyrdom complex. A bit affected, but with a large heart. In her early 30s.

JOSEPH SCHILLINGER—Russian émigré, composer, and musical innovator. Founder of Russian Jazz music, a visionary, and a mathematician. In his 30s or 40s.

LUCY ROSEN—Wife of a millionaire, Theremin's admirer and lover. She is a romantically disposed woman, who is attracted to strong personalities, but completely out of touch with reality. In her 30s or early 40s.

WALTER ROSEN—American banker, music lover, and philanthropist. In his 50s or early 60s.

AMTORG 1—An "employee" of Amtorg Trading Corporation, a front for the Soviet GRU (Military Intelligence), Theremin's handler.

AMTORG 2—His assistant

RESTAURANT OWNER

RADIO HOST

SETTING

The play takes place between 1927 and 1938 in various locales in New York City.

NOTE ON STAGING:
The staging of the play relies on continuous stage action. The different spaces, such as the apartments of the different protagonists, the offices of Amtorg Trading Corporation, the backstage of Yankee Stadium, etc. don't need to be specifically defined. Major scene changes would only break the continuity of the plot.

NOTE ON MUSIC:
Music is an important part of the play. The director/producer is encouraged to compose or choose his or her own for the incidental music where indicated in the text. However, the original compositions for the "Concert at Yankee Stadium" and the "Musical Transformation of the Market" are part of the license agreement and must be used in their original form. The scores and/or recordings of the two pieces are available upon request.

ACT ONE

MUSIC. Lights come up on an exclusive private club/restaurant in New York City in the 1920s. Several tables and chairs, covered with furniture covers. A waitress, LAVINIA, *is uncovering the furniture. As she takes off the last sheet, she uncovers* GOLDBERG *and* THEREMIN *sitting at a table.*

Offstage a woman's laughter is heard. The laughter comes closer, and LUCY ROSEN *and her husband* WALTER ROSEN *enter.* LAVINIA *and the* CLUB OWNER *receive them, take their coats, and lead them towards an empty table. As the* ROSENS *pass they pay little attention to* GOLDBERG *and* THEREMIN. GOLDBERG *jumps from his seat and makes a formal introduction.*

GOLDBERG: Good evening. My name is Hans Goldberg. Professor Theremin's business manager. This is Professor Theremin. (*To* THEREMIN.) Walter Rosen, the owner of the transatlantic liner, which brought us here . . .

ROSEN (*taken aback by such a sudden introduction, but showing signs of recognition*): Ah . . . yes . . . Good evening.

GOLDBERG: . . . and his wife.

THEREMIN: Good evening.

LUCY: Your concert was . . . how should I say . . . it . . . was fantastic, Mister . . .

GOLDBERG: Professor Theremin.

LUCY: Mr. Theremin.

THEREMIN: Thank you.

ROSEN: I've never seen anything so . . . I don't know how to put it . . .

LUCY: Modern perhaps?

ROSEN: So . . . alive.

GOLDBERG: In England and in France the response to Professor Theremin's concerts was absolutely exceptional. When he played the Paris Opera more than three hundred people had to be turned away. Yes. Paris received us extremely kindly.

LUCY: And what about Russia? Is it true that the Bolshevik revolution introduced free love?

THEREMIN: Well, not exactly.

LUCY: That's what everybody here believes. We are trying to catch up with Russia in that regard. New York, of course, is absolutely amoral.

GOLDBERG: But what about Prohibition?

LUCY: Oh, that's only a game. We got bored *just* drinking, so now we drink in secret.

The OWNER *is taking their orders.*

ROSEN: New York's nightclubs are notorious. Women wrestling in popcorn for example . . . Have you ever seen anything like that?

GOLDBERG: No.

LUCY: Well in that case, you must come along with us one day. As a matter of fact, my husband actually owns several such clubs.

ROSEN: It's only one of my many business ventures.

LUCY: Or are they maybe brothels, darling?

ROSEN: No. They are nightclubs.

LUCY: Yes. They are nightclubs. Hardly different from brothels, but—they are nightclubs. Have you ever been in a New York brothel, Mister . . .

GOLDBERG: Goldberg. No, I have not.

LUCY: I believe that one day the whole of New York will meet in one gigantic bed. The only question is who will build it, and how much it will cost.

Everybody laughs. Then there is a moment of awkward silence. Fortunately SCHILLINGER *enters.*

SCHILLINGER: Sorry I'm late. I even missed the concert.

LUCY: You made a big mistake. It was . . . it was absolutely phenomenal. Mister . . .

GOLDBERG: Professor Theremin.

LUCY: Mr. Theremin gave an unbelievable performance.

ROSEN: Absolutely.

GOLDBERG (*introducing* SCHILLINGER *to* THEREMIN): Joseph Schillinger—Leon Theremin.

THEREMIN: Pleasure to meet you. I've heard a lot about you.

SCHILLINGER: Same here. Your instrument is already becoming a legend. They say that you pull your sounds literally from the ether. I'm sorry I couldn't see it in action so to speak . . . It's the only non-contact musical instrument in the world. I mean, you can play it, without touching it at all, am I right?

THEREMIN: Yes.

GOLDBERG: We would like you to have a look at it. And maybe even write some music for it . . .

THEREMIN: . . . even though the sound is still far from perfect.

SCHILLINGER: It's not about how the instrument sounds at this point, but what sort of possibilities it opens. And the same goes for Ondes Martenot, electrophon, sphaerophon, or your thereminvox.

LUCY: I talked to Astor about the concert today.

SCHILLINGER: What did he say?

LUCY: He was disgusted. And if Astor is disgusted by something, then we of course should pay attention to it. Am I right, Walter, darling?

ROSEN: Of course. We are tired of the same old sounds, the same old dusty baroque instruments. But your instrument is something fascinating.

SCHILLINGER: Not to mention that the thereminvox may be the only instrument for which it will be possible to compose music completely mechanically.

LUCY: I beg your pardon?

SCHILLINGER: The recent spread of radio is so fast that if it continues, sooner or later there won't be enough music to satisfy its demands. So it's clear that in the next few years, there will be a need to develop a machine that actually composes music. The music will be broadcast in real time as the machines compose it. The ultimate goal is to produce music of such style and precision that goes beyond anything that humans are capable of.

LUCY: You are a crazy dreamer, Joseph. But an endearing one.

GOLDBERG: Our aim is to organize a concert tour in America. For the exclusive circles, as well as for the general public.

ROSEN: I could arrange something at Carnegie Hall.

LUCY: Or maybe in one of your little brothels, darling.

Everybody laughs. The ROSENS *are ready to leave.* GOLDBERG *and* THEREMIN *exchange a significant look.*

GOLDBERG: You wouldn't believe all the places where Leon Sergeievich has performed.

ROSEN: Is that so?

GOLDBERG: All sorts of really interesting places . . . not to mention the concert where it all started, so to speak.

ROSEN: Which one was that?

THEREMIN: It doesn't matter.

GOLDBERG: They're asking. (*To* ROSEN.) A concert in Lenin's office, in 1922.

Musical accent.

SCHILLINGER: You played for Lenin?

THEREMIN: Well, it wasn't really a concert in the classical sense of the word.

LUCY: But you met him in person?

THEREMIN: It was a very ordinary meeting.

LUCY: What sort of a person was he? Tell us something about him.

GOLDBERG *nods at* THEREMIN. *Their well-rehearsed shpiel is ready to start.*

GOLDBERG: He was a remarkable man. But he had a reputation of being an unpredictable eccentric.

LUCY: Why don't you let Mr. Theremin speak?

GOLDBERG: He doesn't like to talk about it. He's too modest.

LUCY: You don't need to be shy with us.

SCHILLINGER: I didn't know that Lenin was interested in electric music.

GOLDBERG: He was interested in everything that had to do with electricity.

THEREMIN: That is true.

GOLDBERG: Lenin ordered the instrument's presentation at exactly eleven in the morning. Leon Sergeievich had already set off at nine. He, and his assistant. It is a cold and gray November day, last few leaves on the streets . . .

THEREMIN: Cut it short, Hans.

GOLDBERG: But this is important—to set the stage . . . a cold and gray November day, the last few leaves swirling in the wind on the streets, and he and his aide ascend the monumental stairs to the Kremlin. Lenin was about an hour late, but he received Theremin warmly. Theremin explained the theoretical underpinnings of his instrument, and then Lenin asked him to perform a piece.

THEREMIN: I used the fact that his secretary played the piano, and I asked her to accompany me.

GOLDBERG: He played "The Lark."

SCHILLINGER: By Glinka!

THEREMIN: Very clumsily.

GOLDBERG: But Lenin was excited. Right away, he wanted to try it as well.

SCHILLINGER: That's incredible, *Lenin* played the thereminvox?

THEREMIN: Yes. Actually . . . at first I had to lead his hands.

LUCY: What do you mean?

THEREMIN: I was afraid, that Vladimir Ilyich would get angry if he played badly, but he actually did very well.

GOLDBERG: Leon stood behind Lenin, and grasped his hands like this. (*He demonstrates on* LAVINIA, *who is just about to serve their food.*) Allow me please . . . (*He leads her hands as she struggles with the plates.*) Like this . . . The hands of the most powerful man in the eastern hemisphere. Leon Sergeievich is perhaps the only person in the world ever to hold both of Lenin's hands.

ROSEN *gets up and makes a toast. The others join him.*

ROSEN: Gentlemen, to Lenin!

LUCY: But I still don't understand why you held his hands.

THEREMIN: So that I could lead them. It's that's simple.

LUCY: But it was you who played the instrument, wasn't it?

THEREMIN: We played together.

LUCY: But did you touch the instrument or did he?

THEREMIN: Neither.

LUCY: Neither?

THEREMIN: Yes, neither. Since, as you know, the thereminvox, is a non-contact musical instrument.

ROSEN: Naturally.

THEREMIN: As you clearly saw during the concert tonight . . . (*pause*) Or didn't see?

LUCY: We were a bit delayed . . .

ROSEN: Actually, I believe we owe you an apology. We were delayed due to an important business dinner, and when we finally got there, it was all over. The audience was just leaving the ballroom. So, to make a long story short, we completely missed it. I hope that you won't be offended.

LUCY: But the people who were leaving . . . they seemed very . . . interested. And I heard Astor saying that it was . . .

THEREMIN: . . . horrible.

LUCY: Yes, horrible. So naturally we got very interested. But we really are sorry that we couldn't be there ourselves.

It is clear that nobody actually saw the concert. Uncomfortable silence.

GOLDBERG: Well, I'm sure that there will be many other opportunities. Next week we'll be playing at Pabst's on Broadway.

ROSEN: Yes, yes. We'll be there for sure. We are great admirers.

SCHILLINGER: Actually this is quite amusing. We meet here to honor Mr. Theremin, but none of us has seen him perform.

LAVINIA: If you'll allow me, I've seen Mr. Theremin perform. Last year in Paris. It was magnificent. You played "The Swan" and "The Lark" . . .

SCHILLINGER: . . . by Glinka!

LAVINIA: . . . and later some Russian elegies.

THEREMIN: You were at the Paris Opera?

LAVINIA: Yes, my aunt is one of the assistant stage managers there.

GOLDBERG: It was a phenomenal concert. Three hundred people had to be turned away.

LAVINIA: I wanted to find you and ask for an autograph, but there were so many people around you that it wasn't possible. But today, when I saw you here I thought . . .

THEREMIN: What an interesting coincidence!

LAVINIA: Exactly.

THEREMIN: We would be honored if you joined us, Miss . . .

LAVINIA: Williams. Thank you, but I can't. As you see, I work here.

THEREMIN: But there are many other waiters here.

LAVINIA: I'll ask, but I don't think it will be possible. (*She looks at the* OWNER *who doesn't react.*)

THE OWNER (*to* THEREMIN): It's impossible.

THEREMIN: Why?

LUCY: It's against their policies.

THE OWNER: We don't serve Negroes in our club, Sir.

THEREMIN: I beg your pardon?

GOLDBERG: You heard it. She cannot join us because she's a Negro.

THEREMIN: Excuse me?

THE OWNER: Our establishment is "whites only." It's that simple, Sir.

LUCY: Exactly.

THEREMIN: This is silly.

THE OWNER: I have to respect the other customers, Sir.

THEREMIN: Very well. (*Addressing the "other" imaginary customers.*) Would any of you be offended if I invited this young lady to join us at the table?

GOLDBERG: Sergei, that's enough.

THEREMIN: Just let me. (*To the* OWNER.) You see, nobody cares.

THE OWNER: There is nobody else here, Sir.

THEREMIN: Exactly. We are the only ones.

GOLDBERG: Leo, stop it!

THEREMIN: Wait. You should be on my side. Today they forbid me to sit at a table with a Negro woman, and tomorrow they'll ban Jews from restaurants.

THE OWNER: You are exaggerating, Sir.

The OWNER *ends the discussion and is about to leave, but* THEREMIN *has no intention of giving up.* LAVINIA *wants to leave as well, but* THEREMIN *won't let her go.*

THEREMIN: Wait. And you, Miss Williams, stay here. This is a matter of principle. Ms. Rosen, a few minutes ago you asked me what exactly was our aim. I'll tell you: Our goal is to change the world. Mr. Goldberg, please correct me if I am wrong. And not only that: We need to change *ourselves* so that we will be able to live in such a new world. This is what we must strive for. In, say, ten or fifteen years, every human being will be able to play a musical instrument . . . we'll eliminate all disease . . . why, it is even conceivable that man will be immortal . . . and in such a world no waiter would consider telling his customers whether or not they are allowed to invite their friends to join them at a table.

This is a strange lecture. Nobody knows what to say. ROSEN *claps his hands, and for the sake of decorum* SCHILLINGER *joins him.* LUCY *puts out her cigarette, gets up, making a big sweeping arc, she walks around the table, and on her way she elegantly rinses her mouth with soda water. Finally, she arrives at* THEREMIN*'s chair, and gives him a long kiss on the mouth. Then, as elegantly, she returns to her chair. Taken aback, everybody watches* ROSEN*'s reaction.* ROSEN *gets up from the table and leaves.*

LUCY: So. Where were we?

THEREMIN: We were talking about why Miss Williams is not allowed to join us at the table.

LUCY: Because if she does, she'll be fired.

THEREMIN (*to the* OWNER): Is that so?

THE OWNER: It is.

THEREMIN: In that case, I cannot insist. Miss Williams, I'd like to drink to you, but it seems that the odds are against us.

LAVINIA *slowly takes off her waitress apron and takes a seat at the table.* LUCY *gets up and leaves.* SCHILLINGER *follows suit.*

THEREMIN: Welcome to our table Miss Williams. What would you like to drink? Martini? (*To the* OWNER.) One Martini for the lady, please.

The OWNER *turns around and leaves, never to come back.*

I'm afraid our waiter won't be coming back. In that case, we have to serve ourselves. (*Pours* LAVINIA *a glass of wine from a bottle labeled "Apple Juice."*) How long have you been in America?

LAVINIA: Since I was two. I was born in Haiti. And you?

THEREMIN: This is my first day here.

Time shift. THEREMIN *begins to write a "letter to his father." These letters are always disproportionately full of technical details. In reality their function is to pass information about technological developments in the U.S. to the Soviet secret service operating in America under the guise of a trade organization called Amtorg.*

THEREMIN: Dear Father, Sir. My first month in the New World passed quickly. America welcomed us warmly, albeit with some reservations . . . However, we were able to arrange meetings with several rather important people. Our concert last week at Pabst's theatre on Broadway was well attended. Henry Ford and Jacob Astor were in the audience but they didn't express any interest in my instrument. However, the banker and businessman, Walter Rosen, was kind enough to arrange for me to visit his airplane engine factory in Massachusetts . . .

Enter TWO AMTORG EMPLOYEES. *We are now in the Amtorg offices.*

AMTORG 1: What kind of engines?

THEREMIN (*continues to write*): . . . I wish you could see them, my dear father. Beautiful twelve-cylinder Rolls Royce engines, twenty-four valves, twelve hundred HP . . .

AMTORG 1: And what's the yearly output?

THEREMIN: . . . They manufacture about twenty such engines a year, but without a doubt, they could double if not triple their production on a day's notice . . . But I need to end here. Please send my love to mother, to uncle, and to Vladimir. Hoping to see you soon, your devoted son, Leon Sergeievich.

The AMTORG EMPLOYEES *pour vodka into small shot glasses.* THEREMIN *folds the "letter" and puts it in an envelope. He is about to seal it, but decides otherwise, and leaves it open. The* AMTORG EMPLOYEES *invite him to join them at their table, and welcome him enthusiastically.*

AMTORG 1: We are very interested in the engine factory. It will be necessary for you to go back there and get some pictures. We need to know the kind of airplanes that use those engines, the shape of their wings, also the brake systems, and how the wheels are mounted.

He snaps his fingers, and AMTORG 2 *hands* THEREMIN *a camera.*

THEREMIN: I would only like to mention that I'm not an airplane engineer. It may be better to send somebody who actually studied that kind of thing.

AMTORG 1: On the contrary! You are perfectly suited for this job. You're a quick study. Everybody in Russia holds you in high regard.

THEREMIN: Who in Russia holds me in high regard?

AMTORG 1: The head of the secret service, Peter Yanovich Berzin himself, said that you were a very capable person.

THEREMIN: Thank you.

AMTORG 1: Don't thank us; it's Comrade Berzin's opinion. (AMTORG EMPLOYEES *raise their glasses.*) To Peter Berzin! Long live Peter Berzin!

THEREMIN: Long live Peter Berzin!

AMTORG 1: What's the news about the concerts on your thereminvox?

THEREMIN: The attendance is average.

AMTORG 1: That's not what I'm asking.

THEREMIN: Here are the names of some of the important people who came to our concerts. (*Gives them a sheet of paper with the names.*) But I must say that we got better reception in England and France. The Americans don't want to only listen; they immediately want to try everything themselves . . . several people want me to build a model for them.

AMTORG 1: There is a rumor that Charlie Chaplin ordered one from you.

THEREMIN: Yes, I'm building a model for him. But clearly, I can't satisfy all potential customers.

AMTORG 1: Who says you can't?

He snaps his fingers and AMTORG 2 *begins to demonstrate different statistics using a complicated set of tables and graphs on a blackboard.*

AMTORG 2: Last year, Americans spent thirty-six million dollars on pianos alone. Surprisingly, the second most popular instrument in terms of sales was the cello: twelve million dollars. There is no reason why in a year or two they shouldn't be spending the same money on the theremin.

THEREMIN: How?

AMTORG 1: Very simply. You'll mass-produce it.

THEREMIN: Unfortunately, that's impossible. You know very well how the instrument looks, how it sounds . . .

The AMTORG EMPLOYEES *laugh, for the first and last time in the play. Suddenly, they grow serious.*

THEREMIN: The piano and the cello are very old instruments that proved themselves over a long time. Thereminvox is still in a nascent phase . . .

AMTORG 1: That manager of yours, that German . . .

THEREMIN: Hans Goldberg . . .

AMTORG 1: . . . You said he was quite capable.

THEREMIN: But he can't work miracles. Anyway, for something like that we'd need much more time.

AMTORG 1: You've got plenty of time.

THEREMIN: I only have a two-month visa.

AMTORG 1: That's not for you to worry about.

THEREMIN: My family is in Russia. My mother, my nephew . . . my father.

AMTORG 1: Exactly. (*pause*) You'll best serve your father here. To your father! May he live long!

They toast. The conversation is finished. THEREMIN *has received a clear order from Amtorg. The* AMTORG EMPLOYEES *get up. After a moment* THEREMIN *joins them.*

Pause.

AMTORG 2: By the way, Vladimir Semionovich, your cousin, I believe . . .

THEREMIN: Yes?

AMTORG 2: He was arrested a week ago.

THEREMIN: What happened?

AMTORG 2: It's not completely clear yet. He's under interrogation. All we can hope is that everything will turn out well, isn't that so, *Professor* Theremin?

An ominous drone of the thereminvox is heard. The AMTORG EMPLOYEES *leave;* THEREMIN, *shocked and dumbfounded, stands alone.*

Enter GOLDBERG. *We are in* THEREMIN'*s laboratory, which also functions as the living room in his rather elegant New York hotel apartment.*

GOLDBERG: Tomorrow we are starting with a press conference at three-thirty here at the hotel. We want to concentrate on the right wing press. Then a concert in a small private club on Seventh Avenue. No more than a hundred people. We want to create an impression of exclusivity. Classical repertoire. Rehearsal immediately before the concert.

THEREMIN *is spreading all sorts of electrical parts, such as vacuum tubes, triodes, and other components on the table.*

THEREMIN: Just look at that! Beautiful, isn't it? And I bought it all at one single store, about five blocks from here. You'd never find anything like that in Europe, but they have five stores like that just here in New York.

GOLDBERG: I know.

THEREMIN: You can get everything in America. If somebody wants to build some machine or an instrument, a radio for example, he can just go to a store, and buy all the parts he needs.

GOLDBERG: But why would they do it? Anybody can buy a finished radio.

THEREMIN: Exactly. But not a theremin. So anybody can build one themselves.

GOLDBERG: Right. But there isn't anything we can do about it.

THEREMIN: Well, maybe we could. (*pause*) If we started mass production of it.

GOLDBERG (*ignores* THEREMIN's *excitement*): So, rehearsal immediately before the concert. Henry Ford may be there, but we don't know yet. Bohuslav Martinů is also a possibility. Schillinger's coming for sure.

THEREMIN: So you don't think it's a good idea?

GOLDBERG: You can't just willy-nilly out of the blue start producing an instrument that nobody knows about apart from a few enthusiasts. Don't forget that to the vast majority of people we are nothing more than some sort of exotic musical quacks.

THEREMIN: Now, wait a minute . . . !

GOLDBERG: First of all, we'd need to get a U.S. patent.

THEREMIN: We've got the German patent.

GOLDBERG: Yes, but America is not Germany, where I know whom to talk to and when. For it to work here, you'd have to start a school. Maybe even several schools. Teach students how to play it, cultivate musicians. Persuade composers to write original music for the theremin. And especially, we'd have to find somebody who'd be willing to actually produce it. Some big corporation that could afford to sink several hundred thousand dollars into a new production line.

THEREMIN: You're right. It's nonsense.

GOLDBERG (*in his managerial tone*): A dinner invitation following the concert. Informal atmosphere. Only a handful of people. It's not clear yet who exactly.

THEREMIN: On the other hand, if we managed to pull it off, it would mean a complete revolution in the concept of music as such. Maybe even a bigger one than in 1917.

GOLDBERG: But something like that takes time.

THEREMIN: Weeks? Months?

GOLDBERG: Years. Are you willing to stay here for several years? Your wife is in Russia, your parents, your work at the Institute . . .

THEREMIN: And what about you? Your business partners are in Germany.

GOLDBERG: We came here to play a few concerts.

THEREMIN: Yes.

GOLDBERG: Did we or didn't we?

THEREMIN: A few concerts only.

GOLDBERG: So we'll play those few concerts and return home, to Europe. You'll go to Russia, and I'll go to Germany. And that's it.

THEREMIN: That's it. And until the day we die, we'll regret that we never tried.

Pause.

GOLDBERG: But this goes far beyond our original business plans. As a venture, a project like that is completely insane. If I were to try something like that, I couldn't do it as a businessman but only as a . . .

THEREMIN: As a what?

GOLDBERG: . . . as a human being.

THEREMIN: What do you mean?

GOLDBERG: I'm asking whether we could be friends.

THEREMIN: We *are* friends.

GOLDBERG: No. We are business partners. But what I am asking is, if apart from being that, we could also be friends?

THEREMIN: Of course.

GOLDBERG *is a little moved by this.*

THEREMIN: One thing though.

GOLDBERG: Yes?

THEREMIN: Tomorrow at dinner, we'll leave Lenin out of it.

GOLDBERG: OK. Unless somebody explicitly asks about him.

THEREMIN: Even if they ask.

GOLDBERG: Tomorrow, then . . .

Exit THEREMIN *and* GOLDBERG. *Enter* LUCY *and* HOFFMAN. *We are in* LUCY ROSEN*'s house.*

LUCY: I'm not quite sure how to do this. I'm thirty-five, but I've never hired a private detective before. Unlike my husband. You worked for him, didn't you?

HOFFMAN: For a while.

LUCY: Because of me?

HOFFMAN: No comment.

LUCY: You don't have to tell me. So, enlighten me. What is it that people usually hire you for?

HOFFMAN: A wife may be interested whether her husband really did quit drinking or gambling . . . Of course many clients tend to be jealous people, who suspect that their partners are unfaithful, or I may investigate a client's solvency, and sometimes it's just a simple stakeout . . .

LUCY: What's that?

HOFFMAN: You're just waiting for somebody to come out of some place.

LUCY: I see.

HOFFMAN: Some shadowing jobs, and the occasional lost dog or cat.

LUCY: You even do cats and dogs?

HOFFMAN: Purely out of Christian love.

LUCY: So, do you have a code name or something?

HOFFMAN: "Babe."

LUCY: So basically you like your job.

HOFFMAN: I'm not complaining.

LUCY: What did you do before?

HOFFMAN: A bit of professional sport. Baseball.

LUCY: That's delightful. You'll have to tell me more about it sometime.

HOFFMAN: So, who are we talking about here?

LUCY: His name is Leon Sergeievich Theremin.

HOFFMAN *is taking notes.*

LUCY: You are writing it down?

HOFFMAN: I'm writing in code. Nobody will be able to read it. Theremin. How do you spell it?

LUCY: The way it sounds. T-E-R . . . or maybe T-H-E . . .

HOFFMAN: Who is he? What does he do? Any special characteristics I should know about?

LUCY: He is an inventor. And a musician at the same time. Have you ever seen him play?

HOFFMAN: Negative.

LUCY: He's a well-known person.

HOFFMAN: Russian?

LUCY: Yes. He played for Lenin.

HOFFMAN (*not impressed*): What's your particular interest in him?

LUCY: I'm sorry?

HOFFMAN: What sort of information should I be looking for? Are you interested in him as a potential investment, does he owe you money, does he . . . ?

LUCY: I'm interested in him as a human being.

HOFFMAN: Too general. Concretely, you are interested in what?

LUCY: His hands.

HOFFMAN: His hands?

LUCY: Yes. His hands. What are you writing?

HOFFMAN: I'm writing "hands."

LUCY: You know, he's got those peculiar hands. They're . . . hypnotic . . . almost as if they were eyes . . . as well as a mouth. Those hands . . . they're all of that together.

HOFFMAN: His hands are like his eyes and mouth?

LUCY: Yes. When I first met him I felt as if those hands were talking to me. (*Pause. Then suddenly.*) Ah, forget about it. Maybe it's all nonsense. I apologize—I shouldn't have called you here.

HOFFMAN: No problem. Do you intend to have an illicit relationship with Mr. Theremin?

LUCY *significantly doesn't answer.* HOFFMAN *is finally on familiar ground.*

HOFFMAN: Thank you. We can work with that. Am I correct to assume that you are interested in everything pertaining to Mr. Theremin—especially his personal life: How he lives, his friends and acquaintances, his views—political and otherwise, and so on?

LUCY: Yes.

HOFFMAN: In that case we are not concerned about financial questions, correct?

LUCY: You can leave out financial questions.

HOFFMAN: We are interested in other women in his life, places he goes, what he does in his free time, and so on.

LUCY: Yes.

HOFFMAN: I don't see any problem there. Do we have a photograph?

LUCY (*teasing* HOFFMAN): Now, that is something *we* don't have.

HOFFMAN: No problem.

LUCY: There's his caricature in the paper here.

HOFFMAN: Let's see . . . (*Looks in the paper.*) That's him? Are his ears that long?

LUCY: It's a caricature.

HOFFMAN: Right. Interesting guy. Wow, look at those hands . . .

LUCY: In reality they are smaller too.

HOFFMAN: But it's the hands that you are interested in?

LUCY: Yes.

HOFFMAN: OK. Can I borrow this? It'll be fifty bucks a week plus expenses. You pay three weeks in advance.

LUCY (*hands over the money*): Very well.

HOFFMAN (*counts the bills*): Thanks.

LUCY: So how will you proceed?

HOFFMAN: Can't tell you. Secret of the trade.

LUCY: I'm just asking. Will you rent an apartment close to his? Will you try to visit him? Follow him?

HOFFMAN: Maybe.

LUCY: Mr. Hoffman, do you play a musical instrument?

HOFFMAN: Negative. I'm more of the sports type.

LUCY: Because Theremin invented a new musical instrument.

HOFFMAN: What is it? What is it called?

LUCY: Theremin.

HOFFMAN: I know. But what do you call the instrument?

LUCY: Theremin. Just like Theremin.

HOFFMAN: I get it. Theremin equals theremin.

LUCY: Correct. Right now Mr. Theremin is trying to form an electric orchestra. If he succeeds, it would be something unprecedented in the history of music.

HOFFMAN: We'll cross our fingers for him.

LUCY (*points to the thereminvox in the room*): Coincidentally, I have one of the instruments right here. It's a gift for my husband. An original.

HOFFMAN *examines it.*

LUCY: You play it by changing the distance of your right hand from this antenna, which determines the pitch, and the distance of your left hand from this antenna, which controls the volume. Please.

HOFFMAN: Please what?

LUCY: Go on, try it.

She leads HOFFMAN *to the instrument, stands behind him and holds his hands just like Theremin supposedly held Lenin's. The instrument produces dreadful sounds.* HOFFMAN *is a little frightened; he finds the whole situation unpleasant, and steps back from the instrument.*

HOFFMAN: This is supposed to be an instrument?

LUCY: Yes. It's the only non-contact musical instrument in the world.

HOFFMAN: He built this thing? Remarkable fellow, this Theremin of yours.

LUCY: Yes. Why don't you try again.

HOFFMAN: I'll pass. As I said, music's not really my thing.

LUCY: That's a pity. Because I was thinking that the best way for you to get close to Theremin would be to audition for his electric orchestra.

HOFFMAN: I think I'd rather rent that apartment close to his.

LUCY *exits. We are now in* THEREMIN's *hotel apartment.* HOFFMAN *starts going through the drawers, looks under the carpet, etc.* THEREMIN *enters.*

THEREMIN: Who let you in here?

HOFFMAN: The maid.

THEREMIN: Are you here for a lesson? I only teach on Tuesdays and Thursdays. Today's Wednesday. In any case, you should have waited downstairs in the lobby.

HOFFMAN: I'm not here for a lesson. I write screenplays. Samuel Hoffman . . . From Hollywood . . . Good afternoon.

He extends his hand. THEREMIN *tentatively shakes it.* HOFFMAN *carefully examines* THEREMIN's *hand.*

THEREMIN: Leon Theremin.

HOFFMAN: Mr. Theremin, my congratulations! Your concert at the Pabst last week was phenomenal.

THEREMIN: Many people left before it was over.

HOFFMAN: No, No! It was magnificent. You have hands made of gold.

THEREMIN: Did Goldberg send you here?

HOFFMAN: No.

THEREMIN: He's responsible for the, how do you say it . . . "Public Relations." He's constantly sending over all sorts of reporters and newspapermen. Did Goldberg already tell you about my meeting with Lenin?

HOFFMAN: Negative.

THEREMIN: You should ask him about it, it's an excellent story. We have more success with that story than with the whole thereminvox.

HOFFMAN: I don't know Mr. Goldberg. I came on my own.

THEREMIN: All right. So you are a screenwriter. You write movies?

HOFFMAN: Exactly. In Hollywood.

THEREMIN: And how can I be of service?

HOFFMAN: I'd like to write a screenplay about you.

THEREMIN: Do you have a dog?

HOFFMAN: No . . . ?

THEREMIN: You smell like you have a dog. But that's beside the point. Go on.

HOFFMAN: It would be a biographical movie. I'd like to witness firsthand how you invent, how you live . . . to be part of it.

THEREMIN: And who's going to play me? Fred Astaire?

HOFFMAN: I'm not sure.

THEREMIN: Well, Mr. Hoffman, since I already have you here, I'd like to try something on you. (*Puts his new device in front of* HOFFMAN.) Come and look at this. It's a joy to shop here in America. Isn't it something?

HOFFMAN: Hmm.

THEREMIN: Do you know what this is?

HOFFMAN: Negative.

THEREMIN (*pointing to different parts of the new device*): A condenser. And this is a resistance coil. Another coil. Resistance again. Wiring. And this is again a condenser. And this? Now this is a vacuum tube. And if you put it all together like that—do you know what it is? A lie detector. I wanted to build one a long time ago, but there simply weren't enough components for it in Russia. Would you please sit down here? (*Seats* HOFFMAN *in a chair.*) I discovered that lying alters the skin resistance to an electric current. So if we measure the level of resistance we can determine whether a person is lying or speaking the truth. Of course, I'm talking about deliberate lying. Don't worry, it won't hurt you. (*He fastens two wires on a very uncomfortable* HOFFMAN.) So. Now I'm going to ask you a question, and you answer with a lie. What did you have for breakfast?

HOFFMAN: . . . Eh . . . Eggs.

The device reacts.

THEREMIN: Is that true?

HOFFMAN: No.

THEREMIN *adjusts the device.*

HOFFMAN: What are you doing?

THEREMIN: Calibrating. So. Now, what did you really have?

HOFFMAN: What should I say?

THEREMIN: Tell the truth.

HOFFMAN: I had two waffles.

The device reacts—it's a lie.

THEREMIN: The instrument says that you are lying.

HOFFMAN: Well, maybe I had them yesterday.

The device reacts—it's a lie.

THEREMIN: Did you even have breakfast?

HOFFMAN: No.

The device reacts—it's a lie.

THEREMIN: You had something.

HOFFMAN: OK. I had two shots of whiskey.

THEREMIN: That early in the morning?

HOFFMAN: I have a problem with drinking. I'm an alcoholic. Ha, ha . . .

The device reacts—it's true.

THEREMIN: Seriously?

HOFFMAN: No, I'm just kidding.

THEREMIN: The instrument says that it's true. (*pause*) And now for something completely different. Are you really a Hollywood screenwriter?

GOLDBERG *and* SCHILLINGER *enter.*

GOLDBERG: We've got something for you, Leo.

THEREMIN: So do I. This is Samuel Hoffman, a screenwriter from Hollywood. Hans Goldberg, my friend and manager.

GOLDBERG: Good afternoon. (*introducing*) Joseph Schillinger, composer, musical innovator, and a great teacher. A man, who never wore the same suit more than once. His musical experiments are legendary. He played with an orchestra in the great caves of the Caucasus Mountains.

SCHILLINGER: Pleased to meet you.

HOFFMAN: I've heard much about you.

SCHILLINGER *passes out sheets of music to* THEREMIN, GOLDBERG, HOFFMAN.

SCHILLINGER: Well then, gentlemen.

THEREMIN: Your work?

SCHILLINGER: Yes.

THEREMIN *carefully studies the score. It's obvious that he and* GOLDBERG *are well versed in sight-reading, reading the score as if it were an adventure novel.*

GOLDBERG: Remarkable.

THEREMIN (*laughing*): It's quite witty.

SCHILLINGER: I took advantage of the possibility of sustained tones.

THEREMIN: Exactly! (*Pointing to a particular place in the score.*) Look at this one for example!

GOLDBERG: Absolutely. That's what I'm looking at.

SCHILLINGER: It's sustained throughout the piece.

THEREMIN: Fantastic idea.

SCHILLINGER: Until now, it wasn't possible to do anything like that in music.

THEREMIN: Measure 137—G half flat?

SCHILLINGER: That's a quarter tone.

GOLDBERG (*pointing out another part of the score*): A never-ending crescendo! What an incredible idea.

SCHILLINGER: It's only meant figuratively.

THEREMIN: What's the title?

SCHILLINGER: "The First Airphonic Suite for Two Theremins, Rhythmicon, Piano, and Orchestra."

THEREMIN: Key?

SCHILLINGER: Enharmonically changed F flat major. E major for the laymen.

THEREMIN: Excellent. Let's try it. (*He sets up two theremins.*) Mr. Hoffman here can play the pedal tone.

HOFFMAN: I think I'll pass. I'm more of the sports type.

SCHILLINGER: Music is a sort of a physical activity as well.

THEREMIN: It's only one note. Try it. (*Positions* HOFFMAN *by one of the theremins.*) Like this . . . This hand is the pitch, and this one is volume. OK? You see, you're doing fine.

SCHILLINGER: For the rhythmicon we'll use a typewriter in the meantime.

GOLDBERG: Great idea. Who'll play it?

SCHILLINGER: You.

He puts a beautiful old Remington on the table for GOLDBERG. *In the meantime,* HOFFMAN *manages to wring out the first sound from the theremin.*

SCHILLINGER (*to* HOFFMAN): Bass.

HOFFMAN: I beg your pardon?

SCHILLINGER: The bass note. Keep it going.

SCHILLINGER *sits down at a piano to conduct the whole piece.*

SCHILLINGER: Gentlemen . . .

They start playing . . . It is something that very remotely resembles music, which lasts for about three minutes. GOLDBERG *isn't altogether convinced about the whole affair, and the pause at the end of the piece is long. Finally,* THEREMIN *speaks out.*

THEREMIN: Perfect.

Everybody is relieved.

THEREMIN (*to* HOFFMAN): I'll have to tune your theremin to a lower register though.

HOFFMAN: Thanks, that's very nice.

SCHILLINGER: At this point we are missing the rhythmicon—basically an electric drum set . . . and we also need at least a six-octave range on the theremin. A true glissando over six octaves!

HOFFMAN: And when we get it all, then what?

SCHILLINGER: Then we will forever change the face of contemporary music.

They pour vodka and drink to their success. HOFFMAN *drinks from the flask hidden in his pocket. Everybody, except* THEREMIN *leaves.* LAVINIA *enters. MUSIC.*

LAVINIA: The majority of electronic instruments from the nineteen-twenties have one thing in common. The vacuum tube. It is the integral component of the first RCA radios, of telegraphs, the first amplifiers, and it is also the basis for the thereminvox.

THEREMIN: Correct. Now, what is the essence of the vacuum tube?

LAVINIA: The essence of the tube is that it can transmit electromagnetic waves.

THEREMIN: And those waves were discovered in . . . ?

LAVINIA: . . . 1887. Nine years before you were born.

THEREMIN: Yes. During the reign of Czar Alexander. My father was twenty years old then.

LAVINIA: In 1895, the German physicist Heinrich Hertz demonstrates the ability of those waves to travel through space. In his laboratory he produces a spark jumping between two metal conductors . . .

THEREMIN: . . . between two wires.

LAVINIA: The spark sends out electromagnetic waves, which travel through space and are captured at the other side of the room in the form of another spark . . .

THEREMIN: . . . a much smaller one . . .

LAVINIA: . . . which jumps between two other wires.

THEREMIN: What we have here is basically the first transmitter and receiver. (*To illustrate, he stabs his fork and knife, each representing the anode and the cathode, into his unfinished meat loaf.*)

LAVINIA: The problem, however, is that the receiver is not very sensitive.

THEREMIN: This is why Nicola Tesla takes those two wires and seals them into a vacuum glass bulb. (*He covers the makeshift contraption with a bell-shaped glass dome.*)

LAVINIA: And he calls them anode and cathode.

THEREMIN: And Lee de Forest is the first one to insert a platinum grid between the anode and cathode. Why?

LAVINIA: Nobody knows.

THEREMIN: A coincidence?

LAVINIA: But it works. It significantly increases the sensitivity of the receiver.

THEREMIN: But not enough. So de Forest does one more incredibly important thing . . .

LAVINIA: He connects the grid to the anode . . .

THEREMIN: . . . the wire that receives the flow of the current . . .

LAVINIA: . . . and makes it possible for the received signal to circulate inside the vacuum bulb, thus vastly increasing the amplification of the signal.

THEREMIN: A miracle.

LAVINIA: And so the vacuum tube is complete.

THEREMIN: VACUUM TUBE! The most amazing thing since the invention of the steam engine.

LAVINIA: An invention as important for applied physics as the theory of relativity is for theoretical physics.

THEREMIN: And then Edwin Armstrong makes yet another discovery:

LAVINIA: He notices that he can feed the electric current back to the grid, and strengthen the incoming signal. When he increases the feedback to a high level, the tube, which was originally meant only as a receiver, begins sending out electromagnetic radio waves at high frequencies as well

THEREMIN: And this tube, which is both a transmitter and a receiver, would become the very basis of the radio, TV . . . , everything . . .

LAVINIA: The vacuum tube changes the fate of millions of people on the Earth.

THEREMIN: And it also changes how the Earth appears to an observer from outer space. If someone, somewhere else in the universe were to look at the Earth not through the spectrum of visible light but through that of radio waves, he wouldn't—until the nineteen-twenties—have the slightest idea that it even existed. He would see absolutely nothing, because until only a few years ago, the Earth didn't produce any such waves.

LAVINIA: Copernicus placed the Earth firmly within the solar system, and four hundred years later, de Forest placed it on the radio map of the skies. And when that happened, we were part of it.

THEREMIN: We *are* part of it!

The magic of the moment passes.

THEREMIN: Excellent. You are hired. (*Giving her a piece of paper.*) I wrote a list of components that I need you to buy. And by the way, clean this place up. It's a pigsty.

LAVINIA *exits.* THEREMIN *stays. Enter* HOFFMAN *and later* LUCY *at another part of the stage. MUSIC under the entire scene.*

HOFFMAN: The concerts are successful. Theremin continues meeting important people, but he doesn't pay attention to women. His only correspondence is grant applications and letters to his father, who lives in Russia, as does his mother, sister, a cousin, and his wife Katherine. However, Theremin doesn't keep in contact with her.

LUCY *enters.*

Theremin set up a theremin performance studio. There are about ten students coming to his hotel for regular lessons. All men. Apart from that he hired a female assistant.

LUCY: Aha.

HOFFMAN: A very talented girl. She speaks six languages, studied dance and literature, and she is quite familiar with physics as well.

LUCY: Is she pretty?

HOFFMAN: She's a Negro.

LUCY: No problem then.

HOFFMAN: Ondes Martenot is suing Theremin for a patent for the electric production of sound. The U.S. patent court's decision on that matter is pending.

LUCY: We'll cross our fingers for Mr. Theremin.

HOFFMAN: Theremin's electric orchestra rehearses on Tuesdays. Its members, apart from Theremin, are his manager Hans Goldberg, the composer Joseph Schillinger, and yours truly.

LUCY: Good for you Mr. Hoffman! You followed my advice.

HOFFMAN: I do it out of personal conviction. You know that Leon Theremin really is an interesting fellow.

LUCY *pays* HOFFMAN *and exits.* HOFFMAN *stays. We are now in* THEREMIN*'s apartment again.* THEREMIN *is setting up his thereminvox, and* HOFFMAN *tunes his instrument with a newly acquired air of professionalism. Enter* SCHILLINGER. *He sits at the piano and starts preparing for a rehearsal.* GOLDBERG *enters.*

SCHILLINGER: Twenty minutes late, Goldberg.

GOLDBERG: My apologies, gentlemen.

SCHILLINGER: Ready . . . ? (*Raises his hand to start the music.*) One and two and three, and . . .

GOLDBERG: Gentlemen, I'm going to tell you a number: seven-two-four-eight-five-seven-one. Can you guess what it is?

SCHILLINGER: A phone number of some club?

HOFFMAN: One hell of a triple play?

GOLDBERG: It is the number of the American patent on the thereminvox.

Everybody is excited. They pat GOLDBERG *on his back, embrace him, etc.*

GOLDBERG: Furthermore, based on the patent, RCA agreed to draw up a preliminary contract with us for the mass production of the theremin.

SCHILLINGER: How did you do that?

THEREMIN: Did Lucy Rosen have anything to do with that?

GOLDBERG: No. I managed to persuade them that the theremin is a truly popular instrument. To prove it, I booked a very specific place for our concert in March . . .

THEREMIN: What place?

GOLDBERG: Oh . . . A place in the Bronx

THEREMIN: How many people?

GOLDBERG: Ah well, maybe twenty, twenty-two, maximum twenty-five.

THEREMIN: Twenty-five people? (GOLDBERG *shakes his head.*) Twenty-five hundred people?

GOLDBERG: Thousand.

THEREMIN: Thousand what?

GOLDBERG: Twenty-five thousand people. That's the absolute maximum. The full capacity.

THEREMIN: Twenty-five thousand people? You are crazy Hans! How are you planning to cram twenty-five thousand people into a hall, might I ask?

GOLDBERG: It's not a hall.

THEREMIN: So what is it?

GOLDBERG: A baseball stadium. New York Yankees.

Everybody feels as if they haven't heard it right. But HOFFMAN *perks up.*

HOFFMAN: You mean you booked Yankee Stadium?

THEREMIN: Where did you get the money for it?

GOLDBERG: I got a little loan.

THEREMIN: How did you vouch for it?

GOLDBERG: That shouldn't make a difference.

THEREMIN: It makes a difference to me.

GOLDBERG: I used our non-existent "accounts receivable" as a collateral.

THEREMIN: You are out of your mind.

HOFFMAN: But it's *Yankee Stadium*! You remember the 1921 season? Babe Ruth hit fifty-nine home runs there!

GOLDBERG: Exactly! (*Mixing his sports.*) The best . . . quarterback there ever was.

HOFFMAN (*taken aback, but recovering fast*): Phenomenal affair.

THEREMIN: That's beside the point right now. We . . .

GOLDBERG: No it isn't! For Americans Yankee Stadium is a sacred place. Am I right, Hoffman?

HOFFMAN: You bet it is.

GOLDBERG: Exactly. So the biggest concert in history must be played there.

SCHILLINGER: OK, so you managed to book it, but we won't have enough amplification.

GOLDBERG: What do you mean?

THEREMIN (*points to a rudimentary loudspeaker*): Do you know what this is? This is a loudspeaker. It's been on the market for only the past three years. Do you know its output? Twenty watts. What we'd need is at least twenty *thousand* watts to fill a stadium with sound!

GOLDBERG: Thirty thousand watts!

SCHILLINGER: There's going to be miles of cables everywhere. They will interfere with the sound of the theremins.

GOLDBERG: Not if those cables are insulated.

SCHILLINGER: Are there cables like that?

THEREMIN: No.

SCHILLINGER: That's exactly what I'm saying!

GOLDBERG: We'll build them.

SCHILLINGER: And what if we get feedback? With such huge amplification the people in the first rows would go deaf. And then . . . what?

GOLDBERG: I'm sure Leo will figure it out somehow.

SCHILLINGER: Have you all gone crazy ? What's going on?

GOLDBERG: So you don't believe we can pull it off!?

SCHILLINGER: Impossible. Gentlemen, I refuse to subject my orchestra to such extreme circumstances.

GOLDBERG: So what do you propose?

SCHILLINGER: Cancel the concert.

GOLDBERG: Impossible.

THEREMIN: Why?

GOLDBERG: Tickets already went on sale.

SCHILLINGER: It shouldn't be difficult to return a few tickets.

GOLDBERG: As of today we've sold twelve thousand.

THEREMIN: Twelve thousand what?

GOLDBERG: Tickets. You heard me.

THEREMIN: Twelve thousand tickets?

GOLDBERG: Exactly.

HOFFMAN: We can work with that.

THEREMIN: Hoffman, shut up, just shut up. (*To* GOLDBERG.) Hans, what on Earth did you promise them? Do they know that they won't see a baseball game?

GOLDBERG: Yes. "A Concert of Theremin and Schillinger's Electric Orchestra." The posters are all over the city.

Pause.

THEREMIN (*calls*): Lavinia?

LAVINIA (*enters*): Yes?

THEREMIN: Do you have the shopping list I gave you earlier?

LAVINIA: Yes, Mr. Theremin.

THEREMIN: Add tinfoil to it. About four hundred pounds of tinfoil.

LAVINIA *leaves. The four men sit at the table.*

GOLDBERG: Good. Now, there are several small legal issues with the RCA contract. First, we cannot enter into a contract with them as "natural individuals." We need to become a "legal person." This is why I propose we form a corporation called "Goldberg and Sons, Inc."

THEREMIN: Why "Goldberg and Sons?" You don't have children.

GOLDBERG: It's not meant literally.

THEREMIN: Why not "Theremin and Sons?"

HOFFMAN: What's a "legal person?"

GOLDBERG: I'll explain later.

SCHILLINGER: It's a legal term. The four of us are each a natural individual, but as a group we form a legal person.

GOLDBERG: Let's say that the four of us here will become the partners in the corporation, and will report to the board of directors.

SCHILLINGER: Who will be on the board?

GOLDBERG: Also the four of us. That way we'll be in the ideal situation where we only have to answer to ourselves. I used the same system back in Germany.

THEREMIN (*to* SCHILLINGER): Believe me, he knows what he's talking about.

SCHILLINGER: What are our liabilities?

GOLDBERG: Our non-existent capital, so we don't risk anything.

SCHILLINGER: That's fraud.

GOLDBERG: Yes, I know.

SCHILLINGER: So how do you . . .

GOLDBERG: Don't worry, I'll explain later. But the formal—and I might add—symbolic start-up capital is five dollars per person, which with your permission I would like to collect right now.

They start going through their pockets to find the money.

HOFFMAN (*having second thoughts*): I would just like to mention that I never had the intention to enter into this enterprise . . . I'm a screenwriter solely interested in the person of Mr. Theremin here.

THEREMIN: But you said you wanted to be "part of it."

HOFFMAN: Yes, but . . .

THEREMIN: So now you *are* part of it.

GOLDBERG: You are finding yourself at a turning point of history, Mr. Hoffman. There's nothing you can do about it.

HOFFMAN: Unfortunately, I don't have any cash on me today.

THEREMIN *imitates the "lying" sound of the lie detector. This obviously works on* HOFFMAN. *He pulls money out of his pocket and gives it to* GOLDBERG, *who distributes the founding contracts. Everybody signs them ceremoniously.*

THEREMIN (*calls out*): Lavinia, please come here. This calls for a picture.

LAVINIA *enters. The men form a group—camera flash.* GOLDBERG , HOFFMAN, SCHILLINGER, *and* LAVINIA *exit. We are now in the locker room of Yankee Stadium—backstage.* THEREMIN *is writing another "letter" to his father. MUSIC.*

THEREMIN: Dear Father. As you know, I usually don't get stage fright. Even back home in Petrograd, before my entrance exams for the Polytechnic University I was completely calm. But today, ever since I woke up I've had this strange pressure in my belly . . .

GOLDBERG *enters, putting together the play list for tonight's concert.*

GOLDBERG: "Hebrew Melody" by Joesph Achron; "The Lark," of course; Rachmaninoff's "Vocalise . . . "

SCHILLINGER *enters. He is excited and nervous. As he speaks, he's changing into a new tail coat.*

SCHILLINGER: The streets around the stadium are completely blocked by crowds of people. Traffic is at a standstill, public transportation has collapsed . . . I had to walk here, I'm all in disarray, oh god, I have to change . . . oh god . . .

GOLDBERG: Rachmaninoff's "Vocalise," then that thing by Varèse . . . and then intermission. After the intermission the "First Airphonic Suite."

SCHILLINGER: I talked to Morris Hillquit, the head of the Socialists. He said that they alone are bringing around ten thousand people. By the way, he'd like to speak at the beginning. I think it'd be a wise thing to do.

GOLDBERG (*working on the playlist*): That's sixty minutes. Right now we're at sixty minutes. We need another twenty.

SCHILLINGER: Many people are waving leftist banners. The thing may turn into a demonstration. The whole string section wanted to run. I had to pay them twice what was agreed. Well, they may run away anyway. But right now, they won't get far. The streets are completely blocked by crowds.

LAVINIA *brings* THEREMIN*'s tails and helps him get dressed.*

LAVINIA: I'll pray for you.

THEREMIN: I thought you were a communist.

LAVINIA: I am. But at moments like this it's best to pray. (*facetiously*) In Haiti, before men go to war, do you know what women do to them?

THEREMIN: I'm not going to war, Lavinia. I'm going to give an ordinary concert.

LAVINIA: This won't be a very ordinary concert.

THEREMIN: OK, so what do they do back there in Haiti?

LAVINIA *gently kicks* THEREMIN *in the butt.*

THEREMIN: Ouch.

LAVINIA: I'll think of you.

The band members also perform a similar ritual among each other—each kicking the other's butts. They are like little boys—giddy, excited, and playful, and this boyish ritual is designed to give them courage.

GOLDBERG: Gentlemen, break a leg.

They enter onto the "stage." It's twilight. The crowd roars with excitement.

STADIUM ANNOUNCER (*excited*): Ladies and Gentlemen! Leon Sergeievich Theremin, Joseph Schillinger, and their electric orchestra!

The sound of twenty thousand people. It should remind us of the sound of the rock-and-roll crowds in the sixties and seventies. Then, we hear the first number of the actual concert, a composition for three theremins, drums, and symphonic orchestra. The music lasts for about three minutes. We are "backstage."

Enter GOLDBERG *and* SCHILLINGER. *They are sweating. In the background the concert continues, we hear the audience, etc.*

GOLDBERG: A phenomenal success.

SCHILLINGER: Sound-wise it was of course far from perfect.

GOLDBERG: In terms of production values it was about fifty-fifty.

SCHILLINGER: Most of the lights blew out after the first few minutes.

GOLDBERG: However, as an event, it went far beyond anything that had happened in music until then.

GOLDBERG *exits.* LAVINIA *enters.*

LAVINIA: Nobody could see or hear anything. But still, it was the most beautiful evening in my life. Those four people managed to create something that seemed to exist outside of time and space. And outside the bounds of imagination of that time as well.

SCHILLINGER: The whole way of thinking about music was changed that evening. Everything that has happened in music in the last two thousand years suddenly became the first act only.

SCHILLINGER *exits.* LAVINIA *exits.* HOFFMAN *enters. He frequently takes a sip from his pocket flask.*

HOFFMAN: I used to come here as a little boy. I was right here at this stadium on August 16, 1920, when Ray Chapman died after he was hit in the head by Carl Mays's pitch. And I came here many many more times. And I often imagined myself standing at home plate, the crowd clapping and screaming, and chanting my name. But it sure never even crossed my mind that I'd find myself here as a musician. Let alone with an instrument like that. But suddenly you are there, standing on that stage, ten or twenty thousand people in front of you, and the whole experience completely changes you. Whatever you may think about it at that moment is not important, but when you get back to the locker room, you become another person. Well, this whole thing happened thanks to these three fellows, Theremin, Goldberg, and Schillinger—they pulled off something that nobody ever managed before: they elevated music to the level of baseball. And that's how they changed history. And that's a fact.

GOLDBERG *runs in.*

GOLDBERG: Sam, come back.

HOFFMAN: What are we playing?

GOLDBERG: You just keep the bass.

They leave, going back onto the "stage." The crowd goes crazy. MUSIC continues, lights are slowly changing.

End of MUSIC.

Enter THEREMIN, GOLDBERG, SCHILLINGER, HOFFMAN, *and* LAVINIA. *A post-concert celebration in the locker room. Everybody's hugging. WALTER ROSEN enters with a bottle of champagne, which he opens with a bang. Everyone toasts.*

ROSEN: Extraordinary evening gentlemen. (*toasting*) To modern music!

SCHILLINGER: To the second act!

ROSEN: By the way, congratulations are in order for the court victory over Martenot. So the patent is yours.

GOLDBERG: I guess somebody with influence put in a good word.

ROSEN *individually congratulates each member of the orchestra.* LUCY *enters.*

LUCY: Excellent, Mr. Hoffman.

HOFFMAN *looks proudly around.*

You know, you're too talented to be just a private eye.

Everybody looks surprised. LUCY *realizes she made a mistake, but doesn't lose a beat and starts congratulating the band members.* HOFFMAN *is about to sneak out, but* THEREMIN *stops him. He suspected something about* HOFFMAN *all along.*

THEREMIN: Sam! Good concert. Thank you.

HOFFMAN: Oh no, thank *you.*

THEREMIN: Wasn't too bad, was it?

HOFFMAN: The Airphonic Suite caught on.

THEREMIN: I'd say that the Airphonic Suite was the home run of the whole concert.

HOFFMAN: Exactly. And the whole concert was the most phenomenal grand slam of all modern music.

THEREMIN: And now for something completely different: It's OK.

HOFFMAN: Thank you. Mr. Theremin.

HOFFMAN *exits.* LUCY *is leaving, too. To* THEREMIN.

LUCY: See you at the club.

All except THEREMIN *and* GOLDBERG *exit. An awkward pause. Then* THEREMIN *pulls a strange device out of his bag.*

THEREMIN: I meant to show you something.

GOLDBERG: What is it?

THEREMIN: Altimeter. It measures elevation. Either from sea level or from the ground you're standing on.

GOLDBERG (*points to the gauge*): Is that where you read it?

THEREMIN: Exactly. When you climb onto the table, you'll be able to tell how high you are.

GOLDBERG: Nice. When did you build it.

THEREMIN: This morning.

GOLDBERG: This morning?! While tens of thousands of people were streaming into Yankee Stadium, you were sitting at home building this?

THEREMIN: Yes.

GOLDBERG: You are a . . . an extraordinary person, Leo.

THEREMIN: I just threw together a few parts.

GOLDBERG: No, you are a genius. And I knew it, I knew it already in Munich back in twenty-five.

THEREMIN: Did you know that that concert . . . it was supposed to be my last one.

GOLDBERG: Really?

THEREMIN: We thought that we'd demonstrate the thereminvox to a handful of enthusiasts at the convention, and go back to Russia. The plan was to end it there. But then you appeared—out of nowhere—and everything completely changed.

GOLDBERG: I came to see you in the dressing room.

THEREMIN: Your Russian wasn't bad.

GOLDBERG: I used to sell flour to Russia.

THEREMIN: But you were never there.

GOLDBERG: I remember you told me that you traveled in "the direct service of electricity."

THEREMIN: And you asked me to travel around Europe in the service of "new music." But of course at that time I already had three hundred concerts under my belt.

GOLDBERG: Which of course, I didn't know then.

THEREMIN: Did you know what my first concert was like? Ukraine, fall of 1922. I was supposed to play in the town square, but that year winter came early so they moved it into a church turned warehouse. The whole town showed up.

GOLDBERG: The attendance was compulsory of course.

THEREMIN: Yes, but some came of their own accord. It was clear that they were all extremely poor. Some of them hadn't eaten for days. There was this quiet couple standing in the far corner. Husband and wife, skin and bones just like everybody else, but I sort of had the feeling that those two people really *heard* my music. And the official in charge of the concert, he must have seen that I was looking at them all the time, and after it was over he came to me and said: "That guy and the woman in the corner . . . they're going to be hanged tomorrow morning." And I asked what they did, and he just tells me: "They ate their kids." He just said it, just like that. "They had five kids and they ate them all. They started with the youngest. The older kids would eat the younger ones with them. Until they ate them all. They'll be hanged tomorrow morning. They were supposed to do it today, but we didn't want to spoil your concert, comrade Leon Sergeievich."

GOLDBERG: How did they find out.

THEREMIN: They were Christians. They went to confession, and the priest informed the authorities.

GOLDBERG (*makes a toast*): To a better world in the future!

THEREMIN (*toasting*): To electricity!

They take a shot. Enter AMTORG 1 *and* AMTORG 2.

AMTORG 1: Wonderful concert, Leon Sergeievich. You made us proud.

They shake hands with GOLDBERG.

THEREMIN: Thank you.

AMTORG 2: By the way, your cousin, Vladimir . . .

THEREMIN: Yes. What about him?

AMTORG 2: Everything has been cleared up. His arrest was a mistake after all.

THEREMIN: That is good news. Thank you.

AMTORG 1: Good news, yes. He sends his love to you.

BLACKOUT. MUSIC.

The living room/lab in THEREMIN's *apartment in the hotel.* THEREMIN *enters from his bedroom. He is sleepy, he can barely walk, and for the first time in the play, his outer appearance is messy.* LAVINIA *is picking up and cleaning. There is a tray with coffee and some breakfast food on the table.*

LAVINIA: I noticed that you are running low on three-sixty-sevens. And we're almost out of pewter as well.

THEREMIN: Oh Lavinia, what would I do without you? I completely forgot to write the shopping list yesterday. We had a little celebration, you know.

LAVINIA: The concert was magnificent.

THEREMIN: Thanks.

LAVINIA (*ostentatiously picks up the tray*): Would Mrs. Rosen like to have her breakfast in bed?

THEREMIN: Actually, I . . . I'm not sure. I haven't seen her for quite some time . . . I . . . I don't think so.

LAVINIA (*puts the tray on the table again*): Well, I'll leave it here, in case she should be starved.

LUCY *enters from the bedroom.*

LUCY: Good morning. (*pause*) What happened last night . . . this night . . . I mean, what happened during the *whole night* . . . Well, I don't regret it.

THEREMIN: Absolutely not . . .

LUCY: I only regret that it didn't happen earlier.

THEREMIN: So do I.

LAVINIA *exits. She whistles the "Internationale."*

LUCY: From now on, everything will be different. First of all, I'll get you a good manager.

THEREMIN: Goldberg is pretty good.

LUCY: Goldberg is nothing but a little insecure Kraut with a chip on his shoulder. He doesn't even know how to feed you properly. You are so incredibly gullible, Leo! But I'll look after you; I'll protect you from all those leeches and opportunists. I'll take care of you. You don't believe me? No? You just wait, and you'll see how the two of us together will achieve great things—we'll play all around the world. You and me playing the theremin . . .

THEREMIN: You know how to play the theremin?

LUCY: I'll learn. Because of you.

THEREMIN: Thanks.

LUCY: But we won't play for the working class anymore. We'll be playing for the most distinguished people in the world. Or we'll just run away from civilization. Yes! We'll run away to Panama.

THEREMIN: To Panama!?

LUCY: Exactly. You don't believe me? No? We'll work! We'll make our living with our hands!

THEREMIN: But Lucy, you've never worked. You've never even taken the subway.

LUCY: For you, I'd even take the subway. But you have to excuse me now, I have to fix myself up a bit. I'm a mess.

LUCY *leaves. Enter* GOLDBERG. *He is a little hung over.*

GOLDBERG: Your wife is here.

THEREMIN: What wife?

GOLDBERG: What do you mean "what wife?" Your wife, Leo! Katherine.

THEREMIN: But she's in Russia.

GOLDBERG: Well, I just talked with her. She's in New York.

THEREMIN: Katherine is in New York? Where is she staying?

GOLDBERG: I don't know.

THEREMIN: Well, find out, and I'll go see her.

GOLDBERG: She's here. She's waiting in the lobby downstairs. I saw her when I was picking up the mail.

THEREMIN: So . . . Where's the mail?

GOLDBERG: Oh yeah, the mail . . . I forgot it downstairs.

THEREMIN: Pull yourself together Hans. Go downstairs, pick up the mail, and send Katherine up here.

GOLDBERG (*notices a bra on a chair*): I think you should probably move this.

THEREMIN: Right.

GOLDBERG *leaves.* THEREMIN *stuffs the bra out of sight, and tries to prepare for the meeting with his wife.* KATHERINE *enters.*

THEREMIN: Katherine!

They embrace.

Is everybody all right? Dad, Mom, Vladimir . . .

KATHERINE: Yes. They arrested Vladimir, but they let him go. Everything's fine. Apparently it was only a silly misunderstanding. They even offered him your job at the Institute.

THEREMIN: That's good, that's good. (*pause*) You should have let me know that you were coming.

KATHERINE: A letter would've taken longer to get here than I.

THEREMIN: Right. (*pause*) So, where are you staying?

KATHERINE: Nowhere. I got off the boat this morning. I left the baggage at the port. The ground's still swaying beneath my feet.

THEREMIN *gives her something to drink.*

KATHERINE: You look good. The papers are full of stories about you. You're famous. So famous that there are even cartoons about you. I saw one where your hands were huge, with those long fingers—like a vampire's. I couldn't wait for those hands to stroke me. (*pause*) Did you know that not a single one of your letters was delivered to me?

THEREMIN: I didn't write to you.

KATHERINE: Well, then that's good news. I was afraid they really wouldn't deliver them. Russia is so full of lies nowadays.

THEREMIN: Yes.

KATHERINE (*looks around, noticing all the different machines and devices in the room*): This is a nice place. I see you're still working . . .

THEREMIN: I am. (*He shows her the different devices.*) This is an altimeter—it measures elevation, theremin . . . but you know that one . . . electrical hen-house heater, and this is a lie detector.

He turns on the lie detector, which begins to buzz quietly.

KATHERINE: You haven't changed at all. I was afraid I would never see you again . . . Every week I'd write to the Ministry of the Interior to get an exit visa, I talked to the head of the Institute, I tried everything I could, but you know how things work in Russia. And then, all of a sudden I got it. I got the exit visa. I don't know why, but maybe somebody with influence put in a word for me.

THEREMIN: Goldberg will find a place for you to stay. I'll talk to him. I live in the hotel here, but as you can see it's also my lab. It's barely big enough for one.

LUCY *enters from the bedroom.*

THEREMIN (*awkwardly*): This is my wife, Katherine Theremin—Lucy Rosen.

LUCY *exits.*

THEREMIN (*to* KATHERINE): Excuse me for a minute.

He follows LUCY *out of the apartment.*

KATHERINE: Leo!

THEREMIN *stops, turns around, and comes back.* KATHERINE *hugs him—maybe for the last time in their lives.* THEREMIN *leaves. Enter* GOLDBERG.

GOLDBERG: We are in luck, Katherine. The big apartment on the third floor will be available on Tuesday. Until then you can stay in the bedroom here. We'll move the theremins into the room next door . . .

KATHERINE: Mr. Goldberg, would you please find out for me when the next boat is leaving for Europe.

GOLDBERG: But why? As I said, on Tuesday the big apartment will be free . . .

KATHERINE: Do you know why they didn't let me come to America with you?

GOLDBERG: Well, you were in medical school . . .

KATHERINE: They kept me in Russia as a guarantee that he'd come back. Leo is an immensely valuable asset for Russia, and America is a land of many temptations. I was simply insurance for them.

GOLDBERG: That's demeaning.

KATHERINE: Those are the rules.

GOLDBERG: But you're here now, so . . .

KATHERINE: Yes. I'm here. But you know why? Because my husband doesn't love me any more. I'm not important for him any more. So there was no reason to keep me in Russia any longer.

GOLDBERG: That's nonsense.

KATHERINE: I could tell from his eyes.

GOLDBERG: We got a bit drunk last night . . . we were celebrating a concert.

KATHERINE: It's not that . . .

GOLDBERG: It is! We were drunk. (*pause*) But even if the Russian secret service assumes that such is the case, there is absolutely no reason that you should believe it too.

KATHERINE: You think you know him, but you don't. He is a very pragmatic man—you could even call him cruel. Cruel to himself as well. When it's necessary, he's able to stifle love in himself. To kill it in the name of something that he himself puts above it. Science for example. So, would you be so kind and find out when the next boat to Europe leaves? Thank you.

KATHERINE *exits.* THEREMIN *enters. He has overheard the conversation.*

THEREMIN: Everything she told you . . . it's nonsense . . .

GOLDBERG: Are you sure?

THEREMIN: And even if it were the case . . . Who could have told them that I didn't love her any longer?

GOLDBERG: You did.

THEREMIN: I never talked about Katherine with them.

GOLDBERG: Exactly. In the last two years you haven't written her a single letter.

THEREMIN: I was busy.

GOLDBERG: Of course. I'm not blaming you for anything.

THEREMIN: Hans, I simply cannot afford to be dependent on women.

GOLDBERG: Maybe you should have let her know.

THEREMIN: Maybe. But I was sure they wouldn't let her visit me. So I thought that when I returned to Russia everything would somehow take care of itself. (*pause*) We'll give her some monthly allowance, we'll find some place for her to stay, get her a job . . .

GOLDBERG: You mean that *I* am supposed to find her place to stay, that *I* ought to get her a job . . .

THEREMIN: You are my manager.

GOLDBERG: But this isn't a business matter.

THEREMIN: And my friend.

Pause.

GOLDBERG: Actually, why I really came here today was to give you some good news. RCA finally signed the contract for the mass production of theremins.

THEREMIN: There you go, you see.

GOLDBERG *leaves. Enter the* RADIO TALK SHOW HOST. *We are now in a radio studio.*

RADIO HOST: Good evening, ladies and gentlemen. This is Billy Watts, and you are listening to WZY radio, New York. My guest tonight is Leon Sergeievich Theremin. He came to us directly from Russia, and some of you may actually know his face from posters and newspaper cartoons. In any case, I think it is safe to say that his presence here in New York has been the cause of much excitement. Good evening.

THEREMIN: Good evening.

RADIO HOST: What we want to do here tonight is to introduce your musical instrument—the thereminvox—to a wider public. All I will say, is that it is the only non-contact musical instrument in the world, and that one plays it by pulling the sounds, one could say, literally out of the ether. Am I correct?

THEREMIN: More or less.

RADIO HOST: The RCA Victor Company is the manufacturer, and the instrument will be available in stores sometime next month. I have one of their trial models here in the studio—and I do have to admit that it is a *very* unusual musical instrument to say the least—but I think I've said enough . . . I'll let Professor Theremin talk.

THEREMIN: Of course, we are talking here about an experiment. But if the instrument takes off, it could mean a complete change in the general approach to music.

RADIO HOST: In what regard?

THEREMIN: Well, the theremin is a very . . . democratic musical instrument.

RADIO HOST: What do you mean by that?

THEREMIN: It is an instrument that can be played by just about anybody.

RADIO HOST: And the other instruments can't?

THEREMIN: Not really. Let us assume that the Russian Revolution in nineteen seventeen abolished inequality between people in Russia. Possibly not entirely in practice, but certainly in theory. What followed was land reform, collectivization, and the nationalization of industry . . .

RADIO HOST: Mr. Theremin, this is a Catholic radio station.

THEREMIN: Of course. But we still have to deal with the last remaining inequality between people. Talent. If we are to draw the argument about inequality to its logical conclusion, we must consider talent as something that continues making people fundamentally unequal.

RADIO HOST: This is a very . . . remarkable idea.

THEREMIN: So from that point of view, it is obviously ridiculous to leave music-making solely in the hands of a small group of talented—and therefore somewhat unfairly chosen—artists.

RADIO HOST: Are you seriously proposing that even those who don't have a God-given gift should have the right to make music?

THEREMIN: Exactly. That's the philosophy of our instrument. The thereminvox marks the end of the aristocratic understanding of music-making. It will erase the difference between the virtuoso and the occasional hobbyist.

RADIO HOST: And you seriously believe this?

THEREMIN: I do. Take me, for example. I came here tonight, to this studio, in order to play the theremin for you and your listeners. Yet I personally have absolutely no musical talent whatsoever. As a theremin player, I'm average at best.

RADIO HOST: Really?

THEREMIN: Our electric orchestra has four members, and only one of them—Joseph Schillinger—has actually studied music. All of the others are self-taught. People, who don't have any musical talent, yet who play regardless! They play, simply because they decided to play.

RADIO HOST: And your electric orchestra is successful?

THEREMIN: Judging by the thousands of people who see our concerts . . .

RADIO HOST: Which at the same time function as communist gatherings.

THEREMIN: A revolution in music must by definition be a political revolution as well.

RADIO HOST: So you could imagine a world where every bank clerk or stevedore simply comes home after work, plugs his theremin or a similar electrical musical instrument into a socket in the wall, and begins to play music, which then spills out of the window and fills the streets with sounds?

THEREMIN: I can.

RADIO HOST: Are you sure?

THEREMIN: Well . . . Maybe you are right. It may not be possible without God.

RADIO HOST: Is that so? Well, I think that we should just go ahead. Be my guest, Mr. Theremin. The radio waves are yours.

THEREMIN *stands by the instrument and starts playing. The recital lasts for about two minutes, depending on the actor's skill. MUSIC to be chosen.*

MUSIC ends, exit THEREMIN *and* RADIO HOST.

Enter SCHILLINGER. *He brings in a blackboard, and starts a lecture.*

SCHILLINGER: Just like everything else in nature, music can be expressed by formulas. Notes are only one of the many ways of writing down music. Another possibility of notating it is the mathematical formula. And vice versa—an equation can be made into music. A cobblestone pattern on a sidewalk could be transcribed as a simple melody or rhythm, as could the way one is dressed. (*beat*) Let us now conduct a simple experiment. I'll take today's papers. The Business section of the New York Times. It may seem that nothing could be farther from music than the stock market report. But as I will demonstrate that is not so. Let us imagine that there exists a machine, which can assign a sound of an individual musical instrument to each of the columns of the stock market report as printed in the business section. Each advance or decline of an individual company in the market will equal the distance of the tone from the absolute musical zero, namely the 440. Obviously the same company's stock will have a different melody at the opening and closing. That's where the harmonies come from. As for the rhythm of each instrument, a simple algorithm will express it. (*He writes a mathematical formula onto the blackboard.*) A week has seven days. The five weekdays are five beats, Saturday and Sunday are pauses, because on the weekend the stock market is closed. Monday, Wednesday, and Friday are downbeats, Tuesday and Thursday are upbeats. Gentlemen, if you would, please . . .

We hear a simple rhythm.

Monday, Wednesday, Friday, Saturday, Sunday. We'll begin with United Steel. I'm sure that a careful listener already knows how the melody will sound.

We hear a single instrument . . . the composition is a minimalist one, the instrument keeps repeating the musical phrase over and over. SCHILLINGER conducts "the orchestra," as one by one, the other instruments join in.

SCHILLINGER (*to himself*): Monday, Wednesday, Friday . . . We obviously need to work with approximation, round up the values since the smallest interval on the ordinary instruments is the semitone. The only instrument where approximation is not necessary is the theremin. (*conducting*) And here comes J.P. Morgan Bank . . .

Another instrument joins in. The first instrument continues repeating the original phrase in the lower registers.

You are listening to a musical dialogue between U.S. Steel and J.P. Morgan Bank . . . an ongoing weekly stock market report. 3.57, 3.46, 3.57 . . .

The next instrument to join will have a descending line.

And now, the Paramount Studios, which—as you'll clearly hear—hasn't been doing too well recently . . .

We now hear the thereminvox.

. . . and to complete the picture, here is RCA Victor, the manufacturer of the actual theremin. You are listening to the "First Stock Market Cacophony" dated October 24, 1929. Tonal transformation of the market.

SCHILLINGER *waves his hands above the newspaper, as if it were the score. He points into the space in front of him conducting the invisible members of an invisible orchestra. Everything works smoothly as a machine. The music is minimalist, inverted, strange . . .*

Suddenly, everything stops. Lights change abruptly. All we hear is a low buzz and rumble of the subwoofers. This is the stock market crash.

Enter HOFFMAN, GOLDBERG, *and later* THEREMIN.

HOFFMAN: What happened?

GOLDBERG: Stock Market Crash. Thursday, October 24, 1929. In one single day, the market has lost more than fourteen billion dollars.

SCHILLINGER: My apologies, gentlemen. I'm all in disarray. I didn't even have time to change. I was up the whole night.

GOLDBERG: Bad news?

SCHILLINGER: There is a real danger that my stock will become worthless.

Enter THEREMIN. *The ominous drone continues.*

THEREMIN: Hans, what are we going to do?

GOLDBERG: I don't mean to get ahead of myself, but it could be quite serious.

THEREMIN: Does it mean any trouble for us?

GOLDBERG: It could mean lots of trouble for our investors and backers.

THEREMIN: Maybe it's just a temporary thing.

GOLDBERG: Maybe.

SCHILLINGER: But the vast majority of stocks continue sliding. Last I checked, the market had lost yet another four billion. Which is similar to transposing an entire piece by twelve tones.

THEREMIN: How?

SCHILLINGER: In descending order, of course.

THEREMIN: What about RCA?

GOLDBERG: It probably won't collapse completely. It's a big corporation with connections to large New York banks.

THEREMIN: And the theremins?

GOLDBERG: They started mass production last week.

THEREMIN: How many did they make?

GOLDBERG: Fifteen thousand.

THEREMIN: Excellent. How many are sold?

GOLDBERG: About ten at this point.

THEREMIN: Ten thousand sets? That's very good!

GOLDBERG: No, ten. Ten sets.

THEREMIN: Ten sets?

GOLDBERG: You heard me.

THEREMIN: You mean ten, as in ten? The whole week they sold only ten theremins?

GOLDBERG: Exactly.

HOFFMAN: We can work with that.

THEREMIN: SAM!!!

SCHILLINGER: As an overall number it's a disaster.

GOLDBERG: Yes. And from now on, we won't be selling any more at all.

HOFFMAN: Why not?

GOLDBERG: It's simple. People won't have money.

THEREMIN: So, we'll make them cheaper. I can simplify them, redesign some...

GOLDBERG: Leo, shut up, just shut up! Don't you get it? Don't you get anything?

THEREMIN: What did I do now?

GOLDBERG: This isn't just a little inconvenience. This could lead to a complete collapse of the entire American society.

HOFFMAN: Well, I wouldn't paint the devil on the wall . . .

GOLDBERG: I know what I'm talking about, I lived through what happened in Germany in twenty-three.

HOFFMAN: What happened?

GOLDBERG: The economic crisis. The inflation grew at an unbelievable pace. Money that you earned on Monday would turn completely worthless on Tuesday.

SCHILLINGER: The German Crisis was an extreme case, of course.

GOLDBERG: Sure. But it started exactly like this one. In the end, people got paid twice a day. Women would wait by the entrances to the factories, the men would give them the money, and they would literally run to the store to spend it for whatever was on the shelves, because later in the day those morning wages wouldn't buy them anything. The central bank continued printing money with obscenely high nominal value. People who lost everything were committing suicide left and right. At the beginning, a loaf of bread would cost you two Marks; later it was twenty, then *two million marks!* I remember my mother going to buy some potatoes one day, but she needed so much money that she had to carry the bills in a big basket. She put it on the ground in front of the store, but somehow she got distracted, and when she came back, the basket was gone—somebody stole it. But only the basket. You see, the thief just dumped the money on the street so that he wouldn't have to schlep it along. So there's my mother looking at the money swirling in the wind on the street, and nobody even bothers to pick up a single bill. And the basket is gone. America is in danger of reverting to the Middle Ages, gentlemen.

THEREMIN: You mean to say that this is the end of American capitalism?

GOLDBERG: It's possible. In any case, this country will never be the same again.

THEREMIN: In that case, we'll simply return to Russia. We only came to play a few concerts here anyways.

GOLDBERG: But we've been here for two years now.

THEREMIN: From the theoretical point of view, of course, this crisis should actually please us. It's quite possible than in five or ten years America will become a socialist, maybe even communist, country. The stock market won't exist any more. Private ownership will disappear. It will be the final victory of the world revolution. And in a situation like that, it won't really matter whether or not we sell any theremins.

GOLDBERG: Leo, you know the collateral for the loans, and all that?

THEREMIN: Yes?

GOLDBERG: Well, I didn't vouch for it with "non-existent capital."

THEREMIN: You didn't?

GOLDBERG: I used my property.

THEREMIN: But you don't have anything.

GOLDBERG: My property in Germany. My sister's dowry. My parents' home. I mortgaged it all.

HOFFMAN: That's unpleasant.

THEREMIN: Yes. That is unpleasant. But we'll still prevail, no matter what. Gentlemen, let's sing the American anthem.

They sing, but can't quite get it. They keep slipping into other melodies, such as the "Internationale." Then, the real "Star Spangled Banner" fades in from the loudspeakers. They stand while the curtain closes or the lights fade out.

ACT TWO

THEREMIN *is preparing to meet* KATHERINE. *The atmosphere of the scene is reminiscent of a black and white horror movie. We hear the ominous sounds of the theremin. The whole scene is one of fear, ominous anticipation, horror.*

KATHERINE *enters. The atmosphere changes to normal.*

THEREMIN: Katherine.

KATHERINE: Leo.

THEREMIN: I'll be brief. I'm here because I need money.

KATHERINE: What for?

THEREMIN: To buy components.

KATHERINE: What do you mean "to buy components?" Goldberg told me that you owe money left and right, and you want to buy "components?"

THEREMIN: I got an order for a new device, but they'll only pay on delivery.

KATHERINE: What sort of a "device?"

THEREMIN: Metal detector.

KATHERINE: What do you need a metal detector for? Leo, it has been two years since we last spoke. In the five years I've been in New York you only came to see me three times. And now you come to me and want money for those stupid machines of yours? Why don't you ask Mrs. Rosen to lend you some?

THEREMIN: I owe the Rosens two years worth of rent for the lab.

KATHERINE (*sarcastically*): If I loaned you a hundred dollars, would you come back to me?

THEREMIN *slowly accepts* KATHERINE's *refusal, and he is about to leave.*

KATHERINE: Do you hate me?

THEREMIN: I can understand how you might be feeling.

KATHERINE: I'd like you to hate me. Or to love me. Makes no difference. I only wish that you felt SOMETHING!!! That you stopped being only a machine for inventions! Stupid machine that sooner or later will end in the garbage anyways!

THEREMIN: But I *am* a machine for inventions. The day I stop inventing, they'll stop giving me American patents, Amtorg will stop taking care of my immigration status, and the Americans will deport me. I've been here for eight years with a six-month visa. I owe money to just about everyone. I'm trying to persuade the American labor bureau that I mustn't be deported to Russia, because I'm needed by the American industry, and then I go, and try to persuade the Russian intelligence that I'm actually undermining the American industry, and that they should use their sources to intervene with the American labor bureau on my behalf. Goldberg and I are drowning in lawsuits, and nobody, literally nobody, knows how it will all end.

KATHERINE: I'm not moved.

THEREMIN: All I'm trying to explain is that my situation is complicated.

KATHERINE: And how did you get yourself into a "situation" like this?

THEREMIN: That is the question.

KATHERINE: But this is exactly what I'm talking about.

THEREMIN: And how about you? How did *you* get yourself in *your* situation? You live alone in a foreign country, unable to make contacts with people around you. You're begging for love from someone who left you five years ago . . .

KATHERINE: You are my husband, and I love you.

THEREMIN: I'm not your husband. I got a divorce.

KATHERINE: What?! When?

THEREMIN: When did they open the Russian Embassy in New York?

KATHERINE: What . . . ? In 1934.

THEREMIN: Well, then it's been two years.

KATHERINE: You're joking! Didn't you need my agreement?

THEREMIN: We argued Article N1.

KATHERINE: What's "Article N1?"

THEREMIN: According to the Russian Criminal Code, it's the membership in, or association with a fascist organization.

KATHERINE: You told them that I was a fascist.

THEREMIN: No. I just told them that you sometimes attend their meetings, nothing more.

KATHERINE: And they believed it?

THEREMIN: I had some pictures.

KATHERINE: What pictures?

THEREMIN: It doesn't matter.

KATHERINE: What sort of pictures did you have?

THEREMIN (*almost proud of himself*): Well, you see, I made a sort of a montage. I took an old picture of you . . .

KATHERINE: Which one?

THEREMIN: The one, where you wave goodbye to me at the station in Petrograd. I cut you out, and . . .

KATHERINE: You destroyed that beautiful picture?

THEREMIN: I didn't destroy it. I inserted it—I mean I inserted you—into another picture of a crowd at a fascist demonstration. It looked quite amazing.

KATHERINE: Leo!!!

THEREMIN: I figured it'd be easier that way.

KATHERINE: And? Did it work?

THEREMIN: Yes. It made it much easier.

KATHERINE *takes out some money, and throws it on the floor in front of* THEREMIN.

KATHERINE: Help yourself.

THEREMIN *goes on all fours and collects the money from the floor. He gets up, and pulls out some sort of a device from his bag.*

THEREMIN: This is for you.

KATHERINE: What is it?

THEREMIN: Electronic babysitter. Against kidnappings. You fix it onto the crib, here. This is a sensor that can tell when a stranger approaches the baby. It works using the principle of capacitance of space.

KATHERINE: And what am I supposed to do with it?

THEREMIN: You may find it useful when you have children. You're not planning to stay single, are you?

KATHERINE: Just take it back, here, take it.

THEREMIN: Why. What's the problem? What did I do wrong this time?

KATHERINE: Nothing. Everything's fine. You just seem to have forgotten that I can't have children.

THEREMIN: I'm sorry.

KATHERINE: Oh, don't be too hard on yourself. It's OK. It's the way you are, you simply can't change.

MUSIC. KATHERINE *leaves.*

HOFFMAN *enters. We are now in* THEREMIN*'s new apartment/lab. Everything looks quite shabby.*

THEREMIN: Sam. Where were you? The rehearsal is about to start.

HOFFMAN: What rehearsal?

THEREMIN: For tonight's concert. We're playing in some nightclub over in New Jersey.

HOFFMAN: I thought that one was cancelled.

THEREMIN: Not that I know of.

SCHILLINGER *enters.*

HOFFMAN: The concert is cancelled, right?

SCHILLINGER: I don't know. In any case, we don't have the quartet.

THEREMIN: Why not?

SCHILLINGER: Because Goldberg is broke. He can't pay them.

THEREMIN: That's too bad. But we'll manage without them. A piano will have to do.

SCHILLINGER: There's no piano there.

THEREMIN: What do you mean "there's no piano there?" Every nightclub has a piano.

SCHILLINGER: It's not a nightclub.

THEREMIN: It isn't?

SCHILLINGER: It's a former slaughterhouse.

THEREMIN: Goldberg booked us in a slaughterhouse!?

SCHILLINGER: Former slaughterhouse.

THEREMIN: Well, in that case we'll need to sound even more perfect. Gentlemen, get your instruments ready. Let's rehearse.

HOFFMAN *opens his thereminvox. We see wires sticking out of it, some of the tubes are loose and disconnected, and the whole instrument is a complete mess.*

THEREMIN: Sam, what on earth did you do to it?

HOFFMAN: I fell down the stairs.

THEREMIN: You're joking? (*He examines the instrument.*) This will need a major repair. You can't play it tonight. You'll have to use Goldberg's theremin.

SCHILLINGER: And what will Goldberg play?

THEREMIN: He can play the flute.

SCHILLINGER: But he's a terrible flute player.

THEREMIN: I know. But what else can we do. We need to play.

HOFFMAN: I have a solution. (*pause*) If the space is small enough, I could play on my mouth.

THEREMIN: I beg your pardon?

HOFFMAN: I could imitate the theremin with my mouth.

THEREMIN: Unfortunately, that's not possible.

SCHILLINGER (*quickly*): Sure. That's impossible.

HOFFMAN: Why?

THEREMIN: Because it would sound different.

HOFFMAN: Actually, it sounds very similar.

THEREMIN: OK. So theoretically the theremin may sound a little bit like humming, but it's very much beyond doubt that the audience would immediately notice that we were cheating. They'd laugh at us.

HOFFMAN: They won't notice.

THEREMIN: Are you trying to be funny?

HOFFMAN: I played like that once before.

THEREMIN: Where? In your bathroom at home?

SCHILLINGER: Last month. At that veterans' benefit.

THEREMIN: What!? Joseph, you know about this!?

SCHILLINGER: Yes . . . but if he hadn't told me, I wouldn't have noticed. He's really good at it.

THEREMIN: OK. OK. So show me.

HOFFMAN *demonstrates. It's a little bizarre, but he does a relatively good job at it.* THEREMIN *comes close to him, and looks at him intently.* GOLDBERG *enters.*

GOLDBERG: Are you rehearsing?

THEREMIN: No. Sam here is playing on his mouth!

Pause. GOLDBERG *knew about it.*

SCHILLINGER: Can we cancel for tonight?

GOLDBERG: Well, tickets already went on sale, but last I checked, we haven't sold too many.

SCHILLINGER: How many?

GOLDBERG: Two.

SCHILLINGER: In that case, I guess we could cancel.

THEREMIN: OK. Go ahead, cancel it! Why don't we just cancel all our concerts?

GOLDBERG: Actually, that's what I wanted to talk about. It's true that we've been less than successful recently. The concerts are basically empty, we aren't selling anything, the radio doesn't support us, and so on. It's a bit of a disaster.

THEREMIN: That's because RCA doesn't support us.

GOLDBERG: You can't really blame them. They lost hundreds of thousands on the theremin.

THEREMIN: They just didn't know how to market it.

GOLDBERG: Come on, they were the only ones willing to take the risk.

THEREMIN: So? You can find another company.

GOLDBERG: Electric music is dead, Leo.

THEREMIN: Is that so? And who killed it?

GOLDBERG: We did.

THEREMIN: We simply arrived at the wrong moment, that's all. In a year or two everything could change again.

HOFFMAN: I don't see what's the problem. The gig at the lung clinic was pretty good.

THEREMIN: Shut your mouth, Sam!

SCHILLINGER: Well, there is a future for electric music as such, that's for sure. But maybe we just bet on the wrong instrument. Did you hear what Les Paul did with the guitar? He gets the sounds by using a coil to capture the vibrations of a metal string in space. That's quite promising I think. Or Ondes Martenot, for example . . .

THEREMIN: Ondes didn't even get the patent.

SCHILLINGER: Sure. But he's still a remarkable man.

THEREMIN: You know him personally?

SCHILLINGER: I agreed to appear with his orchestra.

THEREMIN: With Martenot's orchestra? What are you going to play?

SCHILLINGER: The Ondes Martenot.

THEREMIN: You can't play the Ondes Martenot.

SCHILLINGER: Why not?

THEREMIN: Because you don't know how to play it. Nobody knows how to play it. It's impossible to play that thing.

SCHILLINGER: Actually, you'd be surprised how easy it is.

THEREMIN (*incredulous*): You are learning the Ondes Martenot?

SCHILLINGER: I learned it in a few hours. It's easy.

THEREMIN: That's treason, Joseph!

SCHILLINGER: Look, I'm not some sort of a traveling theremin salesman. I'm a composer, and I can write music for whatever instrument I chose.

THEREMIN: You actually wrote something for them?

SCHILLINGER: I did. (*proudly*) "The First Polyphonic Toccata for Ondes Martenot and Orchestra in E-Quarter-Minor."

THEREMIN: You are aware that the Ondes is our competition, aren't you?

SCHILLINGER: Sure, but some pieces simply sound better on the Ondes Martenot. You can't deny it.

THEREMIN: You must be joking.

SCHILLINGER: It has a better staccato.

THEREMIN: It may have a better staccato, but it most certainly has a worse vibrato. And I'm not even talking about glissando! You could never play a glissando over four octaves on that thing.

SCHILLINGER: You can. With a little lever.

HOFFMAN: What sort of a lever?

THEREMIN: Sam, would you PLEASE shut up! Is there some "little lever" on the Ondes Martenot that I don't know about?

SCHILLINGER: Well, there is one now.

THEREMIN: And how did it get there?

SCHILLINGER: Ondes installed it.

THEREMIN: Oh, I see. And whose idea was it?

SCHILLINGER: Mine.

THEREMIN: Aha!

SCHILLINGER: That's because he actually *listens* to musicians. Because he actually does what they ask him to do.

THEREMIN: Unlike me, right. Is that what you're saying?

SCHILLINGER: Exactly. You aren't interested in *people*, that's your problem. If you were, you'd try to adjust that awful device of yours so that one could actually play it, rather than making a fool of oneself.

THEREMIN: Good. SO DON'T PLAY WITH US! If the absence of a "little lever" on the theremin offends you so much!

SCHILLINGER: You're simplifying.

THEREMIN: No! I'm talking about human decency. Either we're in this together or we're not!

SCHILLINGER: No. What you're talking about is that the theremin is a Russian instrument and that I had the audacity to play with some Frenchman! But let me tell you one thing: I don't care about Russia! Nothing good *ever* came out of Russia!

THEREMIN: You don't believe that yourself.

SCHILLINGER: Russia can go to hell!

THEREMIN: It's your home!

SCHILLINGER: Not any longer.

SCHILLINGER *is about to leave.* THEREMIN *holds him back.*

THEREMIN: Do you know why it doesn't have any "lever" like the Ondes Martenot? Why it doesn't even have a keyboard or any of those things that you've been so obstinately demanding from me? It's because it isn't a musical instrument at all.

SCHILLINGER: That's exactly what I'm saying!

THEREMIN: It's a signal device.

SCHILLINGER (*joking*): A traffic light?

THEREMIN: It's an alarm system.

GOLDBERG: Now that should be enough. Leave it alone.

SCHILLINGER: Since when?

THEREMIN: From the very start. The whole story about how I met Lenin that Goldberg here likes to tell so much, the whole thing is nonsense.

GOLDBERG: Let's rehearse.

THEREMIN: You're not at all interested in how it really was?

GOLDBERG: No.

SCHILLINGER: But I am. What happened?

THEREMIN: Do you seriously believe that Lenin would receive someone like me? Lenin was somebody to whom an ordinary mortal had no access whatsoever. He was God. Highly placed generals and officials waited for months for an audience with him, and you really think that he'd give the time of day to a nameless inventor with an obscure musical instrument?

SCHILLINGER: So why did he receive you?

THEREMIN: Because I brought him something much more important than some musical instrument. I brought an alarm system that was supposed to protect Lenin's office and the whole of the Kremlin.

SCHILLINGER: All right, so you pretended that the theremin was an alarm. But why?

THEREMIN: Because it *was* an alarm!

Everybody laughs.

SCHILLINGER/HOFFMAN: That's great! That's just too good! This is getting really interesting.

HOFFMAN: So what happened?

THEREMIN: Well, nothing much. While we waited I assembled the alarm on the desk in Lenin's office. Finally he came in with about fifteen people in tow. I explained how it works, and than I asked him to try it. Lenin was of course afraid, so he ordered Berzin, the head of the Russian intelligence to approach it instead of him. Berzin came towards the desk, and the device made a sound. Then each of the others tried it as well, and every time the device buzzed or whistled. Lenin found it monumentally amusing.

GOLDBERG: That figures.

THEREMIN: He even made Lysenko crawl on his belly towards the alarm. And then—as a sort of an off-handed remark—he made a joke about how one could actually play music on it, and advertise the electrification of Russia.

SCHILLINGER: So in the end this whole thing has been nothing more than Lenin's joke?!

THEREMIN: Possibly. But right there in his office nobody dared to laugh.

HOFFMAN: And what happened with the alarm?

THEREMIN: They installed it in Lenin's office about a month later. But at that time I had already been on that infernal concert tour of Russia.

SCHILLINGER: But you've made some adjustments to the instrument since than, haven't you?

THEREMIN: None. I haven't touched it at all.

SCHILLINGER: Do you mean to say that we are playing on the same thing that sat on Lenin's desk?

THEREMIN: Correct.

SCHILLINGER *is lost in deep thought. However, he is a generous man, and he is soon overtaken by his interest in the unusual and his sense for paradox.*

SCHILLINGER: If that's really true, than I believe that we should play in the slaughterhouse tonight after all. Gentlemen, let's rehearse.

THEREMIN: Good. There are at least twenty more concerts in our RCA contract.

GOLDBERG: RCA pulled out of the deal.

THEREMIN: When?

GOLDBERG: Three years ago.

THEREMIN: What? Why didn't you tell us?

GOLDBERG: I was waiting for the right moment.

GOLDBERG, SCHILLINGER, and HOFFMAN exit. MUSIC. Enter AMTORG 1 and AMTORG 2. We are now in the Amtorg offices.

THEREMIN (writing a "letter"): Dear Father, Sir. I'm in a very complicated situation. In the last few years, it has become very difficult to obtain American patents. Apart from that, I ran out of money for my experiments, and most of my potential clients are only willing to pay upon delivery. We lost a bid for the manufacture of metal detectors for Alcatraz, and our electric orchestra fell apart.

AMTORG 1: We can assure you that our situation is not much better either. In Russia, they are discovering a number of traitors at the very heart of the intelligence services, and you can't trust anybody anymore.

THEREMIN: That's sad. Actually, I meant to ask whether, under such circumstances, it was necessary for us to continue meeting.

AMTORG 1: I beg your pardon?

THEREMIN: You haven't even given me any assignments lately.

AMTORG 1: Yes. You're right. To be completely honest, we wouldn't mind if you made your own arrangements here in America.

THEREMIN: I only hope that it won't put my father into any danger. He's an old man, he lives on a modest pension, and I haven't seen him for ages. His life is hard as it is.

AMTORG 1: Well, yes. You know Leon Sergeievich, things are as follows: Your father is dead.

THEREMIN: What? Is he missing? Did they execute him?

AMTORG 1: He died of natural causes.

THEREMIN: How?

AMTORG 1: Heart failure.

THEREMIN: Sure. That's what they always say.

AMTORG 1: Many people in Russia have been dying of heart failure lately.

AMTORG 2: Suddenly, Russian hearts became terribly weak.

THEREMIN: But I did everything I was supposed to. Everything you wanted me to do!

AMTORG 1: Absolutely. Calm down.

THEREMIN: We have thirteen American patents! I infiltrated the aeronautical industry. For years I have been feeding you information about the plane factory in Massachusetts. My altimeter is used in eighty percent of American airplanes! We managed to have the theremin mass-produced, even though everybody said it was impossible. We played concerts for thousands of workers, installed alarm systems in American banks . . . ! What else did you want me to do?

AMTORG 1: Nothing. We are happy with your work.

THEREMIN: So why did my father have to die?

AMTORG 1: He died of natural causes. It had nothing to do with you.

THEREMIN: I don't believe it.

AMTORG 1: So, according to you, how did he die?

THEREMIN: You killed him.

AMTORG 1: Who. Us two?

THEREMIN: I don't know. GRU or GPU, military intelligence, Internal Security . . . How should I know? You made him into an enemy of the state, an enemy of the revolution, a "bourgeois element," or who knows what, and you beat him to death during an interrogation.

AMTORG 2: Was your father an enemy of the revolution?

THEREMIN: No.

AMTORG 2: Well, then there was no reason to beat him. Was there?

THEREMIN: You're right. I'm sorry, I got overexcited. He was an old man. Maybe he did die of natural causes after all.

AMTORG 1: Exactly. Have a drink.

They pour vodka. THEREMIN *takes a shot.*

THEREMIN: I must go back to Russia. I have to arrange for the funeral. My mother is dead, my cousin Vladimir is missing . . . Somebody has to take care of it.

AMTORG 1: It won't be necessary.

THEREMIN: I beg your pardon?

AMTORG 1: Your father died two years ago.

THEREMIN: Why . . . Why didn't you tell me?

AMTORG 1: We didn't want to bother you unnecessarily.

THEREMIN: Where is he buried?

AMTORG 1: We have no such information.

THEREMIN: I'll complain about you two. I'll let comrade Berzin know . . .

AMTORG 2: That won't be possible.

THEREMIN: I can assure you that it *will* be possible!

AMTORG 2: Berzin's dead.

THEREMIN: Heart failure?

AMTORG 1: Heart failure.

They are about to leave.

AMTORG 2: By the way . . . that manager of yours, that German . . .

THEREMIN: Hans Goldberg . . . ?

AMTORG 2: Yes. You don't have to work with him anymore.

Vocoder-generated MUSIC. The AMTORG EMPLOYEES *leave. We are now in* THEREMIN*'s apartment. He takes an electrical cord from his desk and is about to fix it on a pipe on the ceiling and hang himself. But as he does so, he notices some vacuum tubes on his table. He slowly drops the cord and begins to play with the component in his hand. Than he falls asleep. The music lasts for some time. Suddenly* THEREMIN *screams and wakes up with a start.* LAVINIA *runs in.*

LAVINIA: Are you all right?

THEREMIN: I saw them!

LAVINIA: Saw who?

THEREMIN: Those people, who ate their children.

LAVINIA: Calm down. What children?

THEREMIN: In Russia, in twenty-two. I saw them now. I must have had a dream about them. But the church looked different.

LAVINIA *massages his neck, gives him something to eat, etc . . .*

THEREMIN: Ugh! Such dreams! Why do I have dreams like that?!

LAVINIA: Those are just nightmares.

THEREMIN: Lavinia, you are so good to me. I'll miss you.

LAVINIA: What do you mean?

THEREMIN: I can't afford to pay you any longer. I'm broke. I'm sure I already owe you money.

LAVINIA: I'll work for free.

THEREMIN: Why would you do a thing like that?

LAVINIA: Because I respect you.

THEREMIN: That's very nice of you. Well, in that case, could you perhaps lend me some money? Twenty dollars? No. I know. Don't worry about it. Well, you can go home now. Or stay here if you want—it's late, and Brooklyn is not safe at night. You can sleep on the sofa.

LAVINIA (*putting bedding on the sofa*): I was just thinking that in your situation . . . With all those problems with the Immigration . . .

THEREMIN: Yes, I know.

LAVINIA: I thought that maybe a marriage to an American would help . . . I mean in a situation like that.

THEREMIN: Right. That never occurred to me, actually.

LAVINIA: I wanted to say that I'd be able . . . I mean I'd be willing to . . .

THEREMIN: . . . to organize something like that? Do you know somebody who'd do it?

LAVINIA: . . . I wouldn't mind if I did it.

THEREMIN: You are offering me marriage?

LAVINIA: Yes. But only on paper.

THEREMIN: I can't accept that.

LAVINIA: Yes, of course. I'm sorry. It's impertinent of me, of course.

THEREMIN: It's not that. It's just not an option.

LAVINIA: Naturally. What would people say?

THEREMIN: It's not about what people would say. But I'm an awful person. I almost drove Katherine to her death. I have no heart—just ask Goldberg. No, Lavinia, you wouldn't be happy with me.

LAVINIA: Actually, Mr. Goldberg speaks very nicely of you.

THEREMIN: Goldberg speaks nicely of me behind my back?

LAVINIA: He does.

THEREMIN: Well, now you see how sneaky he is. To my face, he laughs at me.

LAVINIA: He respects you.

THEREMIN: And how about you? What do you think about me?

LAVINIA: You're obstinate. Sometimes a little insensitive, but you have a right to be. You are hard on yourself, and you don't ever give up. I like that about you. And, you have an ideal, and you pursue it no matter what.

THEREMIN: What ideal?

LAVINIA: You want to change the world.

THEREMIN: Really?

LAVINIA: Yes.

THEREMIN: Do you have any proof of that?

LAVINIA: Mr. Goldberg told me the story about the bicycle at the institute in Russia way back when.

THEREMIN: What bicycle?

LAVINIA: That bicycle you fixed to generate electricity. In nineteen twenty.

THEREMIN: I don't remember that.

LAVINIA: You experimented with hibernation. You froze some laboratory rats to minus twenty degrees . . .

THEREMIN: Minus thirty-five . . .

LAVINIA: . . . but than there was a blackout that lasted longer than usual, and all your experimental material was in danger of thawing.

THEREMIN: And?

LAVINIA: And you decided to generate electricity by pedaling on those bikes they had there.

THEREMIN: Is that so?

LAVINIA: Yes. You forced everybody in the institute to pedal along. And when they started to tire, you began to sing the "Internationale" to give them strength. One by one they gave up, but you lasted until the very end.

THEREMIN: Yes. That's Theremin for you. And for how long did I pedal?

LAVINIA: For seventeen hours. They literally had to take you off the bicycle since you were paralyzed by cramps. You were in a trance, completely delirious but you went on pedaling.

THEREMIN: So that's what Goldberg tells you?

LAVINIA: He admires you for it.

THEREMIN: Goldberg wasn't there.

LAVINIA: But that's what happened, didn't it?

THEREMIN: First of all: All the bikes at the institute were stolen already by 1917. Second: None of the people who worked there would have lasted longer than five minutes. And finally, we would never have managed to generate enough electricity for all those freezers.

LAVINIA: But still! You had an ideal even then. And you were willing to sacrifice for it.

THEREMIN: It wasn't an ideal. It was despair. Don't mix them up.

LAVINIA: For me, they are the same.

THEREMIN: Look Lavinia, here in America it's easy. If you need some part or a component, you go to a store and you buy it. But do you know how we shopped for it in Petrograd or in Moscow in the twenties?

LAVINIA: No.

THEREMIN: We went to a market.

LAVINIA: What sort of a market?

THEREMIN: An ordinary flea market. Rough fir planks thrown over two sawhorses, and everybody's selling whatever they have to offer. Most of the vendors are villagers. There are potatoes, turnips, live chickens, herring, and mushrooms, and here and there you may see somebody selling, say, a condenser or a triode. But you can't tell what sort of a triode or a condenser it is, and you certainly cannot be sure that they would sell the same thing tomorrow. Every so often somebody would bring something from abroad, the Institute would sometimes order this or that, but it was all immensely tedious, and in most cases what we got was not what we wanted or needed anyhow.

LAVINIA: Then it's even more admirable that you managed to build anything at all.

THEREMIN: But we never had a plan! We simply built our equipment out of what was available, out of things we found between a chicken and a turnip.

LAVINIA: I think you're exaggerating.

THEREMIN: Do you know why I was working on cryonic hibernation then?

LAVINIA: Because you wanted to challenge death, challenge God himself.

THEREMIN: Because somebody at the Institute somehow managed to procure two incredibly efficient freezers. That's all. My colleague Petrofimov experimented with x-rays for the same reasons.

LAVINIA: What reason?

THEREMIN: He found an x-ray machine at a flea market. It wasn't us who determined the course of science, it was the available parts and components that did that for us.

LAVINIA: And you expect me to believe that?

THEREMIN: I only want you to understand that an inventor is an awfully unfree human being.

LAVINIA: But you're more than an inventor, you're . . .

THEREMIN: I'm what?

LAVINIA: You're a Bolshevik.

THEREMIN: Yes, of course. That's what you all see in me: the very incarnation of the revolution. But imagine if you'd find out that I've been doing it all only for the money. I bet you wouldn't like me so much, would you?

LAVINIA: I still would.

THEREMIN: And what if I told you why I did what I did, told you what was behind it all?

LAVINIA: What was it?

THEREMIN: If I told you that there was nothing.

LAVINIA: What do you mean, "nothing?"

THEREMIN: Nothing. No ideal. No vision. No obstinacy, not even greed. If I told you that there wasn't even fear behind it all, or cunning . . . nothing.

LAVINIA: So why would you have done all those things?

THEREMIN: Because I enjoy tinkering with those little parts and components.

LAVINIA: Well of course, I know that about you, but there must be more to it.

THEREMIN: No. That's all there is to it.

LAVINIA: You're joking.

THEREMIN: I'm serious. What if you found out that I was a completely empty human being? A toy of fate. A man without will and without future.

LAVINIA: Then you'd have to kill yourself.

THEREMIN: Absolutely. I'd have to. I'd go to a coffeehouse, figure out how to do it, then I'd come home and I'd tie a piece of cable on that pipe up on the ceiling, I'd take the stool here by the desk . . . but as I'd be passing the desk I'd notice the components on it, and something would catch my attention. I'd put the stool back, grab one of the triodes and I'd begin to twirl it in my fingers, and get an idea—something I'd like to try. An instrument one could play by simply looking at it. I have actually been thinking about it for some time, but I couldn't find the appropriate lenses. And two days later Goldberg shows up and says what's this cable hanging from the ceiling? And I tell him I have no idea, and then I show him that new invention of mine.

LAVINIA: You are a horrible person.

THEREMIN: So, you see. A marriage with me wouldn't be worth it.

LAVINIA *leaves.* LUCY *enters.*

LUCY: There are ten thousand dollars in this envelope. It should cover most of your debts and the purchase of some basic stuff.

THEREMIN: What stuff?

LUCY: Everything we'll need in Canada. Picks, saddles, . . .

THEREMIN: What picks? What saddles?

LUCY: America is too dangerous for both of us Leo. Somebody shot at my car last week.

THEREMIN: Did you tell Walter?

LUCY: I suspect it was one of his men. You can't trust anybody anymore.

THEREMIN: But I can't go to Canada. I have a wife here.

LUCY: You and Katherine are divorced.

THEREMIN: Another wife.

LUCY: You got married? Who is she?

THEREMIN: Actually, you know her.

LUCY: Is it the RCA secretary? The woman that Walter had an affair with, or the one who lived with Edison for a while? No . . . I hope it's not the girl that helps you in the lab. That Negro woman . . .

THEREMIN: Lavinia is not a . . . She has Irish ancestors . . . and Haitian.

LUCY: So it is her?! Jesus Christ . . . ! Oh well, that's no problem. You'll just assume a new identity.

THEREMIN: That's out of the question.

LUCY: Out of the question?! OK, so let me put it differently. In America you're gone and forgotten. Everybody's laughing at you. Schillinger has had it up to here with you, as had Goldberg. You're under mountains of debt, and it's been two years since you got your last patent. And to top it all off, now you married a *Negro!!!* I'm the only chance you've got Leo. So now, listen carefully: I have one last proposal for you. And think *really* hard before you answer. You take these ten thousand dollars, and you go and see this man, who'll get you a fake passport. (*She writes the name and the address of the man on a piece of paper and gives it to* THEREMIN. *Then she begins to "change his identity"—glasses, a fake mustache, perhaps a hat.*) We'll pretend that you left for a business trip to Panama, but in reality we'll flee to Canada. Both of us under assumed names. I'll tell Walter not to look for me. He's a reasonable man, so he'll listen. You do the same with Goldberg. We'll lead a simple life on a farm, far away from other people. Of course we'll have to give up many things that we've been taking for granted—theatre, movies, cars, parties . . . all that will have to go. You'll have to leave all your inventions behind, including the theremin. But our whole life will be filled with love and work from now on.

THEREMIN: But you don't love me.

LUCY: I used to.

THEREMIN: When was that?

LUCY: In the spring of thirty-one. For four whole months. But of course you didn't notice.

THEREMIN: I'm sorry.

LUCY: So, now you take this envelope and do as I say. Otherwise it's deportation from the U.S. or debtors' prison.

THEREMIN (*taking the envelope*): OK. Where will we meet?

She hugs THEREMIN *and leaves. Enter* GOLDBERG. THEREMIN *quickly removes his "disguise."*

GOLDBERG: Hi.

THEREMIN: Come in. Sit down. (*He spreads the blueprints of his devices on the floor and points to them.*) Altimeter, theremin, lie detector.

GOLDBERG (*reaches into his pocket and pulls out a wad of money*): Three hundred dollars. That's all I have, really.

THEREMIN: I don't want money for it. Care for a drink?

GOLDBERG *indeed does care for it.* THEREMIN *pours him a glass. They take a shot.*

GOLDBERG: I found a company that's willing to invest fifty thousand dollars in the development of television. I mentioned your name to them.

THEREMIN: That's over now.

GOLDBERG: Television has future.

THEREMIN: I'm not an inventor anymore.

GOLDBERG: You're my friend. The two of us will still accomplish great things,.

THEREMIN: The two of us won't accomplish anything any longer.

GOLDBERG: And who was it that shouted how in ten years the world will be a different place?! How all disease will be eliminated, how man will be immortal?! Who proclaimed that we'd be able to make music without God's gift?

THEREMIN: Come on, we never believed that nonsense.

GOLDBERG: I did.

THEREMIN: Yes. You did.

Pause.

GOLDBERG: They are asking for a minimal resolution of at least a hundred and twenty lines, and a minimum of a five-foot diagonal picture. But they'd give us an advance.

THEREMIN: You are a terrible romantic, Hans.

GOLDBERG: Are you saying that I'm naïve?

THEREMIN: Exactly.

GOLDBERG: So, why did *you* do it at all? Tell me. For the money? Because of women? I don't think so.

THEREMIN: It was simply an assignment. That's what I'm saying.

GOLDBERG: What "assignment?'

THEREMIN: To invent.

GOLDBERG: An assignment to invent. Who gave it to you?

THEREMIN: The Institute, Amtorg, the Russian intelligence.

GOLDBERG: That's nonsense. You can't invent on command.

THEREMIN: Oh yes. You can.

GOLDBERG: You need a gift to invent.

THEREMIN: A gift from whom? From God? You see, I never had anything like that. All I had was an order.

GOLDBERG: So they ordered you to invent.

THEREMIN: Yes. You saw me going to that office every week.

GOLDBERG: But I thought that it was just a game you were playing with them.

THEREMIN: Not at all. I went there to give them my reports, and they were giving me my orders. Nothing more, nothing less. It was them, who wanted us to start the mass production of the theremin for example.

GOLDBERG: But that was your idea!

THEREMIN: No. That was their idea. And then they said: we want you to get to know the American air industry. So I went and built the altimeter in order to gain access to the airplane factories. And the same goes for everything else.

GOLDBERG: You mean to say that when you accepted my offer back in twenty-five, that was their idea too?

THEREMIN: Yes. It was an important decision, wasn't it?

GOLDBERG: And with Katherine . . . when you wanted to marry her, did you have to get their OK first?

THEREMIN: No, not exactly. It was their idea that I marry her.

GOLDBERG: In that case, you are really pitiful.

THEREMIN: Yeah.

GOLDBERG: But how did that happen?

THEREMIN: What was my first assignment?

GOLDBERG: You tell me.

THEREMIN: 1922. A visit in Lenin's office.

GOLDBERG (*for the first time getting very angry and upset*): FUCK YOU and your FUCKING visit with Lenin!

THEREMIN: But this is *your* visit with Lenin as well.

GOLDBERG: It's not my damn visit with Lenin. It's YOUR FUCKING visit with Lenin, FUCK!!!

THEREMIN: It's got more to do with you than you think.

GOLDBERG: Because for ten years I've been playing on an alarm bell?! Is that why?!

THEREMIN: That too. But look at it from the other side. What if I'm not going to the Kremlin on that memorable day to show Lenin an alarm system? Or what if it isn't *only* an alarm system? What if I have yet another task, a very secret task, let say from Berzin, the head of the intelligence? Berzin and Stalin are pals, so it's clear that Stalin knows about it as well. Everybody thinks that I'm bringing a signal device, but only Berzin, the director of the Institute, Ioffé, and Stalin, know what it really is.

GOLDBERG: And you, too.

THEREMIN: Yes. And me.

GOLDBERG: So what is it?

THEREMIN: A listening device. A bug. A gadget that makes it possible for certain members of Lenin's cabinet to find out what that paranoid madman really thinks. So: it is a cold and gray November day, the last few leaves swirling in the wind on the streets . . .

GOLDBERG: Cut it short.

THEREMIN: This is important—to set the stage . . . the last few leaves swirling in the wind on the streets . . . and my assistant and I ascend the stairs to the Kremlin.

GOLDBERG: He, of course has no idea what is going on.

THEREMIN: No. He thinks that we are bringing an alarm system.

GOLDBERG: But it is still the one and the same device.

THEREMIN: Exactly. Devices don't change, only their use does.

GOLDBERG: Where is the microphone?

THEREMIN: The speaker is the microphone.

GOLDBERG: And how do the sounds leave the room?

THEREMIN: The device functions as a simple transmitter. All you do is tune a radio to a certain frequency a few blocks away, and, *voila*, you can hear everything happening around the thereminvox.

GOLDBERG: The alarm.

THEREMIN: The bug.

GOLDBERG: Ingenious.

THEREMIN: It's simple. Either we pull the sound from the ether, or we send it into it. Two sides of the same coin. And, once again, the hero of the story is the vacuum tube.

GOLDBERG: The triode.

THEREMIN: Yes. But this time it's a matter of life and death. If Lenin's not interested, I fail my assignment from Berzin. And that could have far-reaching consequences. Lenin may be paranoid and obsessively fearful about his safety, but the alarm is a novelty. Is he going to trust that novelty? Or is he going to examine the whole thing, and have us shot on the spot? Or maybe the whole affair is a trap set up in order to get rid of Ioffé, the director of the Institute? Whatever it may be, the fact is that I am the first up in the firing line. This is what goes through my head as I slowly climb the stairs to the building.

GOLDBERG: But everything turns out well.

THEREMIN: Marvelously. Lenin likes the alarm, and he even jokes that one could play music on a thing like that.

GOLDBERG: And he has the alarm—I mean the bug—installed.

THEREMIN: Exactly. And this way, we monitor Lenin's conversations until his death in twenty-four! But by then, I'm already gallivanting around Russia on my concert tour.

GOLDBERG: Katherine said that after you returned to Petrograd from the tour nobody in the Institute would even say hello. They reproached you that amid all that horror and famine in Russia, all you did was wave your hands over that instrument of yours.

THEREMIN: Yes. They never said it directly, but that's what they were thinking. But none of them knew what this was really about.

GOLDBERG: While at that time you already know *too* much.

THEREMIN: Exactly. It's like a time bomb. They have me completely in their hands. They can do anything they want with me. But my father can live a little longer.

GOLDBERG: Why couldn't he live?

THEREMIN: Because he grew up on the Czar's court. He is an enemy of the revolution of the first order. People like him were exterminated already in nineteen eighteen, right after the Revolution—with few exceptions. So here I am, bribing them with all those inventions so that they'll leave him in peace. Bribing them with our American patents, too. Thank God, you've been so clever all this time.

GOLDBERG: You mean to say that everything that we've been doing here, the hundreds of concerts, all those thirteen years of work . . . all that was really only about saving your father.

THEREMIN: Yes.

GOLDBERG: Is that what was behind it all?

THEREMIN: There is always something behind it all, and behind that all there is something else again, and so on, and so on.

GOLDBERG: I thought that we were writing a new chapter in the history of music.

THEREMIN: We saved a human being. That's something.

GOLDBERG: Yes. (*pause*) Only we didn't save him.

THEREMIN: Right. Only we didn't save him. But still, I wanted to thank you for everything.

GOLDBERG: But Leo, if all of this is true, then your whole life you've been a terribly unfree human being.

THEREMIN: And if I had done it for money, or because of women, would I have been any freer? (*pause*) Do you remember how we used to say that electricity would replace God?

GOLDBERG: I do.

THEREMIN: I think about that often now. My parents were believers. Russian Orthodox. We used to go to mass every Sunday and we said grace before every meal.

GOLDBERG: So did we.

THEREMIN: Will you pray with me?

GOLDBERG: If I still remember how to do it.

MUSIC. They go down on their knees.

THEREMIN: What was your family like?

GOLDBERG: My father was a successful businessman, a member of the Munich Chamber of Commerce. A deeply religious man. How about you?

THEREMIN: A respected Petrograd family. My grandfather on my father's side was the Czar's barber.

GOLDBERG (*after a pause*): I don't believe you.

THEREMIN: It doesn't matter. But you understand me. (*He gets up and leaves.*)

Enter LAVINIA.

LAVINIA: Leon Sergeievich is gone!!!

GOLDBERG: What?

LAVINIA: Leon Sergeievich disappeared!!!

GOLDBERG: What do you mean: "disappeared?"

LAVINIA: He hasn't come home for three days. I called the police but they don't know anything. They may have kidnapped him.

GOLDBERG: Lavinia, this is New York. They can't just willy-nilly kidnap a person.

LAVINIA: I'm not sure. But I'm terribly afraid . . . you know how they are.

GOLDBERG: Calm down, I'll take care of it. (*He dials a number on the phone, and speaks. It is clear that he isn't able to take care of anything.*)

Enter HOFFMAN.

HOFFMAN: What's going on?

GOLDBERG: Theremin disappeared.

LAVINIA: He hasn't come home for three days.

HOFFMAN (*his P.I. instincts take over*): Did he tell you where he was going?

LAVINIA: He didn't.

HOFFMAN: Where did you see him last?

LAVINIA: Here in the apartment.

HOFFMAN: Did he behave strangely? Was he dressed suspiciously?

GOLDBERG: Cut it out, Hoffman!

HOFFMAN: What did I do?

GOLDBERG: This is not a lost dog or cat.

HOFFMAN: I don't need your advice. I know exactly what to do in situations like this. We must inform the Russian Embassy.

GOLDBERG: I've been trying to call them for an hour.

HOFFMAN: Did you call Schillinger?

GOLDBERG: I did.

LUCY *enters.*

LUCY: I'm sure there's an explanation.

SCHILLINGER *enters.*

SCHILLINGER: Gentlemen, ladies, good day to you. I talked to my contact from the Russian Embassy. According to his information, Theremin left the United States of America. He boarded a liner in the direction of Petrograd. Old Bolshevik.

GOLDBERG: It's not as clear-cut as that . . .

SCHILLINGER: That's the name of the ship.

Everybody tries to process the new information.

SCHILLINGER (*to* GOLDBERG): Do you have any idea why he left?

GOLDBERG: I'm not sure.

SCHILLINGER: I haven't seen him for a long time. Has he changed?

GOLDBERG: Not at all. He stayed exactly the same. His head was as full of plans as ever.

SCHILLINGER: In that case he must have gone mad.

GOLDBERG: I don't think so.

SCHILLINGER: But only a madman would go back to Russia nowadays.

GOLDBERG: I think that it was his free choice.

Pause.

HOFFMAN: I propose that in memory of Leon Sergeievich we play his favorite piece.

GOLDBERG: A requiem for Theremin? Is he dead? No. Right now, he is standing on the deck of some liner, looking at the waves, and he's happy and content.

HOFFMAN: From what I know about Russia, he's not going to survive there for more than a few months.

LUCY: Oh please!

SCHILLINGER: When he dies, we most likely won't even find out about it.

Pause.

LAVINIA: What do you think we should play?

HOFFMAN: How about "On the Moscow River Bank?"

LAVINIA: He never liked that.

LUCY: He did. It was the only one he really loved.

LAVINIA: No, he liked "Moscow Evenings."

LUCY: Well, as far as I know "Moscow Evenings" was far from his favorite.

HOFFMAN: OK, so which one is it?

LAVINIA: "Moscow Evenings."

SCHILLINGER: How about the "First Airphonic Suite?"

HOFFMAN: He didn't like that one for sure.

SCHILLINGER: How would you know? Actually it'd be a perfect piece for this occasion.

LUCY: Ugh. I'd be more willing to play even "The Lark."

SCHILLINGER: By Glinka!

LAVINIA: He played "The Lark" for Lenin.

HOFFMAN: OK, but did he like Lenin?

SCHILLINGER: What does Lenin have to do with it?

Pause.

GOLDBERG: You're right. It's difficult to know what he really liked.

HOFFMAN *goes to a theremin, ready to play.*

SCHILLINGER: Do you want to play it on the theremin?

HOFFMAN: Of course. On what else?

SCHILLINGER: But did he like it? We don't want to play in his memory on an instrument that he couldn't stand.

HOFFMAN: Fellas, we are in a stalemate here.

GOLDBERG: Absolutely. It may be best not to play at all.

LAVINIA *hums the melody of a famous Russian folksong "The Wide Steppe" or some other recognizable Russian melody. The others gradually join in. After about half a minute,* SCHILLINGER *interrupts.*

SCHILLINGER: That's a sixth-note, Mr. Goldberg, a sixth.

He goes to the piano and absolutely demolishes the entire song cum requiem with his attempt at perfection. Gradually the "Internationale" sung by a children's choir fades in from the loudspeakers. The "final credits" roll in.

SCHILLINGER: In 1943, Alfred Hitchcock was looking for some strange, fright-awakening musical instrument for his movie *Spellbound*. He found out that a certain Samuel Hoffman was listed with the Hollywood musicians' union as a "Theremin player." He invited him to record the long, eerie, and fright-filled sounds of the instrument for the film. *Spellbound* eventually became a great hit, possibly because of the instrument itself. And Samuel Hoffman went on to record the theremin for hundreds of horror movie scores in the fifties and sixties.

GOLDBERG: Singularly, Hoffman has done more for the popularization of the theremin than all of us combined. He died in 1967, a relatively rich man.

HOFFMAN: Hans Goldberg died in 1975. In the early forties, he was Schillinger's business advisor and later, he successfully managed the musical careers of some of Schillinger's students.

LUCY: In 1986 the name Leon Sergeievich Theremin finally appears as an entry in the Encyclopedia Britannica. Father of electronic music. The man, about whom Robert Moog once said that without him, he himself would have never been able to construct his synthesizer.

SCHILLINGER: Such an unfree human being, and yet he changed the world.

GOLDBERG: But for a brief moment he *was* free. That one day, in thirty-eight, when he decided to go back to Russia, he made a free choice.

SCHILLINGER: Perhaps the only one in his life.

LAVINIA: And we were part of it when it happened.

GOLDBERG: We *are* part of it.

MUSIC. They all stand and listen to the music.

Fadeout.

THE END

Play Production Histories

Lenka Lagronová

Miriam premiered on March 24, 2005, at the Pražské komorní divadlo (Divadlo Komedie), directed by Jan Nebeský with stage and costume design by Jana Preková, and music by Martin Dohnal. The cast was: Lucie Trmíková, Gabriela Míčová, Pavel Magda Pražák.

Selected plays:

Nouzov (*Poortown*) 1989, premiere 1990, DISK–Divadelní studio DAMU, Prague
Pokoj (*Room*) 1992, premiere 2002, Pidivadlo, Prague
Antilopa (*Antelope*) 1993, premiere 1995, A Studio Rubín, Prague
Terezka (*Thérèse*), written and premiered 1997, Divadlo Komedie, Prague
Království (*Kingdom*) 2002, premiere 2006, DISK–Divadelní studio DAMU, Prague
Miriam (*Miriam**) 2003, premiere 2005, Divadlo Komedie, Prague
Nikdy (*Never*), written and premiered 2003, Činoherní studio, Ústí nad Labem
Etty Hillesum 2005, premiere 2006, Divadlo Na zábradlí, Prague
Jan Pavel II. (rozhovory) (*John Paul II.* [*dialogues*]) 2006
Pláč (*Crying*) 2007

Miriam was presented as part of Immigrants' Theatre Project's readings series *Czech Plays in Translation IV* on May 9, 2005, at The Public Theater, New York City. Marcy Arlin was the director and Irena Kovarova was the dramaturg. The cast was:

MIRA	Lanna Joffrey
VERA	Adriana Gaviria
STAGE DIRECTIONS/MAN	Frank Camacho

* Translated into English

Egon Tobiáš

Slíbil jsem to Freddymu (*I Promised Freddy*) premiered on May 29, 2002, at Divadlo Na zábradlí Praha (Eliadova knihovna), directed by Jan Nebeský. The cast included: Howard Lotker, Tomáš Žižka, Žan Loose, Pavel Štorek, and Ladislav Soukup.

Selected plays:

Cizinec (*A Stranger*) 1989, premiere 1994 A–Studio Rubín, Prague
Vojcev 1990, premiere 1992 divadlo Labyrint, Prague
Smokie 1992, premiere 2000 Činoherní studio, Ústí nad Labem
*Jaurès** 1994, premiere 1997 Činoherní studio, Ústí nad Labem
Slíbil jsem to Freddymu (*I Promised Freddy**) 1999, premiere 2002 Divadlo Na zábradlí, Prague (staged reading)
Mal D'or, written and premiered 2000 Divadlo Komedie, Prague (part of the Marta project)
*JE SUiS**, written and premiered 2001 Divadlo Na zábradlí, Prague
Je na čase, aby se TO změnilo (*It's Time for IT to Change**), written and premiered 2002 Divadlo Komedie, Prague
Solingen: Rána z milosti (*Solingen: Merciful Blow**) 2003, premiere 2004 Divadlo Komedie, Prague
Vyšetřování pokračuje (*Investigation continues*), written and premiered 2006 Divadlo Komedie, Prague

I Promised Freddy was presented as part of Immigrants' Theatre Project's readings series *Czech Plays in Translation II* on March 24, 2003, at New York Theatre Workshop, New York City. Kaipo Schwab was the director and Maxine Kern was the dramaturg. The ensemble was:

Gregg Mozgala, Evan Lai, Debora S. Craig, Alessandro Colla, Matthew Johnson, Sevrin Anne Mason, Esra Gaffin, Daniel Stowell, Rachel Neuman, Ron Domingo, Andrew Eisenman, John Fukuda, Daniella Chiminelli, Keo Woolford

Jiří Pokorný

Taťka střílí góly (*Dad Takes Goal Kicks*) premiered on January 22, 1999 at Činoherní studio, Ústí nad Labem. The production was directed by the playwright, with stage design by Petr B. Novák, costume design by Zuzana Krejzková, and dramaturgy by Markéta Bláhová. The cast featured: Marie Spurná, Zbyněk Roubal, Jan Bidlas, Veronika Rašťáková, Leoš Noha, Tomáš Krejčíř, Matúš Bukovčan, Zdeněk Novák, Martin Finger, Roman Zach, Marta Vítů, Richard Němec, Petr Olin Hocke

Plays:

Valašská čtverylka (*The Wallachian Quadrille*) 1993, premiere 1994 Činoherní studio, Ústí nad Labem (under the pseudonym Fást J. L.)
Odpočívej v pokoji (*Rest in Peace**) 1996, premiere 1999 Činoherní studio, Ústí nad Labem
Taťka střílí góly (*Dad Takes Goal Kicks**) 1997, premiere 1999 Činoherní studio, Ústí nad Labem
Plechovka (*Can*), written and premiered 1999 Činoherní studio, Ústí nad Labem (under the pseudonym Jarol Ostraval)
Denis (Epilog k Monologům vagíny) (*Denis* [*Epilogue for The Vagina Monologues*]), written and premiered 2003, Dejvické divadlo, Prague (staged reading)
Milada, written and premiered 2007, Divadlo Na zábradlí, Prague

Dad Takes Goal Kicks was presented as part of Immigrants' Theatre Project's readings series *Czech Plays in Translation III* on June 21, 2004, at The Public Theater, New York City. Marcy Arlin was the director and Irena Kovarova was the dramaturg. The cast was:

JENDA	Tibor Feldman
MITEK	Piter Marek Fattouche
RENATA	Adriana Gaviria
BLÁŽA	Ching Valdes-Aran
SLÁVEK	Andrew Guilarte
DUŠÁN	Trevor Osvalt
BRONĚK	Michael Anderson
VELEBORSKÝ	Oscar de la Fé Colon
STAGE DIRECTIONS/POLICE/PARAMEDIC/DOCTOR	Tony Wolf

* Translated into English

Iva Klestilová Volánková

Minach premiered January 11, 2002, at HaDivadlo in Brno, directed by Arnošt Goldflam. The cast was: Pavel Liška, Mariana Chmelařová, Tomáš Matonoha, Marek Daniel.

Plays:

Všichni svatí (All Saints) 1997
Zisk slasti (Gain of Bliss) 1999, premiere 2000 Festival Les divokých sviní, Činoherní studio, Ústí nad Labem (staged reading)
trilogie minach (Minach*) 2000, premiere 2002 HaDivadlo, Brno
Stísněná 22 (Encroachment*) 2001, premiere 2003 Národní divadlo, Prague
3sestry2005.cz (3sisters2002.cz*) 2002, premiere 2005 Divadlo Rokoko, Prague
Taking off, written and premiered 2003 Dejvické divadlo, Prague (staged reading)
HRA(J)! (PLAY/!/) 2003, premiere 2004 HaDivadlo, Brno
Benefice (A Ticket Night), written and premiered 2005 Činoherní studio, Ústí nad Labem
Barbíny (Barbies) (together with Valeria Schulczová), written and premiered 2005 Divadlo Na zábradlí, Prague
Hrdinové (Heroes), written and premiered 2006 Projekt Bouda, Národní divadlo, Prague
Usměj se, mami (Smile, Mum), written and premiered 2007 in the Theatre U Valšů, Prague

Minach was presented as part of Immigrants' Theatre Projects readings series *Czech Plays in Translation II* on April 28, 2003 at New York Theatre Workshop. New York City. Marcy Arlin was the director and Maxine Kern was the dramaturg. The cast was:

SISTER/KAREN	Melissa Leo
WOMAN	Nilaja Sun
BROTHER/MAN	Tzahi Moskovitz
LOUIS	Vaneik Echeverria

David Drábek

Akvabely (*Aquabelles*) premiered on April 30, 2005, at Klicperovo divadlo, Hradec Králové directed by Vladimír Morávek, with stage design by Martin Chocholoušek, costume design by Tomáš Kypta, music by Michal Pavlíček, choreography by Michal Němeček, and dramaturgy by Martin Velíšek. The cast featured: Petr Vrběcký, Filip Richtermoc, Ondřej Malý, Pavla Tomicová, Jan Sklenář, David Steigerwald, Eva Leinweberová.

Subsequent productions of *Akvabely* opened November 12, 2005 at JAMU Studio Marta, Brno, directed by Marián Amsler, and October 1, 2006 at Divadlo J.K. Tyla Plzeň (Divadlo v klubu), directed by Vilém Dubnička.

Selected plays:

Hořící žirafy (*Burning Giraffes*) 1993, premiere 1995 Divadelní společnost Petra Bezruče, Ostrava
Jana z parku (*Joan of the Park*) 1994, premiere 1995 Moravské divadlo, Olomouc
Kosmická snídaně aneb Nebřenský (*Space Breakfast or Nebřenský*) written and premiered 1997 Moravské divadlo, Olomouc
Švédský stůl (*Snack Bar*) 1998, premiere 1999 Klicperovo divadlo, Hradec Králové
Kostlivec v silonkách (*Skeleton in Nylons*), written and premiered 1999 Moravské divadlo, Olomouc
Embryo čili Automobily východních Čech (*Embryo or East Bohemian Cars*) 2002, premiere 2004 Divadelní společnost Petra Bezruče, Ostrava
Akvabely (*Aquabelles**) 2003, premiere 2005 Klicperovo divadlo, Hradec Králové
Žabikuch (*Stabber*) 2004, premiere 2005 Studio Citadela, Prague
Sněhurka—Nová generace (*Snow White—The New Generation*) 2004, premiere 2006 Divadlo Minor, Prague
Náměstí bratří Mašínů (*Mašín Brothers Square*) 2007

Aquabelles was presented as part of Immigrants' Theatre Project's readings series *Czech Plays in Translation IV* on May 16, 2005, at The Public Theater, New York City. Terrell Robinson was the director and Irena Kovarova was the dramaturg. The cast was:

Ron Jones and Students from Henry Street Settlement

* Translated into English

Ivana Růžičková

As of publication, *Otvírám zásuvku a vyndávám nůž* (*Opening the Drawer and Pulling out the Knife*) has not been produced in Czech.

Plays:

Hra na někoho jiného (*Playing Someone Else*) 1999
Zničit sebe sama (*To Destroy Herself*) 2000, premiere 2001 Les scénických čtení Universal NoD–Roxy, Prague (staged reading)
Noční tance (*Night Dances*) 2001
Chvíli před tím, než jsem otevřela zásuvku a vyndala nůž (*The moment before I opened the drawer and took out the knife*) 2002, premiere 2003 Divadlo Na prádle, Prague (staged reading)
Otvírám zásuvku a vyndávám nůž (*Opening the Drawer and Pulling out the Knife**) 2003, premiere 2004 The Public Theater, New York (staged reading)

Opening the Drawer and Pulling Out the Knife was presented as part of Immigrants' Theatre Project's readings series *Czech Plays in Translation III* on June 7, 2004, at The Public Theater, New York City. Gwynn MacDonald was the director and Irena Kovarova was the dramaturg. The cast was:

WOMAN/PUPPETEER	Teresa Linnihan
WOMAN/PUPPETEER	Michelle Beshaw
WOMAN	Jeanne Darst
MAN	Haynes Thigpen

Petr Zelenka

Teremin (*Theremin*) premiered November 17, 2005, in a production directed by the author at Dejvické divadlo, Prague. Stage design was by Martin Chocholoušek, costume design by Renata Weidlichová, Music by Karel Holas, with Dramaturgy from Klára Lidová. The cast featured: Ivan Trojan, David Novotný, Jiří Bábek j.h., Martin Myšička, Vendula Křížová, Jaroslav Plesl, Eliška Boušková, Lenka Krobotová, Petr Koutecký, Pavel Šimčík, Václav Jiráček, Jaroslav Plesl.

Plays:

Příběhy obyčejného šílenství (*Tales of Common Insanity**), written and premiered 2001 Dejvické divadlo, Prague
Odchody vlaků (*Departures of Trains**—inspired by Michael Frayn´s *Chinamen*) 2003, premiere 2004 Divadlo Astorka-Korzo '90, Bratislava (Slovakia)
Teremin (*Theremin**), written and premiered 2005 Dejvické divadlo, Prague
Očištění (*Coming Clean**), written and premiered 2007 Narodowy Teatr Stary, Cracow (Poland)
Herci (*Actors*—a new version of *Train Departures*), written and premiered 2008, Divadlo Ta fantastika, Prague

Theremin was presented as part of Immigrants' Theatre Project' readings series *Czech Plays in Translation V* on May 16, 2006 at The Public Theater, New York City. Marcy Arlin was the director and Irena Kovarova was the dramaturg. The cast was:

LEON SERGEIEVICH THEREMIN	Thom Rivera
HANS GOLDBERG	Tibor Feldman
JOSEPH SCHILLINGER	Robert Baumgardner
LAVINIA WILLIAMS	Lanna Joffrey
LUCY ROSEN	Nannette Deasy
AMTORG/STAGE DIRECTIONS/	
RADIO HOST/RESTAURANT OWNER	Kitty Chen
KATHERINE THEREMIN	Rita Wolf
WALTER ROSEN/AMTORG	Jonathan Smith

* Translated into English

NEW CZECH PLAYS IN TRANSLATION: THE NEW YORK SERIES
Presented by Immigrants' Theatre Project,
in collaboration with the Czech Center New York,
and the Theatre Institute (Prague)

Year I: 2001/02
Hosted by Henry Street Settlement; Maxine Kern, Dramaturg

November 19: *The Insect Play*, by Karel and Josef Čapek
Translated by Paul Selver, with Nigel Playfair and Clifford Bax;
additional translation by Alex Zucker
Director: Marcy Arlin

January 14: *Cat on the Tracks*, by Josef Topol
Translated by George Voskovec and Christine Voskovec
Director: Rasa Allen Kazlas

March 25: *Largo Desolato*, by Václav Havel
Translated by Tom Stoppard
Director: Marcy Arlin

May 13: *Little Pitfall*, by Markéta Bláhová
Translated by Jiří Topol
Director: Marcy Arlin

Year II: 2003
Hosted by New York Theatre Workshop; Maxine Kern, Dramaturg

January 13: *The Girls' Room*, by Jan Antonín Pitínský
Translated by Michael Branwell
Director: Marcy Arlin

February 24: *Tales of Common Insanity*, by Petr Zelenka
Translated by Robert Russell
Director: Gwynn MacDonald

March 24: Two plays by Egon Tobiáš, Translated by Sodja Zupanc Lotker and
Howard Lotker
I Promised Freddy: A Collector's Unbelievable Story
Director: Kaipo Schwab
It's Time for It to Change
Director: Jaye Austin Wiliams

April 28: *Minach*, by Iva Klestilová Volánková
Translated by Alex Zucker
Director: Marcy Arlin

Year III: 2004
Hosted by The Public Theater; Irena Kovarova, Dramaturg

May 3: *22 Anxiety Street*, by Iva Klestilová Volánková
Translated by David Nykl
Director: Daniela Varon

May 24: *I'm Still Alive with a Coatrack, a Cap, and a Signal Disc*, by Samuel Koeniggratz
Translated by Alex Zucker
Director: Jaye Austin Williams

June 7: *Opening the Drawer and Pulling out the Knife*, by Ivana Růžičková
Translated by Ivana Růžičková
Director: Gwynn MacDonald

June 21: *Dad Takes Goal Kicks*, by Jiří Pokorný
Translated by David Short
Director: Marcy Arlin

Year IV: 2005
Hosted by The Public Theater; Irena Kovarova, Dramaturg

May 2: *Three Sisters*, by Iva Klestilová Volánková
Translated by Štěpán Šimek
Director: Daniela Varon

May 9: *Miriam*, by Lenka Lagronová
Translated by Petr Onufer and Mike Baugh
Director: Marcy Arlin

May 16: *Aquabelles*, by David Drábek
Translated by Don Nixon
Director: Terrell Robinson

May 23: *JE SUiS*, by Egon Tobiáš
Translated by Sodja Zupanc Lotker and Howard Lotker
Director: Gwynn MacDonald

Year V: 2006
Hosted by The Public Theater; Irena Kovarova, Dramaturg

May 1: *The Conspirators*, by Václav Havel
Translated by Carol Rocamora and Tomas Rychetský
Director: Gwynn MacDonald

May 8: *Bikini*, by Zuzana Jochmanová
Translated by Zuzana Jochmanová
Director: Andreas Robertz

May 15: *Theremin*, by Petr Zelenka
Translated by Štěpán Šimek
Director: Marcy Arlin

Year VI: 2007
Hosted by the Bohemian National Hall; Irena Kovarova, Dramaturg

December 3: *Britney Goes to Heaven*, by Petr Kolečko
Translated by Kristina Molnárová
Director: Victor Maog

December 10: *The Elle Girls*, by Radmila Adamová
Translated by Michaela Pnačeková
Director: Marcy Arlin

Year VII: 2008
Hosted by the Bohemian National Hall; Irena Kovarova, Dramaturg

June 2: *Miracle in the Darkhouse*, by Milan Uhde
Translated by David Short
Director: Gwynn MacDonald

June 9: *Dorotka*, by Magdalena Frydrychová
Translated by Michaela Pnačeková
Director: Andreas Robertz

June 23: *The Time of the Cherry Smoke*, by Kateřina Rudcenková
Translated by Heather Benes-McGadie
Director: Cosmin Chivu

ARTISTS WHO PARTICIPATED IN *CZECH PLAYS IN TRANSLATION:*

Directors

Marcy Arlin / Jaye Austin Williams / Cosmin Chivu / Rasa Allen Kazlas / Gwynn MacDonald / Victor Maog / Andreas Robertz / Terrell Robinson / Kaipo Schwab / Daniela Varon

Dramaturgs

Maxine Kern / Irena Kovarova

Actors

Jeanine Abraham / Jolly Abraham / Michael Anderson / Clayton Apgar / Mary Q. Archias / Francesca Mantani Arkus / Pun Bandhu / Laurie Bannister-Colon / David Barlow / Spencer Barros / Robert Baumgardner / Michelle Beshaw / Collin Biddle / Michael Borrelli / Elisabeth Bove / Buzz Bovshow / George Brouillette / Christopher Burris / Frank Camacho / Sunilda Caraballo / John Cariani / Louis Changchien / Jay Charan / Kitty Chen / Snezhana Chernova / Daniella Chiminelli / Leonid Citer / Ron Cohen / Alessandro Colla / Debora S. Craig / Jeanne Darst / Oscar de la Fe Colon / Nick De Simone / Nannette Deasy / William Demeritt / Ron Domingo / Lisa Dove / Sandra Duque / Vaneik Echeverria / Andrew Eisenman / Sam Eliad / Tibor Feldman / Joe Fuer / John Fukuda / Esra Gaffin / Andy Gaukel / Adriana Gaviria / Edwin Lee Gibson / Lindy Jamil Gomez / Brad Gore / Rahti Gorfein / Mari Gorman / Andrew Guilarte / Michael Hammond / Reba Herman / Anita Hollander / Susan Hyon / Malcolm Ingram / Joan Jeffri / Lanna Joffrey / Matthew Johnson / Ron Jones / Kathryn Kates / Mia Katigbak / Rana Kazkaz / William Koch / Jeroen Kuiper / Jocelyn Kuritsky / Evan Lai / Melissa Leo / LiJun Li / James Hiroyuki Liao / Theresa Linnihan / Piter Marek Fattouche / Aric Martin / Sevrin Anne Mason / Victor Maxwell / Elena McGhee / Caroline McNeely / Jordan Meadows / John Michalski / Chelsea Miller / Jeremiah Miller / Martina Milo / Michael Morris / Tzahi Moskowitz / Gregg Mozgala / Kevin Napier / Rachel Neuman / Jane Nichols / M.C. O'Connell / Peter O'Conor / Kevin Orton / Trevor Osvalt / Howard Overshown / Andy Pang / Erica Pazel / Ryan Pierce / Ralph Pochoda / Andy Prosky / Anna Tulia Ramirez / Gita Reddy / Thomas Regan / Jennifer Rice / Francisco Rivela / Thom Rivera / Jerry Rockwood / Kaipo Schwab / Christina Shipp / Elaine Smith / Jonathan Smith / Robert Sonderskov / Christopher Speciale / Jenny Sterlin / Daniel Stowell / Jelena Stupljanin / Nilaja Sun / Haynes Thigpen / Laura Tietjen / Eve Udesky / Krisztina Urbanovitz / Ching Valdes-Aran / Christopher VanDyck / David Van Leesten / Max Vogel / Sturgis Warner / Rita Wolf / Tony Wolf / Francine Wong / Keo Woolford / Chris Wright / Mara Zhi

Special Thanks for Support in Presenting
Czech Plays in Translation: The New York Series

New York City Department of Cultural Affairs /// New York Theatre Workshop: James Nicola / Linda Chapman /// The Public Theater: Peter DuBois / Oskar Eustis / Maria Goyanes / Mandy Hackett / Celise Kalke /// Henry Street Settlement Abrons Arts Center: Jonathan Ward /// Arts and Theatre Institute in Prague: Lukás Matasek / Sodja Zupanc Lotker / Don Nixon /// Czech Center New York: Directors Monika Koblerova / Irena Kovarova / Přemysl Pela / Iva Karolina Raisinger // Staff: Radka Křížek / Radka Labendz / Marketa Tessier Novaková / Michaela Palkova-Claudino / Frank Parizek / Kateřina Pavlitová / Jan Žahour /// Immigrants' Theatre Project /// New Georges /// Czech Republic Ministry of Culture /// Bohemian National Hall /// Bohemian Hall, Astoria /// Dilia Literary Agency: Marie Spalová /// Aura-Pont Literary Agency: Jitka Sloupová /// Zdeněk Kříž /// Alex Zucker

Selected Resources on Czech Theatre

Bradbrook, B. R. *Karel Čapek: In Pursuit of Truth, Tolerance, and Trust.* Brighton, England: Sussex Academic Press, 1998.

Burian, Jarka. *Modern Czech Theatre: Reflector and Conscience of a Nation.* Iowa City: University of Iowa Press, 2000.

——. *Leading Creators of Twentieth-Century Czech Theatre.* New York: Routledge, 2002.

Goetz-Stankiewicz, Marketa. *The Silenced Theatre: Czech Playwrights Without a Stage.* Toronto: University of Toronto Press, 1979.

——, Editor. *DramaContemporary: Czechoslovakia.* New York: Performing Arts Journal Publications, 1985. http://mitpress.mit.edu/paj

——, Editor. *Good-bye Samizdat: 20 years of Czechoslovak Underground Writing.* Evanston, IL: Northwestern University, 1992

Havel, Václav. *Letters to Olga: June 1979–September 1982.* New York: Knopf, 1988.

Rocamora, Carol. *Acts of Courage: Václav Havel's Life in the Theater.* Hanover, NH: Smith and Kraus, 2005.

Šimek, Štěpán S. "Karel Steigerwald, Part I." *Slavic and East European Performance,* Vol. 23, no. 3 (Fall 20003): 28-43.

——. "Theatre as 'Temple of the Mind' and The 'Remarkable Moralist': Karel Steigerwald, Part II." *Slavic and East European Performance,* Vol. 24, no. 1 (Winter 2004): 42-55.

Trensky, Paul. *Czech Drama Since World War II.* White Plains, NY: M.E. Sharpe, 1978.

WEBSITES:

http://www.divadlo.cz/
Website of the Arts and Theatre Institute in Prague, Czech Republic, in Czech

http://www.theatre.cz/
Website of the Arts and Theatre Institute in Prague, Czech Republic, in English. The best source of information on Czech theatre, translations, playwright information, etc.

http://www.divadelni-ustav.cz (or http://institute.theatre.cz)
Arts and Theatre Institute, includes on-line database of Czech Theatre and Drama

http://www.vetrnemlyny.cz
Větrné mlýny (Wind Mills) Publishing House and Cultural Agency

http://www.prazska-scena.cz
Pražská scéna (Prague Stage) Publishing House

JOURNALS:

Czech Theatre Magazine
http://www.theatre.cz/go.asp?page=ctm
articles and photos on what's new in Czech theatre

Svět a divadlo
http://www.divadlo.cz/sad/STRANKY/SAD_H.html
In English, *World and Theatre*
http://www.divadlo.cz/sad/STRANKY/WAT_H.html

Let's Play Czechs: Contemporary Czech Drama 1989-2004.
Catalogue of new Czech plays, prepared by Aura-Pont Agency; Dilia Theatrical, Literary and Audiovisual Agency; and Arts and Theatre Institute in Prague. Contact Aura-Pont Agency www.aura-pont.cz, Dilia Theatrical, Literary and Audiovisual Agency www.dilia.cz, or go online to www.theatre.cz.

About the Editors

MARCY ARLIN (Artistic Director, Immigrants' Theatre Project) founded OBIE-winning Immigrants' Theatre Project in 1988, where she has directed over 20 productions and developed over 100 new plays. Recent directing work includes *The First Time*, by Michal Walczak (59E59 Theatre), the German-language translation of Caridad Svich's *Tropic of X*, (Artheater of Koln, Germany) and Jovanka Bach's *Marko the Prince* (Barrow Group Theatre). She is an original member of the Lincoln Center Theater Directors Lab, Core Member of Theatre without Borders, No Passport, and is Fulbright Senior Specialist 2005-09 to the Babes Bolyai University in Cluj, Romania, and Masaryk University, Brno, Czech Republic. Venues where she has worked include: Soho Rep, La MaMa, 59E59, HERE, New Dramatists, Vineyard, EST, NY International Fringe, Dublin Fringe, The Public, NYTW, Barrow Group Theatre, Ellis Island Museum, BAX, Tenement Theatre, Teatrul Imposibil/National Theatre/Romania, Yiddish Book Ctr. Notable plays: *365/365/*Suzan-Lori Parks, *Heresy/*Sabina Berman, *Red Bull/*Vera Ion, (Play Company), *Name Day/*Jovanka Bach; Australian Aboriginal Voices/Andrea James, *Waxing West/*Saviana Stanescu, *Cracking Mud is Pinching Me/*Haya Husseini, *Journey Theatre*-theatre project with survivors of torture (w/ Victor Maog/Ruth Margraff), *A Taste of Freedom/*Aurorae Khoo. She has been the Curator/Director of: *Czech Plays in Translation, Dis-Location/Re-Invention* (The New Group/MESTC), *After the Fall: New Romanian Theatre,* and *Difficult Dialogues*, plays about religion. She has been a Guest Speaker on Immigrant Theatre at the 2003 Prague Quadrennial, Yale University, University of Chicago (her alma mater), Brown University. Marcy is a Lecturer in Theatre and Communications at the City University of New York. Publications include: *Oldish Woman Leaves Earth* 2007/08 Romanian experimental theatre journal Man.In.Fest. (http://maninfest.ro/oldish-woman-leaves-earth-a-play), *Conversations on the Prague Quadrenniale,* 2004—with Maxine Kern, czechtheatre.cz; *Creating Outdoor Museum Theatre*: A Successful Collaboration, Museum Theatre Newsletter; *Garcia Lorca & the American Audience: Cultural Influences on Theatre Appreciation,* College Language Association; *Under Fire: Theatre in Nicaragua*, Theatreworks/International Theatre Institute Library; *Meltdown*, Brooklyn Free Press; *Poems & Drawings from Prison*, by Daymon Cabrera, translation for Amnesty International, Canada

GWYNN MACDONALD is Artistic Director of Juggernaut Theatre Co. and a freelance director and producer of theatre, television and radio. A graduate of Princeton, her theatre work has been featured in *The New York Times, Wall Street Journal, American Theater Magazine*, and WNET. In 2003, she co-directed Juggernaut's First 100 Years: The Professional Female Playwright, a year-long theatre project exploring the work of women who wrote for the English stage in the seventeenth and eighteenth centuries. Looking at contemporary women writers, she contributed the essay "Engaging Social Issues: Expressing a Political Outlook" for *Women Writing Plays* (Alexis Greene, ed., UT Press, 2006). Previously, she worked on *Children of the Night: The Best Short Stories by Black Writers, 1967 to the Present* (Gloria Naylor, ed., Little, Brown and Co., 1995), and her arts writing and reviews have appeared both on the Internet and in print, including: *7 Days Magazine* where she was a reporter, *The Village Voice*, and the *Baltimore Sun*. A member of Lincoln Center Theatre Directors Lab, Women Count, and League of Professional Theatre Women. Fellowships include: Drama League Directors Project, DeGrummond Research Fellowship, Columbia University's Arts Leadership Institute (sponsored by the Arts & Business Council).

The Arts and Theatre Institute (Prague) is an information centre and research institute, whose main mission is to provide the Czech and foreign public with a complex information service in the area of theatre, ballet, dance, puppet theatre, music and other forms of the performing arts. The Arts and Theatre Institute (ATI) was established in 1959 and is a non-profit organization of the Ministry of Culture of the Czech Republic. Since the mid-70s, its offices are located in the Manhart Palace on Celetna street in the very centre of Prague. ATI includes one of the largest theatre libraries in Europe, video library, photo archives, a rich documentation and bibliographical collection, and several on-line information databases. It is also the largest publisher of theatre literature in the Czech Republic—it publishes approximately 15 titles per year. ATI is home of several Czech centers of international non-governmental organizations, of which includes the most recognized International Theatre Institute (ITI). The European Union's project Culture 2000 also has its headquarters here. ATI in Prague, together with the Ministry of Culture of the Czech Republic and other international partners, initiates projects that promote Czech theatre abroad. It engages in international cultural exchanges through its organization of exhibitions, symposiums, seminars and theatre presentations with international festival, venues, companies and other theatre organizations. Its most recognized international project is the Prague Quadrennial—international exhibition of performance design, which it has organized since 1967. For more on Czech theatre, please visit: http://www.theatre.cz

The Czech Center New York, since 1995 has been building dialogue among the Czech Republic and the American public particularly in the areas of culture, business and tourism. The Czech Center New York is primarily focused on presenting the latest and most innovative works of Czech Artists to the U.S. The Czech Center NY is part of a network of 24 Czech Centers abroad under the umbrella of the Czech Centers in Prague. For more information, please visit: http://www.czechcenter.com

Immigrants' Theatre Project (winner 2003 OBIE for Innovative Theater) is a professional non-profit theatre company based in New York City that gives a public theatrical voice to those who are marginalized, promotes the genre of immigrant theatre as a valid American theatre form, and is an artistic model for intercultural relations. Founded in 1988 by Artistic Director Marcy Arlin, ITP presents traditional and experimental plays as full productions and as readings by and about immigrants to the U.S. and worldwide. ITP works with multicultural casts and artistic staff from over 90 ethnicities and nations to reflect the diversity of New York and introduce immigrant and American audiences to challenging theatre works. ITP has presented the American and/or world premieres of over 250 plays, and in addition curates and develops artistic exchange residencies, student and professional development workshops, consultancies for multi-cultural arts programming, and special programs. For more information, contact Marcy Arlin, Artistic Director, immigrantstheat@aol.com, or visit: http://www.immigrantstheat.org

The Graduate Center, CUNY, of which the Martin E. Segal Theatre Center is an integral part, is the doctorate-granting institution of The City University of New York (CUNY). An internationally recognized center for advanced studies and a national model for public doctoral education, the school offers more than thirty doctoral programs, as well as a number of master's programs. Many of its faculty members are among the world's leading scholars in their respective fields, and its alumni hold major positions in industry and government, as well as in academia. The Graduate Center is also home to twenty-eight interdisciplinary research centers and institutes focused on areas of compelling social, civic, cultural, and scientific concerns. Located in a landmark Fifth Avenue building, The Graduate Center has become a vital part of New York City's intellectual and cultural life with its extensive array of public lectures, exhibitions, concerts, and theatrical events. To find out more, please visit: http://www.gc.cuny.edu

The Martin E. Segal Theatre Center (MESTC), is a non-profit center for theatre, dance and film affiliated with CUNY's Ph.D. Program in Theatre. The Center's mission is to bridge the gap between academia and the professional performing arts communities both within the United States and internationally. By providing an open environment for the development of educational, community-driven, and professional projects in the performing arts, MESTC is a home to theatre scholars, students, playwrights, actors, dancers, directors, dramaturges, and performing arts managers from the local and international theatre communities. Through diverse programming—staged readings, theatre events, panel discussions, lectures, conferences, film screenings, dance—and a number of publications, MESTC enables artists, academics, visiting scholars and performing arts professionals to participate actively in the advancement and appreciation of the entire range of theatrical experience. The Center presents staged readings to further the development of new and classic plays, lecture series, televised seminars featuring professional and academic luminaries, and arts in education programs, and maintains its long-standing visiting scholars-from-abroad program. In addition, the Center publishes a series of highly-regarded academic journals, as well as books, including plays in translation, written, translated and edited by leading scholars. For more information, please visit: http://thesegalcenter.org

Ph.D. Program in Theatre, The Graduate Center, CUNY, is one of the leading doctoral theatre programs in the United States. Faculty includes distinguished professors, holders of endowed chairs, and internationally recognized scholars. The program trains future scholars and teachers in all the disciplines of theatre research. Faculty members edit MESTC publications, working closely with the doctoral students in theatre who perform a variety of editorial functions and learn the skills involved in the creation of books and journals. For more information on the program, please visit: http://web.gc.cuny.edu/theatre

The MESTC Publication Wing produces both journals and individual volumes. Journals include *Slavic and Eastern European Performance* (SEEP), *The Journal of American Drama and Theatre* (JADT), and *Western European Stages* (WES). Books include *Four Melodramas by Pixérécourt* (edited by Daniel Gerould and Marvin Carlson—both Distinguished Professors of Theatre at the CUNY Graduate Center), *Contemporary Theatre in Egypt* (which includes the translation of three plays by Alfred Farag, Gamal Maqsoud, and Lenin El-Ramley, edited by Marvin Carlson), *The Heirs of Molière* (edited and translated by Marvin Carlson), *Seven Plays by Stanisław Ignacy Witkiewicz* (edited and translated by Daniel Gerould), *The Arab Oedipus: Four Plays* (edited by Marvin Carlson), *Theatre Research Resources in New York City* (edited by Jessica Brater, Senior Editor Marvin Carlson), and *Comedy: A Bibliography of Critical Studies in English on the Theory and Practice of Comedy in Drama, Theatre and Performance* (edited by Meghan Duffy, Senior Editor Daniel Gerould). New publications include: *BAiT-Buenos Aires in Translation: Four Plays* (edited and translated by Jean Graham-Jones), *roMANIA AFTER 2000: Five New Romanian Plays* (edited by Saviana Stanescu and Daniel Gerould), *Four Plays from North Africa* (edited by Marvin Carlson), *Barcelona Plays: A Collection of New Plays by Catalan Playwrights* (edited and translated by Marion Peter Holt and Sharon G. Feldman), *Josep M. Benet i Jornet: Two Plays* (translated by Marion Peter Holt), *I Am a Mistake: Seven Works for the Theatre* by Jan Fabre (edited and foreword by Frank Hentschker). To find out more, please visit: http://web.gc.cuny.edu/mestc/subscribe.htm